P9-DUI-895

Crash Course in Web Design for Libraries

Recent Titles in Crash Course Series

Crash Course in Children's Services
Penny Peck

Crash Course in Storytelling
Kendall Haven and MaryGay Ducey

Crash Course in Web Design for Libraries

Charles P. Rubenstein, Ph.D.

Crash Course Series

Westport, Connecticut • London

Library of Congress Cataloging-in-Publication Data

Rubenstein, Charles P.
Crash course in Web design for libraries / Charles P. Rubenstein.
p. cm. — (Crash course)
Includes bibliographical references and index.
ISBN 1-59158-366-7 (pbk. : alk. paper)
1. Library Web sites—Design—Handbooks, manuals, etc. 2. Web sites—Design—Handbooks, manuals, etc. I. Title.
Z674.75.W67R83 2007
006.7—dc22 2006033742

British Library Cataloguing in Publication Data is available.

Copyright © 2007 by Charles P. Rubenstein

All rights reserved. No portion of this book may be reproduced, by any process or technique, without the express written consent of the publisher.

Library of Congress Catalog Card Number: 2006033742
ISBN: 1-59158-366-7

First published in 2007

Libraries Unlimited, 88 Post Road West, Westport, CT 06881
A Member of the Greenwood Publishing Group, Inc.
www.lu.com

Printed in the United States of America

The paper used in this book complies with the Permanent Paper Standard issued by the National Information Standards Organization (Z39.48–1984).

10 9 8 7 6 5 4 3 2 1

This Crash Course is dedicated to my parents, who gave me the opportunity to continue my education; my wife Rose, who has encouraged me and made it possible for me to write this text; our three sons—Jaron, Adam, and Scott, who have made our lives worthwhile; and Stephanie, Jaron's wife, who has given Rose and me our first grandchild—Alyssa Michelle.

I am also indebted to my editor, Blanche Woolls, and all the folks at LU who have guided me through the process of bringing this text to life.

Contents

List of Illustrations

Preface

Librarians communicate with their patrons and staff in many ways. These include signs and posters in the library, newsletters to the local community, and now, with Web pages via the World Wide Web. Each mode of communication has its own strengths and weaknesses. Each provides opportunities for you to put your best foot forward. Each is also a publication that requires some common branding elements, such as logos and consistent names.

Posters, newsletters, and other printed materials are fixed publications that cannot easily be modified once created. Web pages can be (and are!) changed nearly instantaneously and updated as errors are discovered, events end, or changes are needed—the Web is a dynamically changing "instant" publication. Your only challenge then is that where most of us know how to use word processors to create print materials, knowledge of the special markup language of Web pages' HyperText Markup Language (HTML) is needed to present your information on Web pages for the entire world to see.

Planning, HTML coding, and publishing Web pages need not prevent you from being creative online. In fact, your page can link to other pages, other Web sites, and even your library's online public access catalog or OPAC. More than merely a text, *Crash Course in Web Design for Libraries* is a gentle introduction to Web design and publishing that takes you on an adventure into the creation of a Web site for the Red Rose Library. Once you have completed this process, you can easily create your own library Web pages.

About the Red Rose Library (http://www.redroselibrary.com)

Rather than obtaining permission to publish dozens of other libraries' Web pages, the author developed a (mythical) Red Rose Library that provides many of the services that you probably have in your brick and mortar library and want to feature on your Web pages. After looking over dozens of online library pages (see "Where Can I Find Library Web Page Examples?," below), think about what kinds of "stuff" might be on, or linked to by, a library Web site. In no real order, this stuff consisted of links from the library's home page to inside or internal page content links covering Ready Reference Q&A, a Children's Section, a Young Adult's Section, a General Patron Section, an OPAC and/or Online Databases Link, a link to the library's online collection(s), the hours of operation, special events, calendar, Library Board and Staff Contacts (including special budget vote information), newsletters and archive, links to the local library system, and links to community and governmental agencies.

Key to your success in this adventure is your creativity, and CONTENT! Great prose makes great pages. Sad, but true, not everyone is a writer or poet, and not everyone is an artist. However fancy your page format is, be aware that like a blank sheet of paper without good content, your Web site could be a wasteland of information-empty files. Although professional looking graphics and marketing techniques are not everyone's cup of tea, clip art is easy to find and use, if you make sure you have copyright permission! And talking to your library's newsletter editor or public relations person (or a friend at another library performing these functions) will give you lots of marketing ideas.

In this text, through the development of a variety of pages for the "Red Rose" Library, you will be guided through creating your own Web pages. Linking these pages together will create a Web site that will function internally on your library's intranet, or when posted on a Web server, be accessible externally on the Internet for patrons anywhere in the world. From paper designs to working Web sites, you'll find tips and techniques on every page where you will discover how to present your library through the broadcast medium of the World Wide Web.

Why Take This Crash Course

So you saw this really neat Web page while surfing the Internet and said how great it would be if your library had a page that looked just like that one. Well, it is certainly possible, and in buying this book you have indicated you are up for the challenge.

While there may be several very complicated pages that you will not be able to replicate because they contain high-level computer science techniques, or others that may use special graphics such as flash movies, after following the procedures and tips in this text you will be able to create a very functional Web page that can do nearly everything "professional" pages can do.

This text is intended to be used as a stand-alone, user-friendly workbook for individuals who have no programming background but have an interest in the rapid development of professional looking Web sites. What you need to begin is lots of paper for designing your page layout. You'll also need lots of words, articles, and other content and ideas. Finally, you'll need a computer and familiarity with creating and using files and folders in a Microsoft Windows™ environment. You'll need a text processor and Internet browser installed on your computer. Although you can use any plain text editor, like Microsoft's Notepad, and any browser (see examples in Chapter 2), examples in this text were created using Microsoft WordPad™ (Version 5) and viewed with Microsoft Internet Explorer™ (Version 6) in the Microsoft Windows™ XP environment. "Cut and Paste" techniques and templates are used throughout as examples of how to create pages without the need to really learn the HTML markup language, and all are downloadable from the text's demonstration Web site.

Finishing this "crash course" in Web design doesn't mean you are an instant Webmaster or Webmistress any more than having oil paints and canvas, an easel, and brushes means you can paint like Picasso. What you will get is the feeling that you know how Web pages fit together, how to create them, and how various Web page tools work with markup languages to make your Web pages come alive.

In fact, our goal is that, in the time it takes you to go through each chapter, you will see the creation of Web pages for the "Red Rose Library," and using those techniques you could easily configure pages for use in your library. Each page will be simple enough for a novice to create and yet have enough choices to make HTML-aware folks happy with their results.

You will be able to create your own personal Web page and one for your library or even a basic library system Web site. You supply the time to practice these techniques and add the content, design, and structure you want; we'll supply the tools, techniques, and markup code snippets that will permit you to design Web pages and sites that combine text, graphics, animation, and multimedia using markup language techniques to control the layout and flow of your information.

The text's focus is on the creation of HTML pages useful in libraries and information centers using the hypothetical Red Rose Library as a demonstration site. Screen shots and code sets/files will be created, and Uniform Resource Locator (URL) links to them will be included in each section of the text. We will show you how to add style to a single page or your entire Web site using program language-like style and cascading style sheet coding.

After completing the text, or participating in an instructor-led workshop, you will understand the Web design cycle, from content development to publishing on the Web, will learn the most essential topics in Web page development, will be able to develop complex Web sites in a short period of time, and will realize some of the benefits and limitations of using HTML to create Web pages.

The good news is that after working the through the exercises in this text, you will be able to create Web pages that can be published on any Web server to show the world all the great things you have in your library.

At your public library, do you have a Web server as part of your local government or school board's electronic resources? If you do, you should see if they can arrange for you to use it to publish your pages.

Where Can I Find Library Web Page Examples?

Not all libraries are on the Web, but most public libraries in the United States that have Web sites can be located using the searchable, and regularly updated, "Libweb—Directory of USA Public Libraries" Web site (© 1995–2005, Thomas Dowling—OhioLINK e-mail:tdowling@ohiolink.edu). On Libweb you'll find library Web sites that vary from single home pages to elaborate presentations offering everything from digital collections to online public access catalog access, some with e-mail and interlibrary loan options. The more sophisticated sites have at least two levels of access: general public and password-protected areas for authorized registered users. Those Web sites with some level of online accessible digital collection are typically interconnected with a special e-commerce or transaction server, which also enables the librarian to process forms and permits document purchases. Not content with only offering access to the public libraries, Dowling's Libweb also has lists (and hyperlinks) to academic libraries, national libraries and library organizations, state libraries, regional consortia, as well as special and school libraries. You'll also find links to library Web sites in Europe, Africa and the Middle East, Asia, Australia, New Zealand, the Pacific, Canada, Mexico, the Caribbean, Central America, and South America as well as to several resource maintainers and mirror sites at **http://lists.webjunction.org/libweb** Libweb's Public Library Resources are available directly at **http://lists.webjunction.org/libweb/Public_main.htm** Libweb is updated daily at midnight, Pacific Time and as of August 25, 2006, listed over 7,300 pages from libraries in more than 125 countries.

About Using Templates

Some are of the opinion that the easiest way to create their own Web pages would be to use an already coded template page. To satisfy their needs, all the examples used in the text and a variety of template styles may be found in the **template.zip** file on the Red Rose Library demonstration Web site at **http://www.redroselibrary.com/template.zip**

Throughout the text discussions are references to looking at specific templates. The names of these templates are included in the figure captions. To use these sample Web pages and templates, save the **template.zip** file on your desktop and extract the **code** folder onto your hard disk. Then whenever you need a template or code example, decide which file to use, open the file up in a text processing program, change the titles, put your text (etc.) in it, and add in images or the HTML destinations (links) for your text or graphics as appropriate. Saving the **code** folder and then copying the individual files or giving them a different filename will allow you to reuse the template files without resaving them from the Web site. (If you accidentally overwrite the original files, relax. Exact copies are still on the Web site for you to download.)

Typographical Conventions

To make use of this text easier, specific typographic conventions have been used. When HTML element or attribute names are used, the name of the element or attribute is shown in boldface. All filenames and Web site addresses (e.g., **filename.htm** or **http://www.redroselibrary.com**) are also in boldface. Graphics used in this text, unless otherwise noted, were created by the author, used with permission, or obtained through the Clipart.com link on the Red Rose Library page. This low-cost service is discussed in Chapter 2. The company permits royalty-free personal and/or commercial use of its graphics, etc., as long as not more than five images appear on any given Web page.

Chapter 1

Quick Start in Web Design

Welcome to a *Crash Course in Web Design for Libraries*!

Our task in this first chapter is to give you the tools to jump right into creating a Web page so you don't have to wait too long to have a page up and running. The remainder of the book is designed to ease you into good design of Web pages using common HyperText Markup Language (HTML) techniques without expensive software.

You won't need much to begin your Web page design. What if all you needed for rapid Web page design was to create a word processed document and then quickly turn it into a simple Web page? In this age of instant gratification, we all want to see results quickly and effortlessly. By the time you finish this chapter, you will have learned a quick and easy way to create Web pages that you can use on your individual computer, on a CD-ROM, on your library intranet, or on an Internet Web server for viewing by the entire world.

To avoid having to learn a new (and possibly expensive) program, we use the popular Microsoft Word™ software program with its built-in word to Web converter, and then create HTML pages from "scratch" using Microsoft WordPad™ and simple HTML elements to "tag" the information. Then we use Microsoft Internet Explorer™ as our standard Web page viewer or "browser."

Setting up a Web Site Shell Directory

Because you will be saving your work on a computer or server somewhere (either locally or through your Internet service provider), it is best to create a Web site "shell" folder on your computer's desktop that you can use to collect all the bits and pieces you'll be using, such as graphics and pictures, audio and other multimedia files, primary and secondary Web pages, and other information. This will keep them in one space. Creating this shell requires a few simple steps.

To create a directory or folder that will be your Web site location and container for all our files on your computer desktop, right-click your mouse anywhere on your desktop. Then select "New" and then "Folder" from the drop down menu that appears. A new folder will appear on your desktop. Use the name "**library**" for your overall shell directory. Then press "Enter."

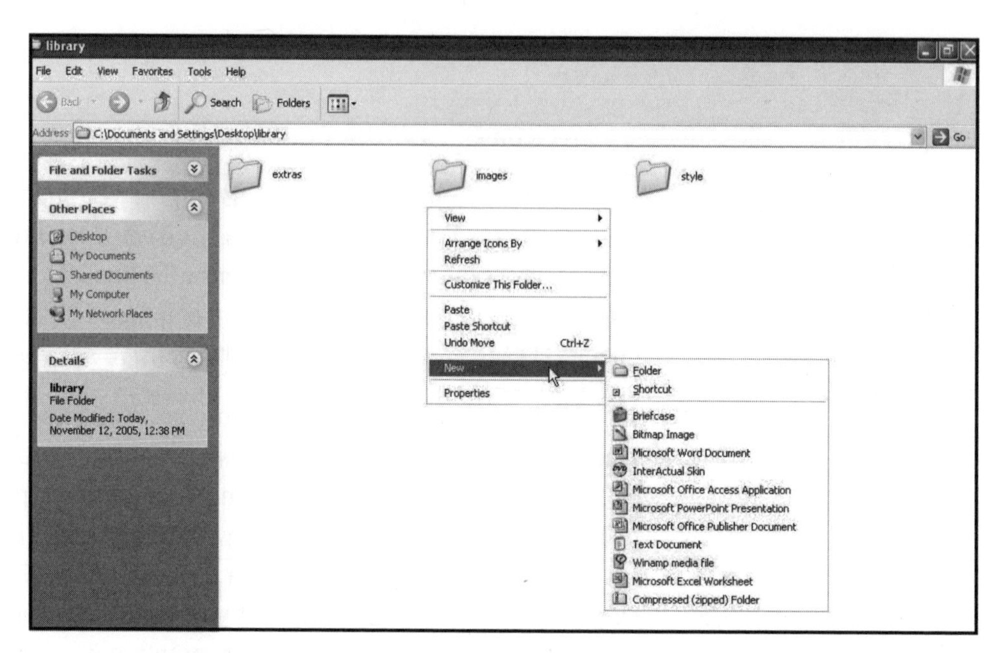

Figure 1.1. Creating Subfolders in a Folder (Directory)

Next create a subfolder (subdirectory) inside "library" named "images." This is where all of your page's graphic, picture, audio, and other multimedia files will be stored. This strategy makes it easy to reference your links to digital multimedia items, and you will always know where they are. Figure 1.1 shows the "New" drop down menu after adding two more subfolders to our structure, named **style,** which will be used for style definition files and **extras** for documents and other files that we might want to have accessed by our Web pages.

The model we use for our library Web site is the single directory, with all Web page HTML files and one set of image, style, and extras subfolders supporting these HTML files, as shown in Figure 1.2.

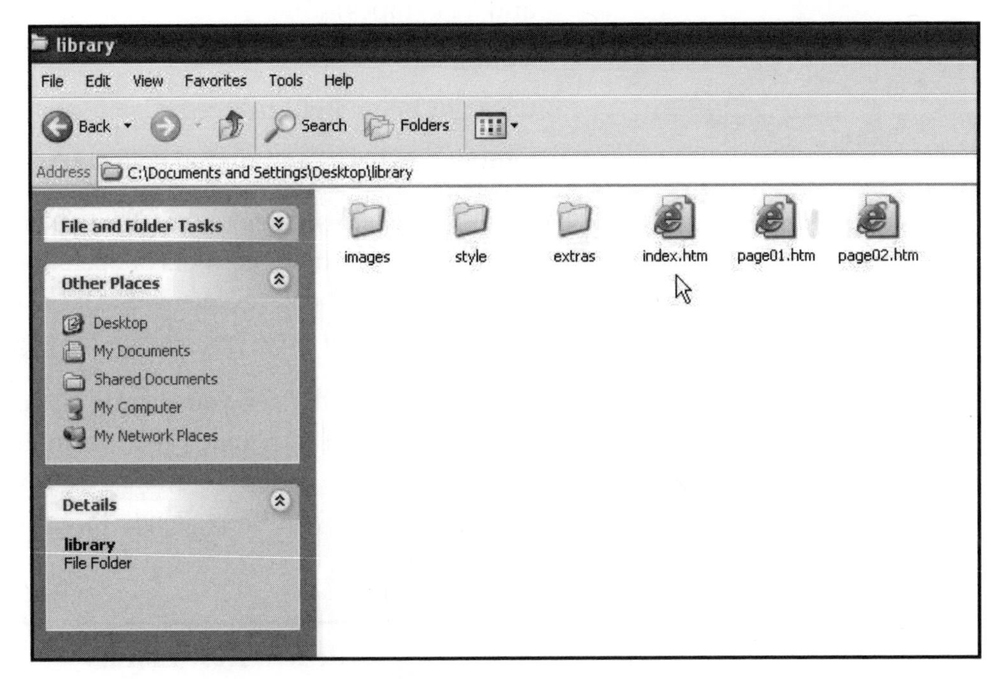

Figure 1.2. Web Site with Common Subfolders

Creating a Web Site

You will be creating a series of Web pages, including the first or home page (often called the index page), for your library. You will want to have some or all of the following "Library Web Site Topics" and information available on your Web site:

Address information (phone and fax, maps and directions)

Hours of operation

Special events

Library board and staff

Library newsletter and archives

Links to local and state library systems

Volunteer page

Ready reference section

Children section

Fiction and nonfiction sections

Audio and video resources (CD-ROMs, DVDs, cassettes, and VHS tapes)

Young adult section

OPAC (Online Public Access Catalog)

Online databases and digital collections

This quick start exercise begins with only five items on your initial, or home page: address information, hours of operation, children's room, young adult services, and special events. We will call our library the Red Rose Library and will want a logo graphic on the page.

If you have a newsletter for your library patrons, your library's Web page/home page will look much like a simple Word document newsletter. For the fictitious Red Rose Library we have created a simple newsletter (see Figure 1.3). It corresponds to a word document file called **code0103.doc**.

The Red Rose Library

18 Rose Street

New York, New York 10010

Telephone +1 212 555-7673

Fall 2006 Newsletter

Open Weekdays 9:00am – 9:00pm   Weekends 11:00am – 6:00pm
Come visit us – we're across from Town Hall

For Young Adults:
Young Adult Services for those in the Red Rose High School - assistance in researching end-of-semester reports, science fair projects, and how to use online databases.

The Children's Room - for even younger adults:
Mommy and Me reading programs: Monday-Wednesday-Friday 10:00am – 12:00noon.
Tuesdays We Read program for kindergarten through second grade 3:30pm – 4:30pm.
Computer and Internet Instruction: Thursdays from 3:30pm – 5:30pm.
NEW! Children's Videos Section (next to the audio tapes)
Come in Fridays after 3:30pm and borrow any video for the whole weekend.

Special Events
(Sorry - our December trip to Radio City Music Hall has sold out.)
Annual trip to the American Museum of Natural History and the Hayden Planetarium.
Sign up now! The bus to New York City will be leaving on Sunday January 14, 2007 at 6:00am. Trip cost is $50 which includes bus tickets, snacks on the bus, lunch at the Museum, and a souvenir. Be sure to make your reservation early as this is a fast sell out! The bus trip is sponsored by the Cultural Committee of the Friends of the Rose Library.

The Red Rose Newsletter - C. Rubenstein, Editor

Figure 1.3. Red Rose Library Newsletter (code0103.doc = redrose1.doc)

Using Microsoft's Word to Create Easy Web Pages

Creating a Word document page layout is usually easy because you already know how to do it. What you may not be aware of is that the later versions of Microsoft's Word have the ability to save your word processed document as a Web page with an **.htm** file extension, and it can be instantly viewed using your browser. The downside of this technique is that speed often results in not exactly a what-you-see-is-what-you-get result, and minor changes require returning to the original file rather than editing the HTML Web page. Another challenge is that there are lots of "droppings" due to Word's desire to keep its entire proprietary markup commands when converting to simple HTML. This will be demonstrated after a discussion of file sizes, because file sizes directly affect patron retrieval.

About File Sizes (Bytes)

If we look at the size of the files for the page in Figure 1.3 (**code0103.doc = redrose1.doc**), we see the doc file is 26,624 bytes. When saved directly as a Web page, its htm file (**code0104.htm = redrose1.htm**) is 11,627 bytes plus another 4,520 bytes for the graphics and other files saved in a **redrose1_files** folder (when you save your files on your computer, the exact number of bytes may vary, but the relative sizes will not). The plain text version of the doc file (**code0103.txt**) is only 1,555 bytes! Even when we add our HTML tags and links, the manually configured HTML file (**code0105.htm = redrose.htm**) you will have designed by the end of this chapter will be less than 5 kilobytes, including the red rose image. (I won't use these number games too often, but they are important.)

File sizes are critical because many of your patrons are still accessing the Internet, and thus your Web pages, via a dial-up connection to AOL or another Internet service provider (ISP). Whereas cable modems and digital subscriber line (DSL) connections are typically fast enough that you don't have to worry about file size, dial-up modems are very slow, and you will want to give your patrons the information they need as quickly as possible, or they may go to another site.

Using the quick Word-to-Web method uses more space, and the page must be edited in the original, but it still gets the job started. Or does it? After converting the newsletter from **doc** into **htm** we look at the result (**code0104.htm = redrose1.htm**) in Internet Explorer and see that the rose images have shifted and now cover up some of our text, as shown in Figure 1.4.

Figure 1.4. Word Document Saved as a Web Page (code0104.htm)

The other, not so quick, way to get your page online uses WordPad to change the text file of your newsletter (**code0103.txt = redrose1.txt**) into an HTML file by changing its extension from **.txt** to **.htm** and accepting the change of extensions. This will result in a nongraphic, continuous stream of words that looks something like Figure 1.5:

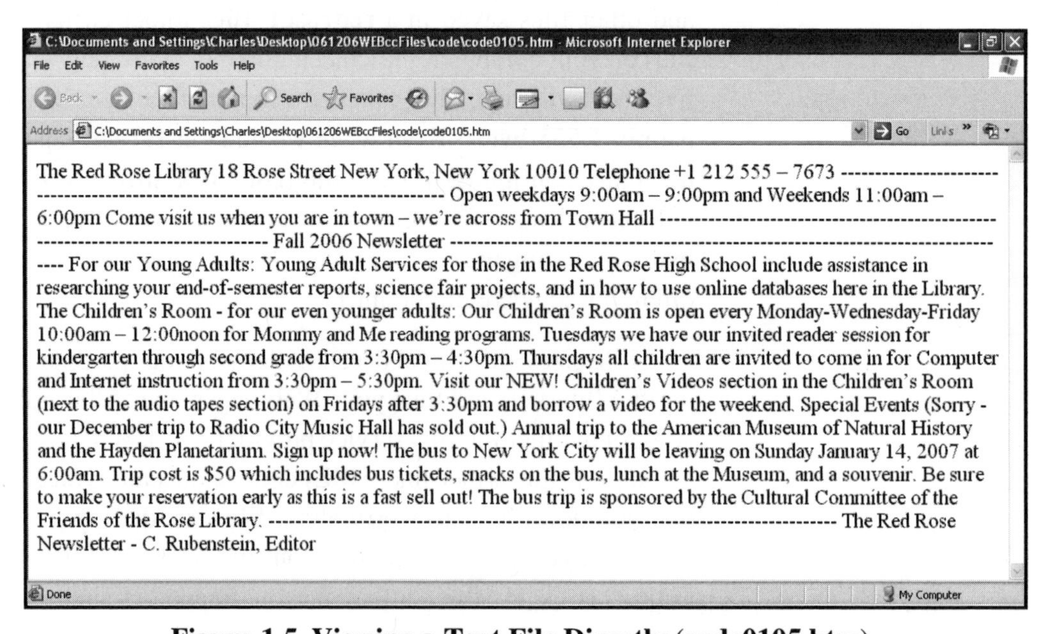

Figure 1.5. Viewing a Text File Directly (code0105.htm)

Okay, it doesn't look pretty. But it does have all the text content of the original word processed page without wasting a lot of file download time. That said, it is not a page that would have your patrons coming back for more. It's time to turn to some very basic markup elements to create your page using HTML Page Structure.

HTML Page Structure

All HTML pages should begin and end with the basic element named **html** to inform the browser that the contents in the file are tagged with HTML elements. These element names are incorporated into HTML tag commands, which can be thought of as switches that turn on and off a particular way your text or images are displayed. Tags usually consist of an opening and a closing tag. Opening tags contain the name of the element and one or more optional "attributes" that can further stylize your display. Closing tags only contain a slash, which precedes the element name. The tags surround your text and images to produce the desired display features.

The basic structure of HTML elements is that they exist in Tags. The opening tag contains any additional attributes or subelements of the element and their values:

<elementname attribute1="0"> = OPENING TAG

The attribute values become defaults during the time that the element is surrounding text, etc., and cease when the closing tag is reached in the document. Note that the closing tag only contains the element's name, as closing the element closes all of its attributes:

</elementname> = CLOSING TAG

The correct way of using HTML element tag sets is to surround the text you wish to redefine by the element and its attributes:

<elementname attribute1="0"> Your Text **</elementname>**

Using the HTML, Title, and Body Tags

The basic HTML page has a head area that usually contains a title tag, and then an optional body tag. Thus, for the "Fall 2006 Newsletter" you should have a starting HTML file structure that looks like Figure 1.6. (Please note that your WordPad display will not have the various

HTML element tags in bold. This has been done to allow you to see them more clearly in this figure).

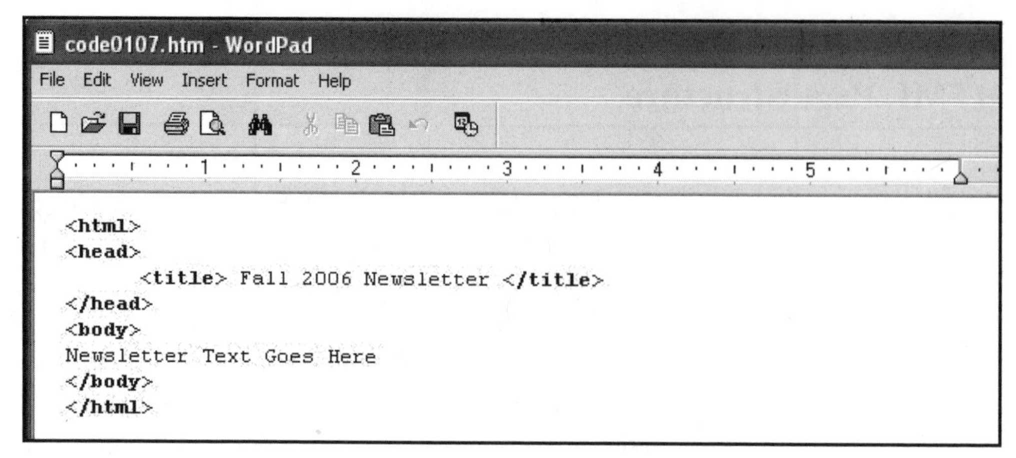

Figure 1.6. Basic Skeleton of an HTML Page (WordPad View of code0107.htm)

Notice the symmetry of the opening and closing element tags in the figure. Proper nesting order is essential so that your browser knows when to start and stop its job of styling your text. Note that although the filename appears in the WordPad window, the page's title appears in the browser window at the top, to the left of the pointer, to announce the name of your page. This simple file structure would be displayed as in Figure 1.7.

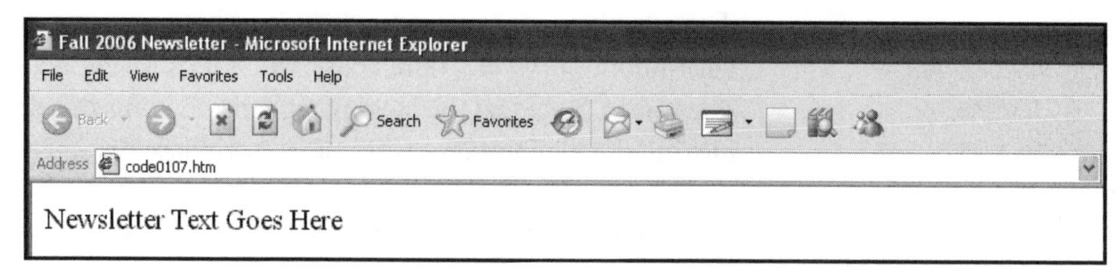

Figure 1.7. Browser View of Basic Web Page (code0107.htm)

Add the contents of newsletter's text file (**code0103.txt = redrose1.txt**) to this basic HTML file structure overlaying the "Newsletter Text Goes Here" line after the opening body tag to create the WordPad file of Figure 1.8 (the added text is shown in bold).

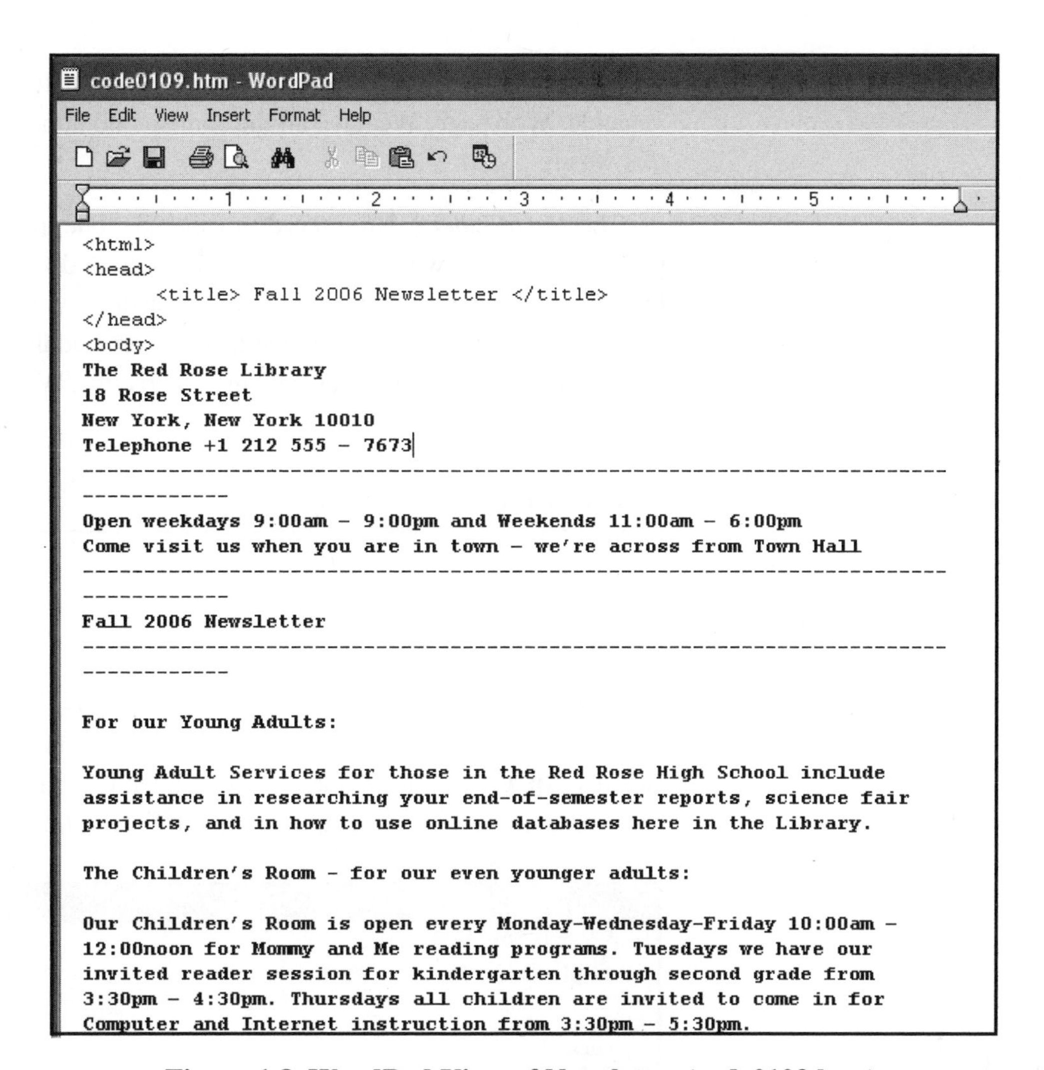

```
<html>
<head>
      <title> Fall 2006 Newsletter </title>
</head>
<body>
The Red Rose Library
18 Rose Street
New York, New York 10010
Telephone +1 212 555 - 7673
----------------------------------------------------------------------
------------
Open weekdays 9:00am - 9:00pm and Weekends 11:00am - 6:00pm
Come visit us when you are in town - we're across from Town Hall
----------------------------------------------------------------------
------------
Fall 2006 Newsletter
----------------------------------------------------------------------
------------

For our Young Adults:

Young Adult Services for those in the Red Rose High School include
assistance in researching your end-of-semester reports, science fair
projects, and in how to use online databases here in the Library.

The Children's Room - for our even younger adults:

Our Children's Room is open every Monday-Wednesday-Friday 10:00am -
12:00noon for Mommy and Me reading programs. Tuesdays we have our
invited reader session for kindergarten through second grade from
3:30pm - 4:30pm. Thursdays all children are invited to come in for
Computer and Internet instruction from 3:30pm - 5:30pm.
```

Figure 1.8. WordPad View of Newsletter (code0109.htm)

The result is an otherwise still pretty ugly Web page that we already saw as Figure 1.5 but, in Figure 1.9, one that has a title appearing in the browser window.

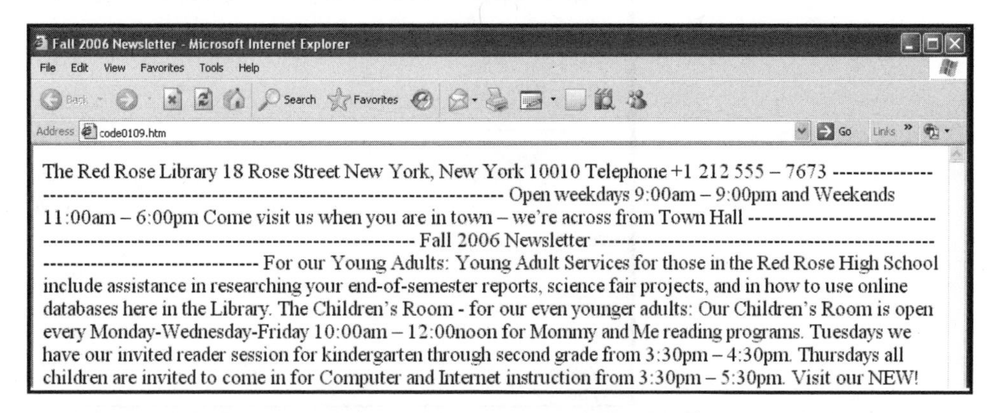

The Red Rose Library 18 Rose Street New York, New York 10010 Telephone +1 212 555 – 7673 -- Open weekdays 9:00am – 9:00pm and Weekends 11:00am – 6:00pm Come visit us when you are in town – we're across from Town Hall -- Fall 2006 Newsletter -- For our Young Adults: Young Adult Services for those in the Red Rose High School include assistance in researching your end-of-semester reports, science fair projects, and in how to use online databases here in the Library. The Children's Room - for our even younger adults: Our Children's Room is open every Monday-Wednesday-Friday 10:00am – 12:00noon for Mommy and Me reading programs. Tuesdays we have our invited reader session for kindergarten through second grade from 3:30pm – 4:30pm. Thursdays all children are invited to come in for Computer and Internet instruction from 3:30pm – 5:30pm. Visit our NEW!

Figure 1.9. Browser View of Newsletter HTML File (code0109.htm)

Clearly this simple solution does not yield an attractive, nor easily readable, Web page. We have all the content and none of the formatting that we are seeking.

Lesson number 1: Browsers do not interpret line spaces or even multiple spaces between words the way a word processor does. Extra spaces and lines (carriage returns) are ignored, resulting in displaying text as a continuous line. We will need to enlist the help of some additional markup elements to create a more realistic, and more attractive, Web page.

Creating a Red Rose Newsletter Web Page

Adding the Preformat Tag

To keep the structure we have in our text file, look to the HTML **pre** element. Merely adding an opening **<pre>** tag before our text and a closing **</pre>** tag after our text dramatically changes the way the browser displays our content, as shown in Figure 1.10.

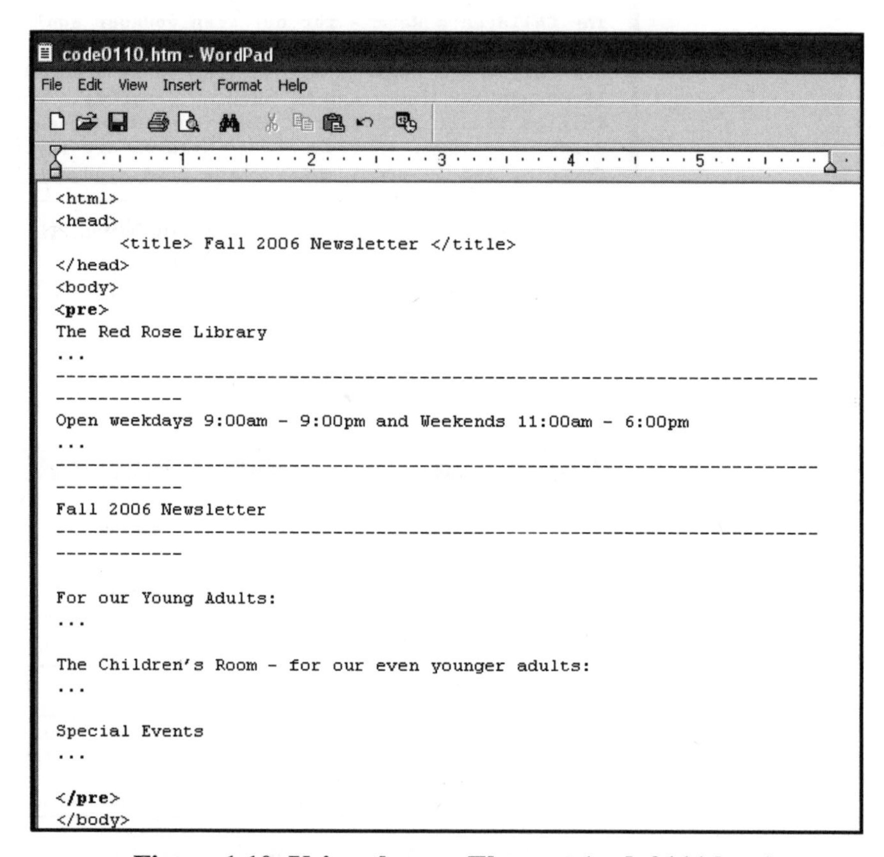

Figure 1.10. Using the pre Element (code0111.htm)

The addition of just the **pre** tag results in a file whose browser display closely resembles that of the original, except it does not have bold or underlining. We're getting closer to the desired effect, but the text for each paragraph still runs across the page and does not wrap, and there still are no rose logos on the page in Figure 1.11.

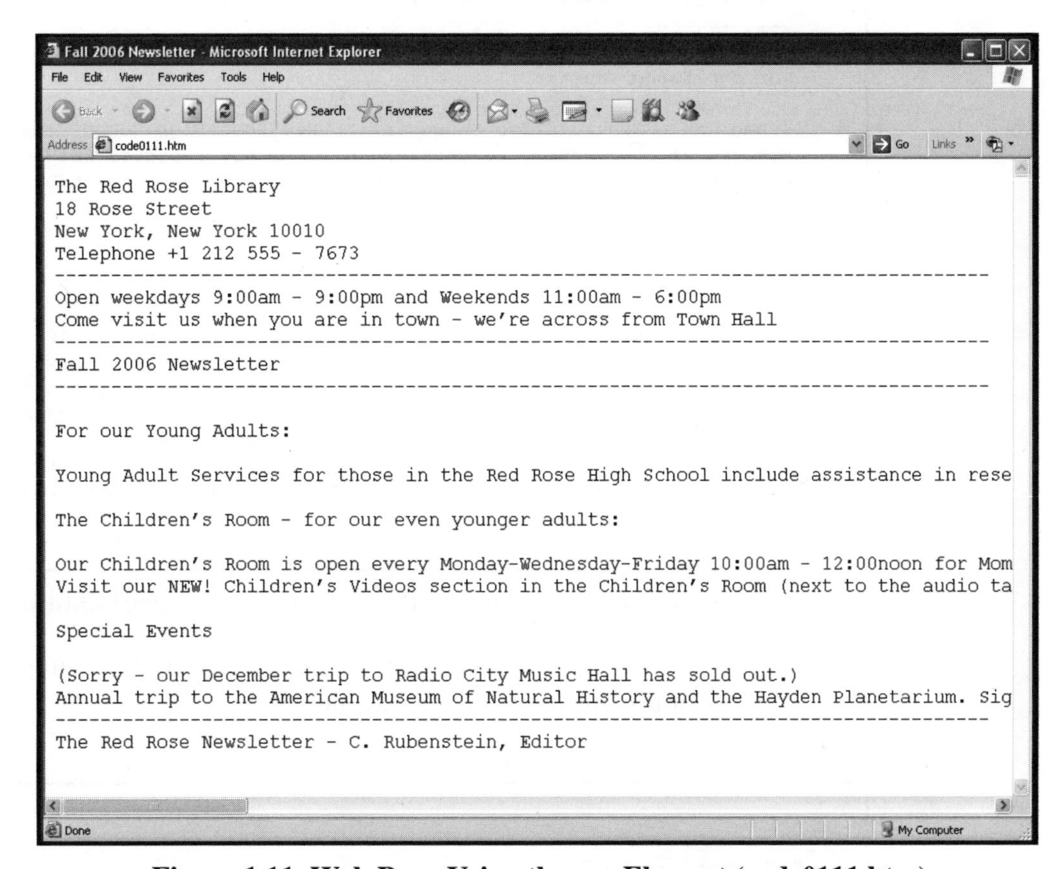

Figure 1.11. Web Page Using the pre Element (code0111.htm)

Adding the Paragraph Tag

Although the **pre** tag added some structure, as seen above, paragraphs tend to run wild, with the text running off the page to the left. Adding the paragraph tag **p** will take care of that problem. To make this change easier to visualize, remove the **</pre>** from the end of the file and place it just before the "For our Young Adults" line. Then add paragraph opening **<p>** and closing **</p>** tags at the start and end of each paragraph, and also around each "heading" to achieve a page that has text wrap to the size of the browser window. Note that most browsers do not require a closing paragraph tag, but as it is proper nesting, we will use it anyway. To make surrounding text by the paragraph tags easier to see in our HTML file, use the TAB key, as shown in the WordPad document in Figure 1.12. Recall that your browser ignores tabs and extra spaces.

```
Fall 2006 Newsletter
------------------------------------------------------------------------
------------
</pre>
For our Young Adults:
        <p>
Young Adult Services for those in the Red Rose High School include
assistance in researching your end-of-semester reports, science fair
projects, and in how to use online databases here in the Library.
        </p>
<p>
The Children's Room - for our even younger adults:
</p>
        <p>
Our Children's Room is open every Monday-Wednesday-Friday 10:00am -
12:00noon for Mommy and Me reading programs. Tuesdays we have our
invited reader session for kindergarten through second grade from
3:30pm - 4:30pm. Thursdays all children are invited to come in for
Computer and Internet instruction from 3:30pm - 5:30pm.
Visit our NEW! Children's Videos section in the Children's Room (next
to the audio tapes section) on Fridays after 3:30pm and borrow a video
for the weekend.
        </p>
```

Figure 1.12. Adding Paragraph Tags (code0113.htm)

Adding paragraph tags to our plain text file is a simple way to get our text file to look better, as shown in Figure 1.13.

```
The Red Rose Library
18 Rose Street
New York, New York 10010
Telephone +1 212 555 - 7673
-----------------------------------------------------------------------------------
Open weekdays 9:00am - 9:00pm and Weekends 11:00am - 6:00pm
Come visit us when you are in town - we're across from Town Hall
-----------------------------------------------------------------------------------
Fall 2006 Newsletter
-----------------------------------------------------------------------------------
```

For our Young Adults:

Young Adult Services for those in the Red Rose High School include assistance in researching your end-of-semester reports, science fair projects, and in how to use online databases here in the Library.

The Children's Room - for our even younger adults:

Our Children's Room is open every Monday-Wednesday-Friday 10:00am – 12:00noon for Mommy and Me reading programs. Tuesdays we have our invited reader session for kindergarten through second grade from 3:30pm – 4:30pm. Thursdays all children are invited to come in for Computer and Internet instruction from 3:30pm – 5:30pm. Visit our NEW! Children's Videos section in the Children's Room (next to the audio tapes section) on Fridays after 3:30pm and borrow a video for the weekend.

Figure 1.13. Effect of Paragraph Tags (code0113.htm)

Adding Center, Bold, and Underline Tags

Three elements that can be used to further enhance our Web page are named **center**, **b** for bold, and **u** for underline. Using these will give text the basic look found in the original document. Figure 1.14 shows in boldface the proper location of these elements, using both opening and closing tags as necessary to create our HTML file.

```
<body>
<pre> <center><b>
The Red Rose Library
18 Rose Street
New York, New York 10010
Telephone +1 212 555 - 7673</b>
----------------------------------------------------------------------
------------
Open weekdays 9:00am - 9:00pm and Weekends 11:00am - 6:00pm
Come visit us when you are in town - we're across from Town Hall
----------------------------------------------------------------------
------------
Fall 2006 Newsletter
----------------------------------------------------------------------
------------
</center> </pre> <u>
For our Young Adults: </u>
<p>
Young Adult Services for those in the Red Rose High School include
assistance in researching your end-of-semester reports, science fair
projects, and in how to use online databases here in the Library.
```

Figure 1.14. Styling with center, b, and u Elements (WordPad View of code0115.htm)

Figure 1.15 shows the improvement in the browser's display by using these elements to create our Web page.

Figure 1.15. Web Page with center, b, and u (code0115.htm)

Adding the Image Tag

Figure 1.16 shows how to place an image on the Web page (**code0117.htm**) where the rose graphic **img001.jpg** is stored in the images folder by using the **img** element.

```
<html>
<head>
      <title> Fall 2006 Newsletter </title>
</head>
<body>
<pre><center> <img src="images/img001.jpg" />  <b>
The Red Rose Library
18 Rose Street
New York, New York 10010
Telephone +1 212 555 - 7673</b>
```

Figure 1.16. Adding the img Tag (code0117.htm)

Figure 1.17 shows the resulting single rose graphic, centered on our almost complete Web page.

Figure 1.17. Web Page with Graphics (code0117.htm)

Creating Structure with Table Tags

Figure 1.18 shows the use of the table elements (**table**, **tr**, **td**) to add a second rose graphic to our Web page **code0119.htm,** where the rose graphics are positioned on either side of text by placing the graphics and text into a table that creates a single row with **tr** tag sets and three "columns" with **td** tag sets. Note that the table element has a width attribute as well as a border attribute. (This is a Wordpad window with highlighting to show the added table elements.)

Please don't concern yourself with the fact that you may have no idea what is happening here. A later chapter on tables will take all the magic out of creating these structures that give form to our pages.

```
<html>
<head>
      <title> Fall 2006 Newsletter </title>
</head>
<body>
<pre> <center>
<table width="640" border="1">
<tr>
<td> <center> <img src="images/img001.jpg" /> </center>
</td>
      <td>
<pre><center><b>
The Red Rose Library
18 Rose Street
New York, New York 10010
Telephone +1 212 555 - 7673</b>
      </td>
<td> <center><img src="images/img001.jpg" /> </center>
</td>
</tr>
</table>
```

Figure 1.18. Adding a Basic Table with a Border (code0119.htm)

Figure 1.19 shows the result of using these **table** elements, and the **border"1"** attribute allows us to see how the table is designed to show two rose graphics. Your initial Web page is almost finished; the borders just need to be adjusted.

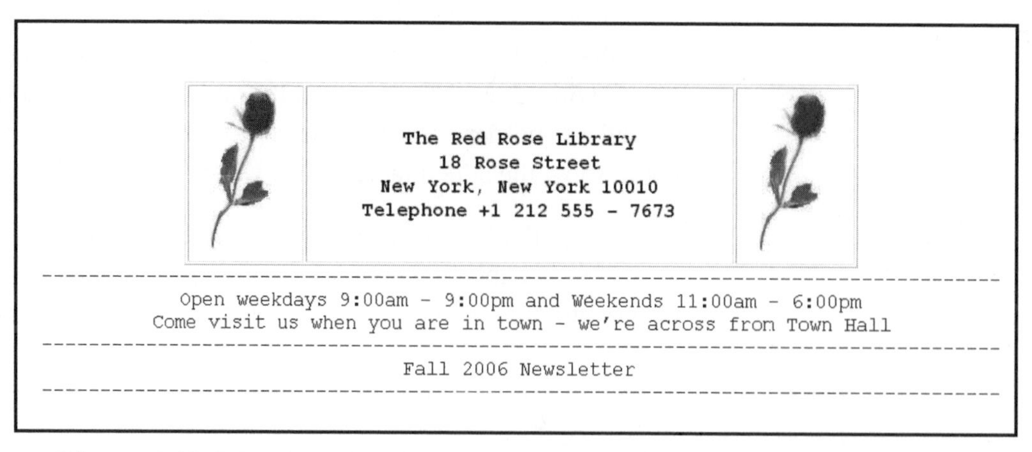

Figure 1.19. Web Page Table with Borders [**border=**"**1**"] (**code0119.htm**)

In Figure 1.20 the border attribute is changed to **border="0"** to show two rose graphics on either side of text, without showing the actual table structure border.

Figure 1.20. The Red Rose Web Page [**border=**"**0**"] (**code0120.htm**)

Of course, an even better result might occur if all of our text was included in the table, as shown in Figure 1.21. If you would like to investigate how this happens, please feel free to look at the code in the file **code0121.htm**. If you aren't ready yet, these techniques will be discussed in a later chapter.

The Red Rose Library
18 Rose Street
New York, New York 10010
Telephone +1 212 555 - 7673

Open weekdays 9:00am - 9:00pm and Weekends 11:00am - 6:00pm
Come visit us when you are in town - we're across from Town Hall

Fall 2006 Newsletter

For our Young Adults:

Young Adult Services for those in the Red Rose High School include assistance in researching your end-of-semester reports, science fair projects, and in how to use online databases here in the Library.

The Children's Room - for our even younger adults:

Our Children's Room is open every Monday-Wednesday-Friday 10:00am – 12:00noon for Mommy and Me reading programs. Tuesdays we have our invited reader session for kindergarten through second grade from 3:30pm – 4:30pm. Thursdays all children are invited to come in for Computer and Internet instruction from 3:30pm – 5:30pm. Visit our NEW! Children's Videos section in the Children's Room (next to the audio tapes section) on Fridays after 3:30pm and borrow a video for the weekend.

Special Events

(Sorry - our December trip to Radio City Music Hall has sold out.)
Annual trip to the American Museum of Natural History and the Hayden Planetarium. Sign up now! The bus to New York City will be leaving on Sunday January 14, 2007 at 6:00am. Trip cost is $50 which includes bus tickets, snacks on the bus, lunch at the Museum, and a souvenir. Be sure to make your reservation early as this is a fast sell out! The bus trip is sponsored by the Cultural Committee of the Friends of the Rose Library.

The Red Rose Newsletter - C. Rubenstein, Editor

Figure 1.21. Web Page with All Content (code0121.htm=redrose.htm)

Recap of HTML Elements Used in Chapter 1

Well, you made it. Hopefully most of your hair is on your head and your headache is subsiding, but you were able to create a simple html newsletter page for your library using **html**, **title**, **body**, **pre**, **p**, **center**, **b**, **u**, **img** and **table**, **tr**, and **td** tags! And this is only your first chapter.

What's Next?

In the next few chapters these basic HTML elements are reviewed in more detail. Examples of a variety of content-specific Web pages that you might want to have in your library are created as examples of their potential use. These examples use additional sets of HTML elements while showing you how to create Web pages you might want to use on your library's Web site.

Chapter 2

Hypertext Markup Language (HTML)

As we saw in Chapter 1, HTML elements have three parts to them: a starting tag with the element's name and a variety of special "attribute" commands that modify the default use of the element, inside a pair of angle brackets: **<tag ...>**; your encapsulated content; and an ending tag with a slash preceding the element's name only (even if attributes were described in the opening tag), also inside a pair of angle brackets **</tag>**:

Standard HTML Element Tag Set:

```
<tag attribute="value" attribute="value">
    your content
</tag>
```

The element's specific structural, presentational, and semantic behavior are predefined in your browser by document type definitions (DTDs). Attributes and styles can be added to the starting tag to modify the way elements re-create your document. Some elements don't surround content. These are called "empty tags." Standard HTML browsers do not require empty tags to have ending tags. For upward compatibility to XHTML or XML (Extensible Markup Language), empty element tags should have either a standard closing tag or a slash before the ending bracket of the opening tag: **<tag />**:

HTML Element Empty Tag Set:

<tag attribute="value" attribute="value"></tag>
or
<tag attribute="value" attribute="value" />

File-Naming Conventions

During the earliest years of the Web, servers used an 8.3 filename specification whereby all filenames were to have no more than eight alphanumeric characters plus a three-character extension to indicate the file's type or application. The filename "**document.doc**" indicates that the resource named "document" is a doc or Microsoft Word file. The original Web servers were programmed to return either a file named "**default.htm**" or the more common "**index.htm**" as the first, or default, opening page of a Web site. Today's Web servers and their operating systems permit files to have "long filenames" as well as long extensions. This has resulted in the most common opening page filename becoming "**index.html**" (note the four-character extension). It is now also common to have long filenames for HTML pages and the documents and graphic files they require.

As our Web sites will be relatively small to start with, and we don't know which server platform you will be using to mount your site, it is recommended that you keep to the original 8.3 file-naming standard:

8.3 File name: **file0124.htm ←Yes!**
Long File Names: **File Version 24.htm ← Don't use here!**

Uniform Resource Locators (URLs)

The URL for a Web server describes the method of transferring information (http, ftp, drive letter, and others), the Web server name, and the name of the file or resource to retrieve. The URL for our library is:

http://www.redroselibrary.com

URLs are a subset of the more general Uniform Resource Identifier (URI) scheme that permits linking to a file on a Web server using a full URL. Links to a file **img001.jpg** in an **images** folder on another Web server require the full (often called an absolute) URL:

http://www.redroselibrary.com/images/img001.jpg

Links to that file on your own Web server, located "relative" to the current (index) page, would not need the **http://www.redroselibrary.com/** preface and would look like

images/img001.jpg

Locations within a Web page (for example, **paragraph3**) are defined on that page with the anchor element **name** attribute. You would insert the **<a name="paragraph3">** tag just before the location on a relatively "long" Web page. When accessed, that portion of the page would be placed at the top of the browser's viewing window.

The location in the Web page where the **<a name="paragraph3">** tag would be located, in the file **filename.htm**, on the Web server **www.servername.com** is fully described using the following URL link:

http://www.servername.com/filename.htm#paragraph3

Now is a good time to remind you that Web server URLs and filenames are case sensitive. Be sure to carefully copy the upper- and lowercase letters of any Internet address.

Web Browsers

Before continuing the construction of more pages for your library, it is important to learn the names of and understand the four most common browsers. Three are graphical user interface (GUI) browsers (Microsoft's Internet Explorer, Mozilla's Firefox, and Netscape's Navigator) that give the common "what-you-see-is-what-you-get" (WYSIWYG) display and printout. The fourth is the Lynx, plain text, browser.

Currently the most popular, Microsoft's Internet Explorer browser, is available for download at **http://www.microsoft.com/downloads/search.aspx?displaylang=en**

The next most popular GUI browser, Mozilla's Firefox, is being used by a growing number of Web surfers. The Firefox browser default starting page is the Google Search page. Firefox is available for downloading at the Mozilla Web site (**http://www.mozilla.org**).

Firefox claims to yield faster downloads and higher security, and includes more spyware and pop-up blockers than either Microsoft's Internet Explorer or Netscape's Navigator (the third and least popular of the common GUI browsers, which is available at: **http://browser.netscape.com**). However, all browsers are nearly identical in their treatment of Web pages as well as in their application design and structure. Most browsers are available in Microsoft Windows, Macintosh, and Linux operating system flavors and in different languages, as can be discovered on the Web pages noted above.

Still available and useful for your sight-impaired patrons, Lynx is a text-based Web browser that creates an eighty-column text output. Note that as Lynx is a non-GUI browser, it ignores the preformat tag (**pre**) in our file. When using graphics, the **img** element tag (see Chapter 5) must include the **alt** attribute to provide information on what the graphic represents; otherwise, your patron will just get the filename of the graphic (e.g., **img001.jpg**) appearing, which probably won't give that person any idea what the image represents. Lynx browsers are often used in conjunction with voice synthesizers to enable blind and sight-impaired patrons to "see" Web pages. Lynx software can be downloaded from the distribution site hosted by the Internet Software Consortium (**http://lynx.isc.org**). There are several online services that let you see how your Web page would look viewed in the Lynx browser. The Red Rose Library Web page in Figure 1.21 was processed by the service at **http://www.delorie.com/web/lynxview.html** with the resulting nongraphic Web page output that would be "seen" by a Lynx browser looking like Figure 2.1.

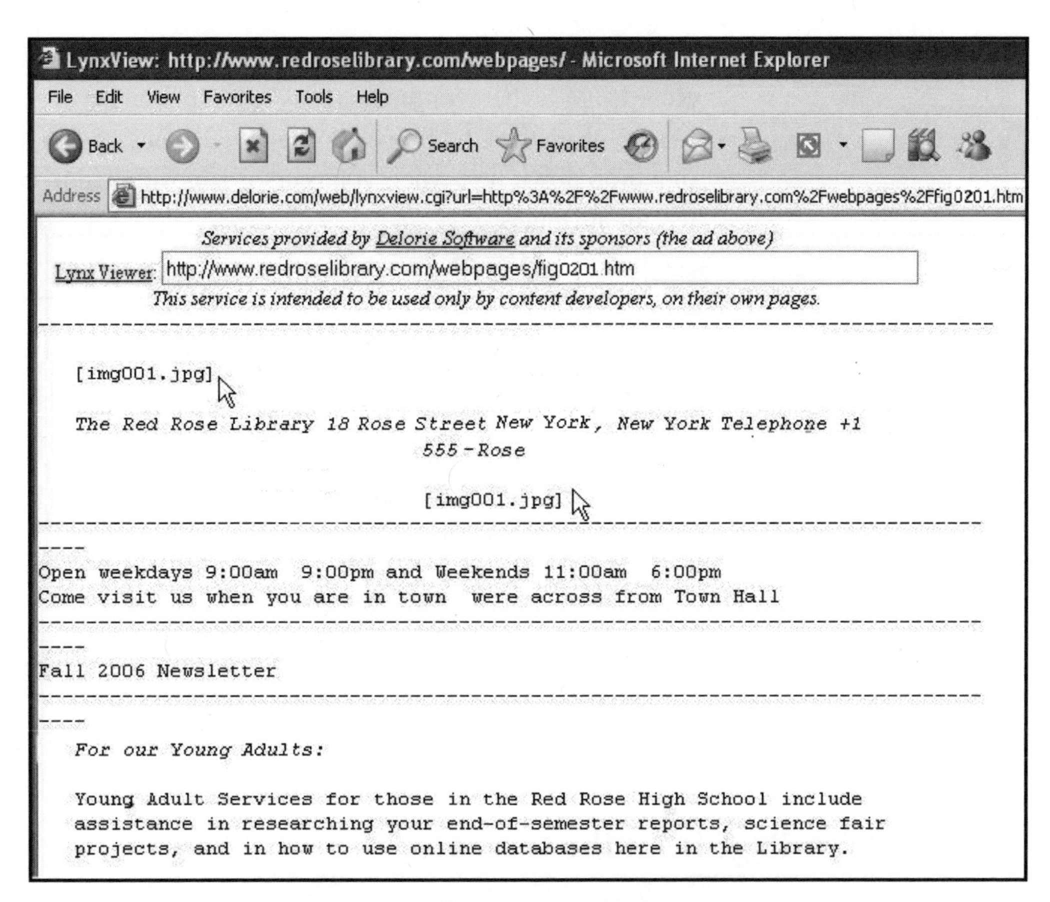

Figure 2.1. Lynx View of Figure 1.21, Red Rose Library Newsletter

Figure 2.2 shows the code snippet where an **alt** attribute was added with the value **"Red Rose Logo"**.

```
<html>
<head>
      <title> Fall 2006 Newsletter </title>
</head>
<body>
<pre>
<center>
<table width="640" border="0">
<tr>
<td>
      <img align="right" height="100" alt="Red Rose Logo"
src="images/img001.jpg" /> </td>
```

Figure 2.2. Inserting the alt Attribute (**code0121.htm** to **code0203.htm**)

With this code change, the Lynx browser displays the value **"Red Rose Logo"** wherever the image is found on the page, as shown in Figure 2.3. With the GUI browsers, the **alt** attribute value normally appears in a drop down box when your cursor is positioned over graphics that use **alt** attributes.

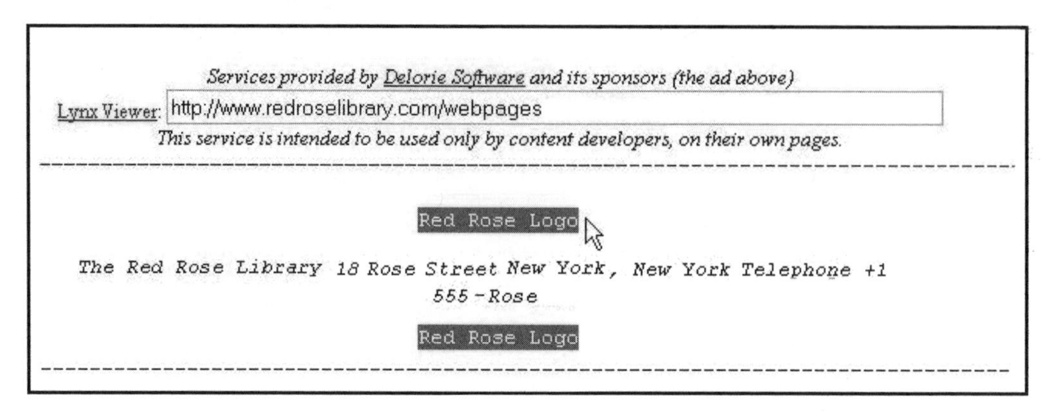

Figure 2.3. Lynx View of Image (code0203.htm)

Saving a Web Page from the Internet

It is presumed that you are connected to the Internet via modem or network card through either an ISP or directly to the Internet using a high-speed leased line connection. What happens next, happens in the computer or server, and you need not understand all the steps. You will have an opportunity to refer back should you need to review the information. With the options for libraries increasing, it is suggested that you check with your IT staff, or the computer vendor that created your Internet connections, to see how your specific facility is constructed.

Open your browser and type a URL (e.g., **redroselibrary.com**) into your browser's Address line. Your browser will automatically add the **http://** access preface, and if not already there, the **www** URL preface that indicates the request is not to your computer's local drives (as we'll be doing when we create our own pages), but to a Web server accessed using the hypertext transfer protocol (http) on the World Wide Web at the full address (**http://www.redroselibrary.com**). In a matter of seconds, your browser displays the Web page you requested in its window. But what really happened?

A Web site's opening page is normally **index.htm** or **index.html** unless otherwise specified (e.g., **http://www.redroselibrary.com/1stpage.html**). Your browser initially sends a request to the Web server named by the URL or address name of a Web site (e.g., **www.redroselibrary.com**) requesting the default or specified file. The server sends that file to your browser using the hypertext transfer protocol (http), then the browser assembles, formats, and displays the file on your computer monitor according to established HTML rules that are already stored inside its program.

If you click View on your browser's taskbar and then select Source, you will be shown the contents of the displayed page's HTML coding. Even if your displayed Web page uses several pictures, sound, or other multimedia files, all you will see in this file is plain text. Portions of that text are surrounded by special markup codes, the HTML element tags. Looking more closely, in the areas where you have graphics on the Web page, you'll see several "**<img ...**" markup tags. On "reading" these markup codes, your browser will actually request additional files one at a time until all images in the HTML file are stored in a temporary Internet file folder on your computer. Then your browser will assemble all requested files and display them as a formatted Web page.

As you probably already know, you can save someone else's online Web page, and all its related files, by clicking on Files on your browser's taskbar and then selecting Save As. Saving a Web page this way normally creates a set of long filename files with an **htm** or **html** extension (e.g., **index.htm**), as well as a folder with all the associated files (e.g., **index_files**) needed to re-create a Web page for offline use (without going onto the Internet to reconstruct the display). This file set is all that is needed to view that Web page any time, anywhere. (Be sure to get permission if you want to reuse the graphics or content of someone else's Web pages.)

Web Site Design

As there is no standard for good Web site design, we will define the one we used in Chapter 1 to make it easier for you to put your site together and to reduce the number of graphics files. First we'll open a new folder, give it an eight-character long name, say **webpages,** and place it on the desktop so you can access it quickly.

Good Web page design suggests reducing the space you use for files on your server by having only one instance of a file on your Web site. The easiest way to do this would be to have a separate folder, with all of your images, which can be shared by your Web pages. We will use this **images** folder for all graphic, audio, or other files. As we plan on using style sheets to give a uniform look and feel to our Web pages, we will also want to have a **styles** folder. In this design all HTML pages would be in the **webpages** folder, which would also have **images** and **styles** folders. If you wish, you can include other semantically named folders for other specific files, such as a **pdf** or **extras** folder or a **text** folder. Figure 2.4 shows the "tree" diagram of this type of folder or directory structure.

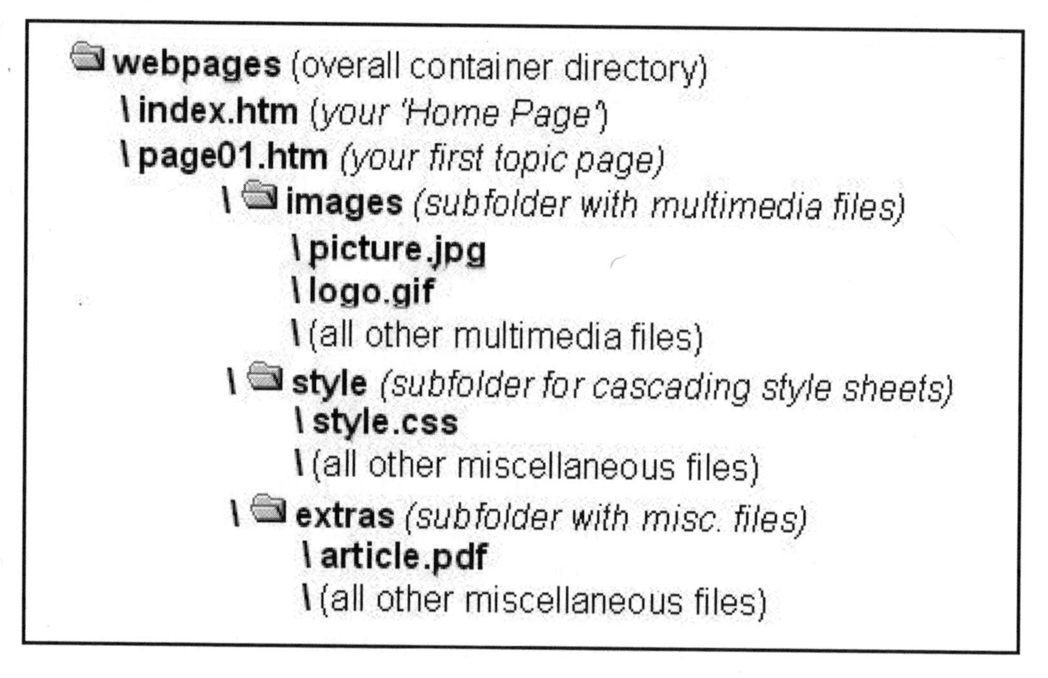

Figure 2.4. Suggested Web Site Directory Tree Structure

Figure 2.5 shows the Windows Explorer view of the suggested standard folder or directory structure.

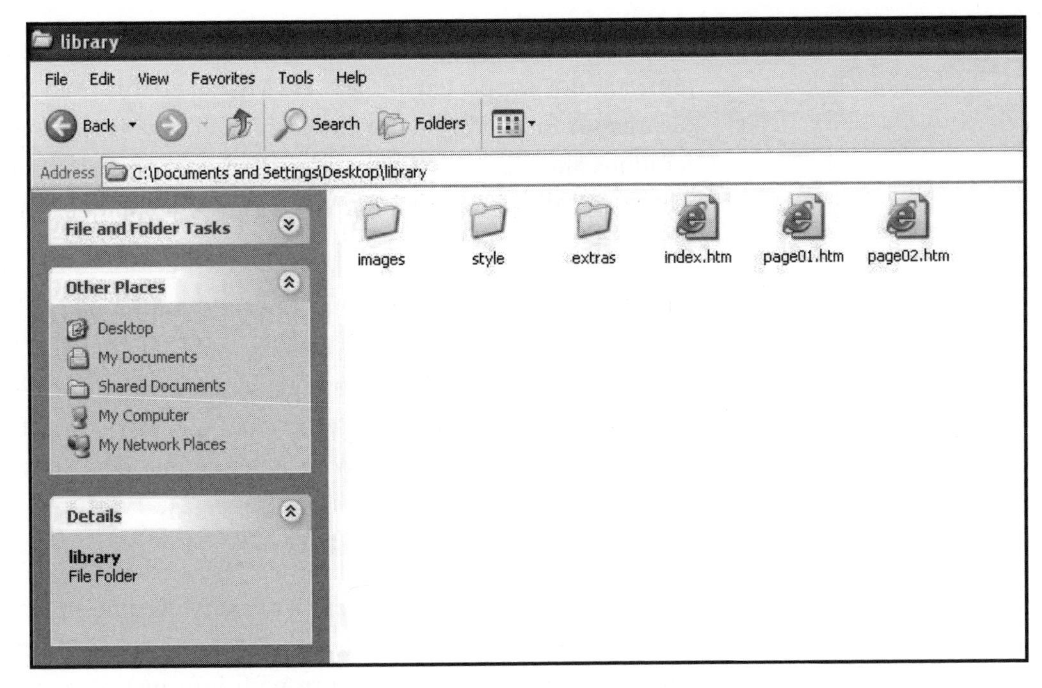

Figure 2.5. Suggested Web Site Windows™ Folder Structure

About Browsers and HTML Standards

Today's browsers bring your Web pages to life. Browsers are a combination of graphical user interfaces, protocol interpreters, and markup language interpreters. Graphical user interfaces are designed to display images (such as **jpg** and **gif**, which will be discussed in Chapter 5 in the coverage of the **img** element). The browser is an interpreter for a variety of **ftp**, **http**, and other Internet protocols. It functions as a markup language interpreter based on a built-in set of rules for formatting text and other digital objects (such as graphics, animation, sound, and movies) according to standardized rules.

Document Type Definitions (DTD)

Each browser's built-in DTD rule set includes decoding rules for HTML elements, their common default attributes, and display styles. Modification of these rules is accomplished by using inline style commands (attributes) or style sheet techniques.

Some browsers do not recognize or display all standard HTML elements and others don't recognize some of the attributes of some of the elements. Still other browsers have their own set of special HTML extensions not supported by the HTML standards. We'll review some techniques for modifying the look and feel of your page using style declarations, in-file embedded style definitions, and external style files. These are all cascading style sheet (CSS) techniques that overlay the DTD rules in your browser.

HTML document type definitions are composed of element tag sets that compose a variety of levels (e.g., HTML Level 4.01) and types (Strict, Transitional, and Frameset) as defined by the W3C or World Wide Web Consortium, an international industry consortium dedicated to building consensus about Web technologies. The latest W3C HTML 4.01 recommendations (dated December 24, 1999) may be viewed at **http://www.w3.org/TR/html401/**

As an aside, Extensible HyperText Markup Language (XHTML) is, as its name suggests, an extension of the basic HTML rules. XHTML was designed specifically for use with information appliances such as cell phones and PDAs (Portable Digital Assistants), to create Web pages that look good on a small screen. The Extensible Markup Language (XML), on the other hand, goes one step further, allowing you to define new and unique document type definitions (yes, new HTML tags!) that supplement the built-in HTML standards. Finding aids and specialty markup language DTDs for music and science are designed using customized XML elements that define the way your browser will treat specially tagged content. Once these specialized XML DTDs are accepted in a particular field, they become de facto standards for specific Web page uses.

Top Ten Library Home Page Links

Although this chapter is mostly background and setup suggestions, we don't want to leave it without at least showing you a hypothetical library home page that contains the top ten links that every library should consider having on its home page. Each of these would link to at least one more HMTL page on your library's Web site.

Figure 2.6 shows a possible home page design with the top ten links called out in it. In later chapters you will see how these linked pages are constructed.

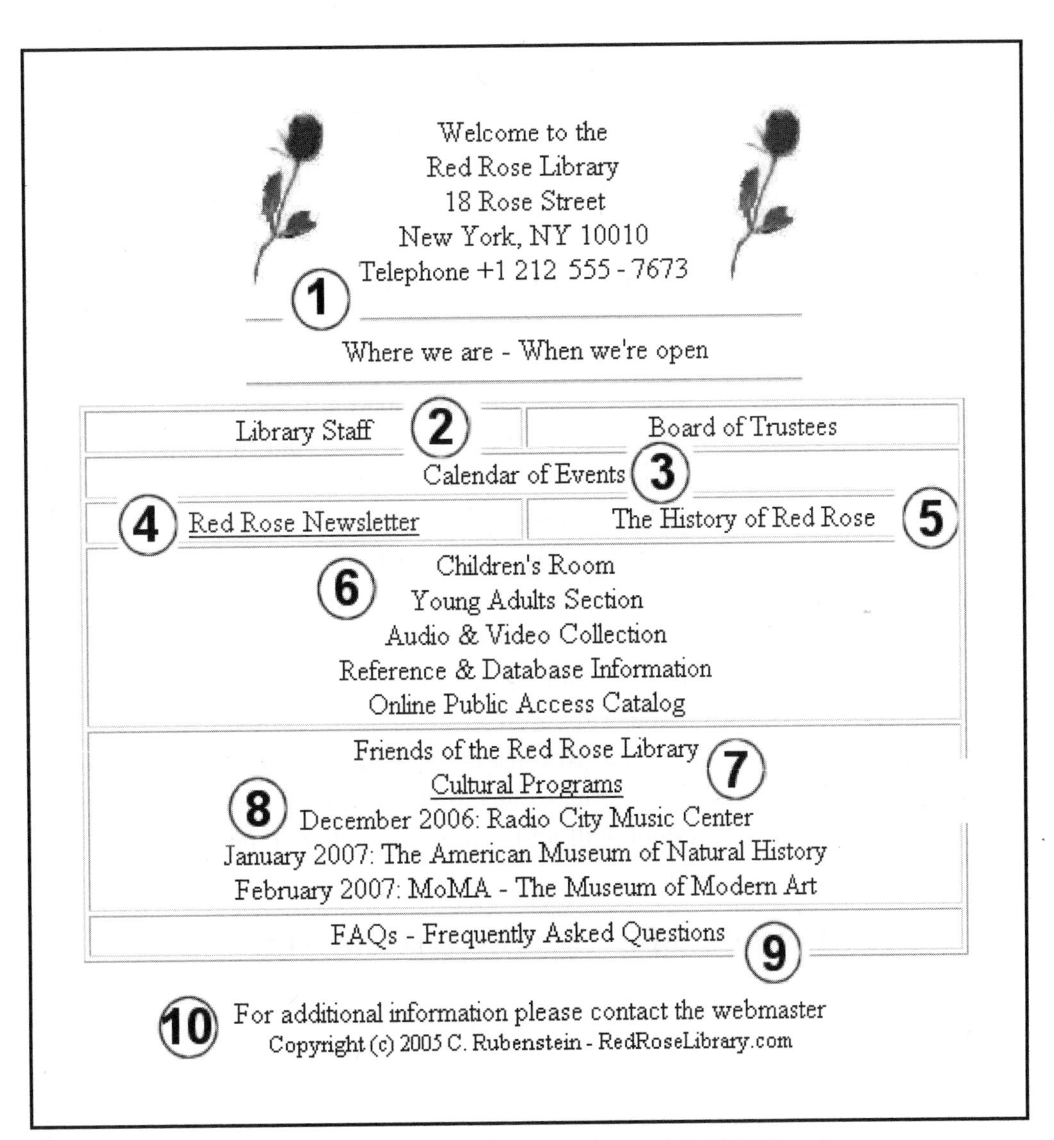

Figure 2.6. Library Home Page (code0206.htm)

This home page file (**code0206.htm**) will be a work in progress for a final home page and is a bit advanced for now. Although the page is pretty bland, with only a pair of rose images to brighten it up now, we will see it come to life as we go through the next chapters using HTML elements. As we create the underlying Web pages, we will come back to this page to link the new files into this page.

Note that the newsletter link is highlighted in blue and underlined (HTML link standard). In Chapter 1 you already put together a basic HTML newsletter page (Figure 1.21) and thus have already created, and can link to, an HTML version of the fourth item in these top ten page links. Please note that there is no hierarchy intended by the order in which the items are discussed.

1. Location and Hours of Operation

If you build it they may come, but they need to know where to go and when you are open!

2. Library Staff and Board of Trustees Contact Information

As library professionals we already know that communication is the key to keeping information flowing between staff and patrons. Be sure to include your staff's "@yourlibrary.com" e-mail addresses, but not any personal information. Some pages, to avoid the problem of Web tools used by e-mail address sellers, spell out the e-mail addresses. Using "webmaster_at_yourlibrary.com" is one example of how this might be done. Don't forget your board of trustees. Post public information about the board, its members, and its meetings. Note that your board is usually made up of volunteers (even if they may be elected) who devote much of their efforts to making it possible for the e-library to grow and succeed. Reward them with their own Web page and photo galleries. Don't release any of their personal information, but a library-based e-mail will let them be in touch with patrons, too.

3. Calendar of Events (Keep It Current!)

Here's where you keep all the current programs on one page so that your patrons can plan their lives around your library.

4. Your Library Newsletter

Posting your library's current newsletter, as well as an archive of past issues, will let your patrons (as well as your board and staff!) plan for the future based on your past programs. Newsletters are often posted in **doc**, **html**, and/or **pdf** formats. Most newsletters are created using a word processing program, like Word, but many librarians don't like the fact that a downloaded word processed file could be altered and thus no longer be a true archiving tool.

You saw in Chapter 1 some of the basic techniques for creating an HTML version of your newsletter. Unfortunately, it requires some effort to create an HTML rendering of even a simple newsletter. **pdf** files can be created using word processor plug-in text to **pdf** file converters that preserve the look and feel of your original newsletter using one of several Adobe products, such as Adobe Print Shop and Adobe Acrobat, or those of other vendors. Some of these **pdf** file creation applications are free; others can cost as much as $300. Either way, the freely available, multiplatform Adobe Reader software can be used to read any standard **pdf** file. The latest version of Adobe Reader (currently 7.0.5) for any platform can be downloaded from **http://www.adobe.com/products/acrobat/readstep2_allversions.html**

5. History of Your Library

A brief overview with major milestones reached and major capital programs underway will give your patrons an insight into your library's importance to the neighborhood and its rightful place as your community's information resource and provider. Don't forget to include a photo archive of its construction or original buildings and personnel.

6. List of Departments

Once they know what programs you have that they want to be involved with, let your patrons contact the staff person in charge so that they can volunteer, or register for your activities.

7. Friends of the Library

If you have one, your FOL group should also get its fifteen minutes of fame. Offer the Friends the same benefits of patron communication you give to your board members.

8. Trips and Special Programs

Many librarians have special programs or sponsor trips; some use them for fund-raising. Place these prominently on your home page so your patrons can easily sign up for them. You might even consider a photo gallery archive for past programs.

9. FAQs

Frequently Asked Questions should be online in one place. Accumulate these and place them on one or more pages for online access.

This way your patrons won't need to go into the building to find out answers to common questions, such as:

How can I get (or renew) a library card?

What are the policies for on-site computer use?

How can I get a Web e-mail address?

What databases can I access from home?

How can I get answers to reference questions?

10. Webmaster Contact Information and Copyright

Again, with communication in mind, you should include a line at the bottom of your home page that will permit the person viewing it to e-mail you or the person helping with your Web site and also to understand that the page(s) are copyrighted.

Web Page Graphics

As you probably recall from your own searching of Web sites, finding what you want easily and quickly is important. Also important are your Web page's graphics. Since you won't be spending time doing original artwork, you may wish to subscribe to one of several online and CD-ROM clip art collections such as Clipart.com. Their service is reasonable, at $49.95 per year. For more information and to order, check the Web site at **http://www.clipart.com**

Purchasing a clip art collection, such as PrintMaster®, provides tens of thousands of images on CDs or DVDs and is often easier than doing online searches. The software allows you to browse the collection offline, and you can also browse the included print catalog of images. PrintMaster® is only one of Broderbund's graphics and publishing products, which include ClickArt® and The Print Shop®. All have online access to even more artwork. For more information and to order, check out the Web site at **http://www.broderbund.com**

Another vendor, Jupiterimage's Animation Factory, hosts an online subscription service for a wide variety of clip art and animated graphics, backgrounds, and PowerPoint™ templates. Memberships are available from $19.95 per month to $99.95 per year. Check out the Web site at **http://www.animationfactory.com/brain/home.cgi**

Also online are a variety of vendors for what are known as stock photos; professionally photographed standard images of babies and workers, farms and cities, tricycles and airplanes, and everything in between. iStockphoto™ provides a nonsubscription service that permits you to upload and download royalty-free stock images. Each download is $1 for low resolution, $2 for medium resolution, or $3 for high resolution stock photos. For more information, go to **http://www.istockphoto.com**

What's Next?

In this chapter we focused on the "**8.3**" naming convention and explained the document type definition (DTD). We also addressed the HTML element and saw how the **alt** attribute can be used to add a title to your **img** elements.

In Chapter 3, the discussion of the process of more completely defining HTML concepts and elements and linking them to HTML Web pages will give you the understanding of how to work with the various elements you used with a "leap of faith" in Chapter 1. Some readers will decide to skip over Chapter 3 now and return to it at a later date to find out how to incorporate header information in their HTML pages.

Chapter 3

The HTML Document and Header Information

From time to time, even in the best of worlds, we have to "pay our dues" in order to go on with what we would rather be doing. In Chapter 3 you will be paying your dues by looking into the structure of an HTML document. It isn't glitzy. It isn't exciting. In fact, this chapter, which covers basic HTML elements and the structure of Web pages, is quite boring.

Those of you who just want to "just do it," please feel free to skip this chapter and jump ahead to Chapter 4. Return some night when you can't fall asleep and review the finer details of HTML's defining elements described herein.

The HTML document is your Web page. Ideally, the page you create using text editors or high-end software programs should work on all browsers. That concept is called *interoperability* and it is the essence of HTML's design. Unfortunately, technology seldom functions ideally, and not all browsers interpret HTML elements the same way. Regardless of what browser they normally view Web pages on, good Web page designers will test the formatting of their pages on at least three browsers: Mozilla's Firefox, Netscape's Navigator, and Microsoft's Internet Explorer.

The basic HMTL page and its header have little to show you. They do their work behind the scene. If you can bear with us until the next chapter, you'll have the information you need to create Web page headers and be ready to add content and display text on your page. To create effective Web pages, it is important to understand tags, elements, and attributes as well as the basic HTML file structure, fonts, and color values.

HTML Tags, Elements, and Attributes

Each HTML "command" is an element type. To provide for future upgradeability to XHTML or XML, each element type must be written in *lower case*. As we saw in Chapter 2, an HTML "tag" consists of the element name placed inside a pair of angle brackets. For example, the opening tag for HTML **preformat** element is **<pre>**. The **preformat** element's closing tag is placed after the text or object the element operates on. The closing tag has a slash preceding the element name in angle brackets, in this case **</pre>**.

Opening tags may include one or more optional "attributes" that stylize the element for the specific set of text they enclose. In Chapter 1 we saw that the **table** element used the **border** attribute. Its opening tag was **<table border="1">**, indicating that the table was to be displayed with a one-pixel thick border. Note that the element attributes defined in the opening tag are NOT included in the closing tag. Thus, although the opening tag for a table with border attributes includes the **border** attribute, its closing tag does not and is simply **</table>**.

"Nesting" is the technique of using tags inside other tags; such as bold inside center, for better styling of our content. We need to be careful to NOT "overlap" tags or we may end up confusing the browser into prematurely closing tags we still want open. It is good practice when you open a series of nested tags (**<tag1><tag2><tag3>**) to close them in the reverse order (**<tag3><tag2><tag1>**), as you'll see below.

Several HTML elements do not actually surround content (e.g., the line break **br**, horizontal rule **hr**, and image **img** elements). These "empty tags" do not require a closing tag, but to maintain upward compatibility, empty tags will be "self-closed" by adding a space after the element name or last attribute and then a slash in their *opening* tag **
. The **img element, for example, is an empty tag that also *must* have attributes inside its opening tag to describe the location or source (**src**) of the graphic file. The rose graphic stored as **img001.jpg** in the **images** subfolder was placed on our page using the tag:

<img src="images/img001.jpg" />

The element's name, which major elements the element can contain and/or where the element might be located, and the elements' common attributes will be noted in the text before each example. Often, in the description of the element, information is included on typical uses and values of these attributes.

Well-Formed Markup Tags

Good markup language practice encapsulates content between "nonoverlapping" opening and closing element tags. Such proper nesting of tags is essential in well-formed pages that can easily migrate to XML, as well as to avoid confusing the browser. Examples of good and improper nesting are:

Well Formed, Proper Nesting of Tags ← *USE THIS STRUCTURE!*
<tag1> stuff, stuff, stuff ←**Open Tag1**
<tag2> text, text, text ←**Open Tag2**
</tag2> ← **Close Tag2** ← *Good Form!*
</tag1> ← **Close Tag1**
Overlapped, Improper Nesting of Tags ← NEVER use this!
<tag1> stuff, stuff, stuff ←**Open Tag1**
<tag2> text, text, text ←**Open Tag2**
</tag1> ← **Close Tag1** ← ***BAD, Tag2 still OPEN!***
</tag2> ← **Close Tag2**

In the second case, **tag1** and **tag2** are turned "on" and then **tag2** turned "off" before **tag1** has been turned "off", resulting in an unreliable interpretation of what you want the browser to do.

Basic HTML File Structure

Quite often, when you download an HTML file from someone else's Web site, your browser will review the file and add a line declaring the **DOCTYPE** of the file. This information is unnecessary for our current needs and there is no reason to include a **DOCTYPE** declaration in your Web pages. Your browser will figure out what HTML type and level you are using without this extra line.

Once you have provided your HTML document with the root **html** element opening and closing tags, it is time to consider the overall structure of your HTML document. HTML documents have three specific sections, the root, the head, and the body.

As noted earlier, the HTML **root** element surrounds the entire document. As can be seen in Figure 3.1, the **root <html>** is followed by the **head** element and section, and the **head** section is followed by the **body** element and section. The **head** section needs to be closed **</head>** before opening the body section. The **body** section should be closed **</body>** when you have finished adding content to the body of your document. Then the **root** element is closed **</html>** to fully close your document. The **head** contains page definition information and other metadata (the data about the data in your document). Most of the elements that can be found in the **head** are shown in Figure 3.1. The majority of your page's content, and all of the other HTML elements, are found in the **body** of your markup file. Each element must be written in lowercase and have a closing tag to be upward compatible with XHTML and XML.

```
<!DOCTYPE ... >                              ← (Optional declaration line)
<html>                                       ← Root element opening tag
  <head>                                     ← Head element opening tag
      <title> Web Page Title </title>        ← Title element tags and content
      <base ... />                           ← Base element empty tag
      <basefont ... />                       ← Basefont element empty tag
      <meta ... />                           ← Meta element empty tag(s)
      <link ... />                           ← Link element pointing to other files
  </head>                                    ← Head element closing tag
  <body>                                     ← Body element opening tag
      Your content would continue written here, left to right, in English.
  </body>                                    ← Body element closing tag
</html>                                      ← Root element closing tag
```

Figure 3.1. Structure of an HTML Document

In Chapter 1 we saw the HTML model structure above used in Figures 1.6, 1.8, 1.10, 1.14, 1.16, and 1.18. Figure 1.10, for example, is repeated here as Figure 3.2.

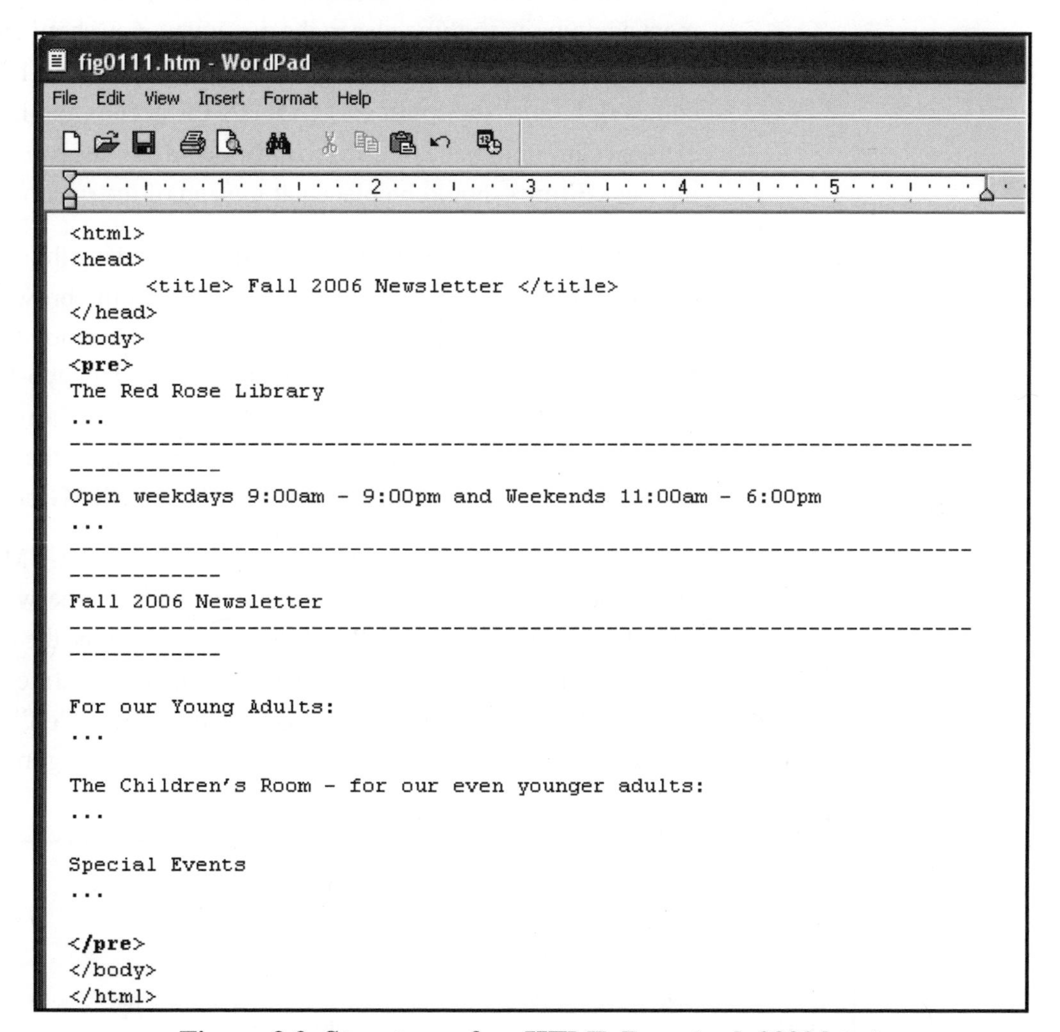

Figure 3.2. Structure of an HTML Page (code0302.htm)

Although at the end of your Web page file, when your browser runs out of content, it automatically closes all open elements, the closing **body </body>**, and **html </html>** tags should be used to properly close your HTML documents.

HTML Elements and Their Attributes

Following the XML concept that the first (outermost) or "root" element contains everything else in the document, you should always begin and end your HTML document with the **html** element. The **<html>** tag comes right after the (optional) **DOCTYPE** declaration line. The **html** element can contain the **head** and **body** elements. The root element closing tag **</html>** should be placed at the end of the document.

The default **html** element can be modified, using the attributes **lang** (language) and/or **dir** (text direction) to inform the browser what language you are using and which document type definition (DTD) should be written into the browser's HTML rules area. The two-letter ISO639 Standard native language default HTML attribute is **lang="en"** (English). For other languages, additional information on the ISO639 standard can be found at **http://www.w3.org/WAI/ER/IG/ert/iso639.htm**

As noted earlier, to assure upward migration to XHTML and XML, all attribute values are enclosed in quotes. Unless otherwise noted, the default text direction is **dir="ltr"** (left to right). Thus, the opening **html** tag, with either the default tag **<html>**, or the fully defined element tag with its default attributes called out, **<html lang="en" dir="ltr">**, would result in the standard English text display of Figure 3.3.

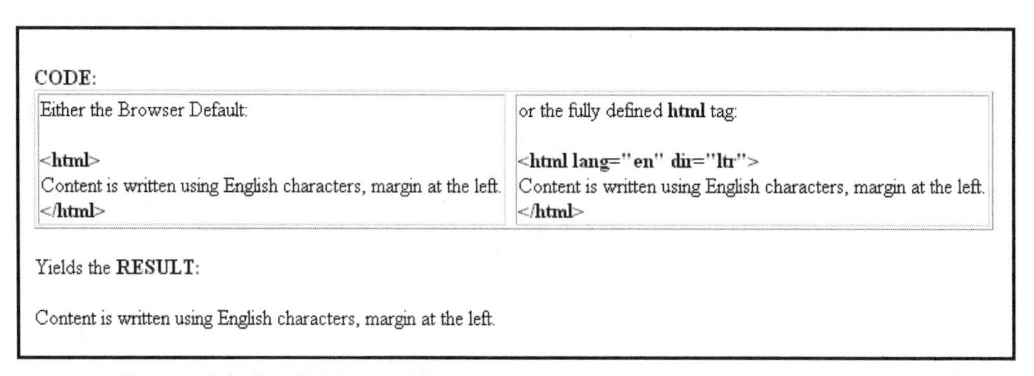

Figure 3.3. Default html Tag and Its Attributes (code0303.htm)

HTML Head Section

The Head Section of your document includes the **head** and **title** elements. Most of the element types contained in the **head** portion of your

HTML document are empty elements, that is, although they may have several attributes and can be a rich source of information for your document, they do not encapsulate anything. In the **head** only the **title** element surrounds content with opening and closing tags. Thus *you* won't see anything happen differently, with or without these other head section tags! Your *browser* will be given information it needs to go to another Web site or to set the font or URL for your page, or a *search engine* will be told what contents you have on your Web page.

Document Header Information

The **head** element encloses the header information in your HTML document. The **head** contains general information about the document and can contain the **title**, **base**, **basefont**, **meta**, **link**, **isindex**, and **nextid** elements. The **head** is located inside the root **html** element.

With the singular exception that the **title** element displays the title in your browser's title window, elements in the document's **head** are ***not*** displayed when the Web page is displayed. Any number of element tags (above) can appear in the **head**, in any order, but only the **title** element is typically used. In the future, it might be expected that use of the **meta** element to describe the Dublin Core description of your Web page would become more widespread as cataloging of Web pages becomes necessary.

Document Title Element

The **title** element specifies the title of your document that is displayed in the browser's title window. It can contain only character data (CDATA), that is, no other tags or elements can be in your title. Although not required to be included in your Web page, the **title** tag must be inside the **head** section if you are using it. When you do not use the title element, the browser will display the full URL and filename of your page, including the path, instead of just displaying the page's title. We already saw this in Chapter 1, in Figure 1.6, without the **title** tag, and in Figure 1.9 with the **title** tag. To add a **title** tag to your Web page, insert the **title** tags and its content inside the **head** of your document:

```
<html>
    <head>
<title>Your Library's Home Page</title>
<!-- Other head elements go here -->
    </head>
<!-- The rest of the document goes here -->
</html>
```

Figure 3.4 shows the contents of a file **code0304.htm** that uses the above code. While this file yields only a blank Web page, it demonstrates how using a **title** tag makes your page more attractive and defines its intended contents as that of "**Your Library's Home Page**."

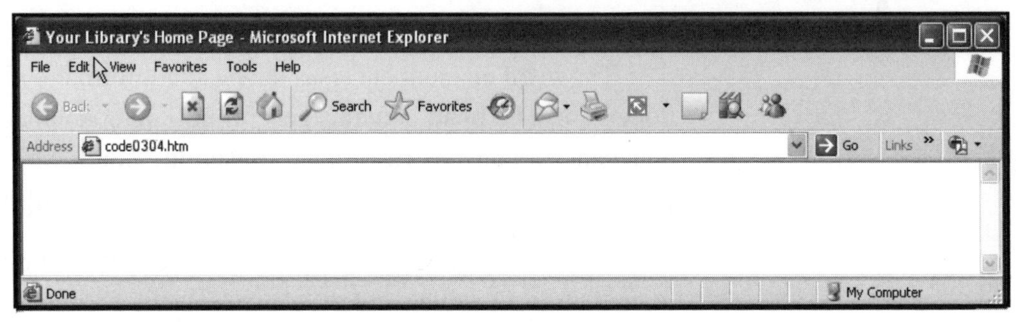

Figure 3.4. Browser Showing Page Title (code0304.htm)

Your Web Site's Base URL

The **base** element is an empty element that is placed inside the **head** and does not require a closing tag. It uses the **href** attribute to specify the server and folder address of the current document. If the **base** element is absent, the browser assumes the **href** addresses in your HTML document point to documents on the same machine. If your Web site is in the folder **lib** on the server **www.yourserver.org**, the base tag would look like:

```
<base href="http://www.yourserver.org/lib/" />
```

Default Fonts for Your Page

The **basefont** element is also an empty element that does not require a closing tag. You can use it inside the **head** section to set the default font characteristics for all the text in your HTML document. You can override the standard default text attributes for **size**, **color**, and **face**, or even a **basefont** default attribute by using **font** tags around specific text. This technique is described in Chapter 4, with the more elegant style sheets method described in Chapter 6. Although either technique will change the appearance of specific text inside of your document, please note that both the **basefont** and **font** tags that specify size color and face attributes will be phased out in lieu of **style** sheet definitions in future HTML versions.

The **basefont**'s **size** attribute can be used to reset default font values from **1** through **7** to override the default "**3**" value. You can also use + or – numbers to change the font size *relative* to the current font size.

The **color** attribute can override the default "**black**" by changing the text default **color** to "**red**" with a "**6**" font **size** **(e.g., <basefont color="red" size="6" />**. The **font face** attribute permits changing the face (e.g., Arial, Times, etc.) using a comma-separated list of font names. Attributes can be in any order and do not all have to be listed.

Defining Color Values

The sixteen common color values are defined by either their color name or their RGB (red-green-blue), two-digit hexadecimal (Hex) values, preceded by the pound sign (#). Two-digit hexadecimal numbers are used to describe the "amount" of each color using the sixteen Hex numbers (0, 1, 2, 3, 4, 5 ,6 ,7, 8, 9, a, b, c, d, e, and f) for 256 shades of each basic color. The color "**white**" contains the full-color spectrum as its two-digit Hex number equals all the red, all the green, and all the blue we can display, or **#ffffff**. At the other extreme is "**black**" (the absence of color), or **#000000**. Pure red contains only red, no green and no blue and thus has the value **#ff0000**. The full set of hexadecimal values from black to white (**#000000** through **#ffffff**) can be used to generate a 24-bit color map with 16.7 million colors!

Note that when the green hexadecimal value is **ff** and red and blue are both **00**, the resulting color **#00ff00** is NOT green but lime (green being rendered by **#008000**), as is illustrated in the sixteen common Web page colors and their RGB values:

Standard Web Page Color Values:

black = #000000	**navy = #000080**	**blue = #0000ff**	**green = #008000**
teal = #008080	**lime = #00ff00**	**aqua = #00ffff**	**maroon = #800000**
purple = #800080	**olive = #808000**	**gray = #808080**	**silver = #c0c0c0**
red = #ff0000	**fuchsia= #ff00ff**	**yellow = #ffff00**	**white = #ffffff**

Unfortunately, color palettes are not consistent between browsers. To help you decide how best to colorize your Web pages, use a color chart or **body** attribute creator service like that offered by

Color Chart Service, **http://www.visibone.com** or

Online Color Chooser, **http://www.clipartconnection.com/colorchooser.php**

Not only will these pages let you see the colors in use, but they will also give the specific **#rrggbb** numeric code, and show how the colors show up on your actual browser. You should be aware that how your browser looks does not guarantee how your page will look to patrons with other browsers, especially if they have alternate color palettes that change the appearance of these codes installed on them.

Describing Your Page with Metadata

The **meta** element is another empty element that hides inside the **head** and does not require a closing tag. This element allows you to include a variety of metadata (the data about your data) in your Web page. The **meta** tag is particularly interesting as it can be used to supply lots of data about your page in the form of descriptors and keywords that search engines find particularly easy to work with. In effect, by using **meta** tags one can look at a Web page as if it were a book and describe the ownership and creator of the page, and other characteristics of your page.

Good practice suggests libraries and information centers *should* be using the Dublin Core ISO Standard 15836 metadata elements (**http://www.dublincore.org/**) to identify the content of their Web pages, using the **name** attribute to describe the specific Dublin Core

(DC) parameter and the **content** attribute to provide keywords for that parameter. The suggested DC metadata set in a head might include one or more of the typical Dublin Core **meta** tags shown here in the **head** section of an HTML document:

```
<head> ...
    <meta name="dc.title" content="Red Rose Library Web Site" />
    <meta name="dc.creator" content="Charles Rubenstein" />
    <meta name="dc.subject" lang="en" content="Library Web Site" />
    <meta name="dc.description" content="Red Rose Library Web Site" />
    <meta name="dc.date" content="05/05/05" />
... </head>
```

The full Dublin Core Metadata Initiative (DCMI) Specification can be found at **http://dublincore.org/documents/dces/** If all the **meta** element tag accomplished was to provide a Dublin Core profile for a Web page, that would be sufficient to make it worthwhile to use.

You might wish to include several non-Dublin Core elements in your pages that are available as values for the **meta name** attribute. These include information about your e-mail address (**email**) or the URL of your site (**url**), or even add keywords to your page (**keywords**):

```
<meta name="email" content="webmaster@redroselibrary.com" />
<meta name="url" content="http://www. redroselibrary.com" />
<meta name="keywords" content="Library Web site, web pages, City, State" />
```

When a software program creates a Web page, it may insert an additional meta tag to note the page's creation (**name="generator"**) by that specific software application:

```
<meta name="generator" content="Adobe GoLive" />
```

Telling Search Engines "Don't Index This Page"

You should know that a search engine can index the contents of your pages. This means that information found in *your* Web pages, such as, names of your board of trustees, goes into the search engine's database and can be used for retrieval by others. Because you have a small library, this is not a likely scenario for your library's Web pages. However, if you **don't** want search engines to index the content of your pages, so that your board members' names cannot be retrieved, the following **meta** element tells search engines to pass over your file:

```
<meta name="robots" content="noindex" />
```

Setting a Freshness Date for Your Page

A Web page is only worthwhile if it is kept up-to-date. If you want to automatically delete dated information, set an expiration date for your page following the model below for your **content="date, time GMT"** after the **name="expires"** attribute, as shown here:

```
<meta name="expires" content="Wed, 30 Nov 2005 23:59:59 GMT" />
```

Don't Cache—Get Me the Latest Page

To instruct your patron's browser to ignore cached (saved) pages and request the latest files from your server, use the **http-equiv** attribute with the value **pragma** and a **content** attribute with a **no-cache** value:

```
<meta http-equiv="pragma" content="no-cache" />
```

Redirecting Your Patrons to a New Web Site

To redirect a viewer from one Web page (perhaps an original page that has been relocated either elsewhere on your server or on another server) to another, use the **http-equiv** attribute with the value "**refresh**", set the **content** attribute to show the amount of time your patron will see the current Web page (in seconds), and after a semicolon provide the protocol and full URL name of where the browser should go to get the next page, as shown here:

```
<meta http-equiv="refresh"
content="10;url=http://www.somewhereelse.com/newpage.html" />
```

After a delay of about ten seconds, the browser will redirect itself to the new server at **http://www.somewhereelse.com** to open and display the **newpage.html** file it finds there. In Chapter 10 we examine other ways to use the **http-equiv** attribute to create a variety of page transitions.

Adding an ISBN

Finally, the **meta** element **scheme** attribute can be used to identify the ISBN for a document, or the Web page referring to it. A review Web page about *Wynar's Introduction to Cataloging and Classification*, Ninth Edition, by Arlene Taylor, might use:

```
<meta scheme="ISBN" name="identifier" content="1-56308-857-5" />
```

Your Page's Relationships to Other Documents

The **link** element is used to establish a relationship between your page and other Web documents. It is found inside the **head**, and its attributes are **rel**, **type**, and **href.** This element is commonly used to link your Web page to another page that has support information needed for proper displaying of your content. Chapter 6 reviews style sheets and you'll see the need to link a cascading style sheet file named **default.css** saved in the **styles** folder on your Web site. The style sheet information **type** in the file is noted by the value "**text/css**" with the file location indicated by the "**styles/default.css**" hyperlink address:

```
<link rel="stylesheet" type="text/css" href="styles/default.css" />
```

What's Next?

In this chapter we reviewed the structure of the HTML document and saw that it included three sections, the **html root**, the **head**, and the **body**. We looked deeper into the various default and configurable subelements of the **head**, specifically the **base**, **basefont**, and **meta** elements. We saw that each element has a variety of default attributes that can, if desired, be revised to better stylize the look of your Web pages.

In Chapter 4 we illustrate the use of the elements that change the way text looks in your browser. You'll see how HTML can format your text using examples you would expect to find on your library Web site.

Chapter 4

Displaying Text in Your HTML Document

Now that you understand the structure and header portion of your HTML document, it is time to see how we can display text. You will learn what you can do in your document, locally and globally, to change the way text is displayed by surrounding the text with a variety of stylizing elements. You need to understand these elements, and you will see how they tell the computer to center something, to make a paragraph, or other commands, all things that you can do more easily working in a word processing program. However, you won't need to be as fast in creating your Web page as you might think you needed to be writing a proposal for funding. Your Web page won't need as much work once you have it started as it will seem right now, when you are trying to absorb a great deal in a short time.

Before we begin, you need to know how to remind yourself what, or why, you used a particular method in a section of your page, through adding comments to your HTML document.

Comments can be included in your HTML document to explain why a particular set of tags or items were included, or suggest future enhancements. You must surround the text with the delimiter set, **"<!--"** and **"-->"** to indicate that comments and notes—not HTML elements—are being presented. The comment can be anywhere, inside or outside the **html** element tag**.** All the text and/or element tags occurring between these two delimiter sets will not be decoded. They will be completely ignored by your browser. Comments can appear anywhere text would normally be allowed. As an example: **<! --** comments about blah-blah-blah … **-->**

Using Comments

Comment delimiter sets can be used inline, highlighted or separated with tabs. Bearing in mind that your browser does not normally display extra spaces, tabs, or lines, the text lines can be broken, and the comment's angle brackets separated from the text and/or markup commands being ignored. This makes for much easier reading:

```
Inline Comments
    <!-- Filename: index.htm          Created by CR, on 05/05/06 -->
Highlighting Comments with Tabs       ← Browsers ignore extra spaces & tabs!
    <!-- Filename: index.htm
             Created by CR, on 05/05/06 -->
Separating the Comment with Tabs      ← Browsers ignore breaks & tabs!
    <!--
             Filename: index.htm
             Created by CR, on 05/05/05
    -->
```

As HTML tags can exist within a comment, you can temporarily delete text and all its formatting by inserting the comment opening delimiter and ending delimiter around all the information you want to "comment out" or want your browser to ignore. Let's see if we can create a page that uses some of the tags we used in Chapter 1, to show how it is done. The code for a simple Web page (**code0401.htm**) with commented out text and HTML elements, where characters in **bold** are not displayed, could be:

```
<html>
<pre>
Use comment delimiters to keep notes <!-- that are hidden and not displayed
in your web page files -->
Comment delimiters can also be used to “remove” html commands
<!--
        <b>This line and BOLD tag will be ignored</b>
        <i>This line and ITALICIZED tag will be ignored</ i>
        <u>This line and UNDERLINED tag will be ignored</u>
-->
</pre>
</html>
```

Note that in the browser view of Figure 4.1, whatever text in **code0401.htm** was surrounded by the comment delimiters is not displayed, and any HTML tags present were not parsed (decoded) by the browser.

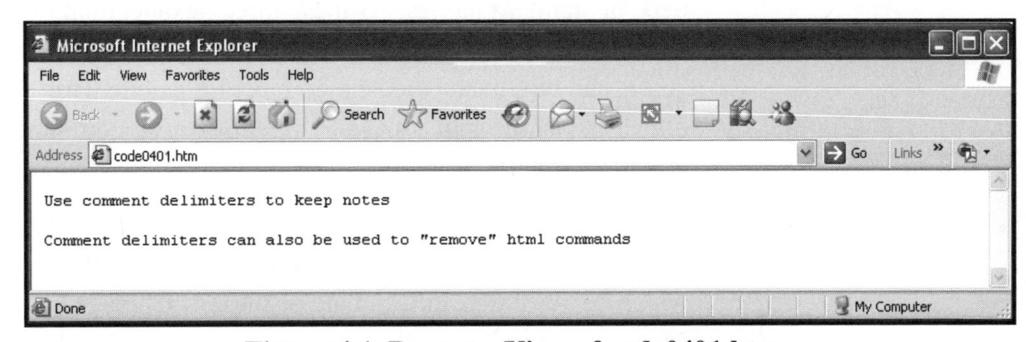

Figure 4.1. Browser View of code0401.htm

The Body of Your HTML Document

From a **head** filled with a **title** and one or more “invisible” empty tags, whose effects are not always apparent, your HTML document opens into the **body** of your page. The **body** element encloses the text and tags comprising the main body of your document.

Your **head** supplied a **title** to your page and a variety of “hidden” metadata and other information about your document. The major portion of your HTML document consists of information surrounded by element tags in the **body**. Elements within the **body** tell the browser how to control appearance and formatting (rendering) of your page’s content. Content must be surrounded by one or more (properly nested) elements that determine what will be done to display the text and graphics of your document.

The displayed text in the **body** section can contain one or more headers (**h#**), paragraphs (**p**), or horizontal lines (**hr**). It can keep its preformatted spacing (**pre**), be displayed as a quote (**blockquote**), or be a list or interactive form.

The **body** element itself can be modified by adding a variety of attributes (**background**, **bgcolor**, **text**, **link**, **vlink**, and **alink**). For example, we may want to specify a URL pointing to an image file to be used to tile the full background of the document-viewing area (**background="Full URL"**), or merely change the color(s) of the page's background (**bgcolor="aqua"**), text (**text="black"**), or the various visited and unvisited hyperlinks (**link**, **vlink**, and **alink**).

In HTML documents, as noted in Chapter 3, when a color is specified the attribute's value is the red-green-blue hexadecimal triplet (e.g., **"#rrggbb"**) derived from standard color tables. You can use the numbers, or standard names. As these three hexadecimal numbers are each capable of displaying 8 bits or one of 256 possible levels of color (red, green, and blue), they create a 24-bit color palette with 16.7 million colors! This is the same palette used by most common scanners and graphics creation programs.

To speed your use of colors in the body tag, several free online services permit you to create color combinations without worrying about which color coding to use. One of these is Clipart Connection's Color Chooser (**http://www.clipartconnection.com/colorchooser.php**). This particular site dynamically shows the effect on background as well as text (link) colors of changing up to three colors at a time and then gives you the correct HTML coding for your results.

The default color of your Web page's background is **white**. If you wanted to change the white background color to **aqua**, you would use the **body** element's **bgcolor** attribute with the hexadecimal triplet color value **#00ffff**. The code that would generate a solid **aqua** background is:

```
<body bgcolor="#00ffff">
The background of this web page is then colored "aqua"
<!— The rest of the document body goes here —>
</body>
```

The file with this example (**code0402.htm**) generates a solid colored background, shown in Figure 4.2.

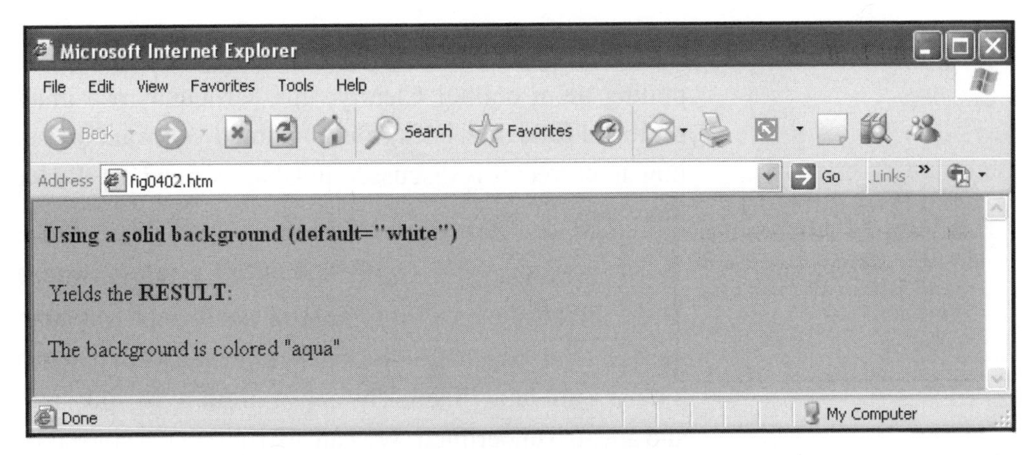

Figure 4.2. Creating a Solid Background

To create a tiled graphic background is equally simple using the **body** element with the **background** attribute pointing toward an image file. The code for using a single red rose graphic **img001.jpg** that has been stored in an **images** folder to create a multiple "tiled" image back drop for your web page using the **background** attribute with an image value (**background="images/img001.jpg"**) is:

```
<body background="images/img001.jpg">
The background of this page is made up of a single graphic 'tiled' or
repeated to fill the background
<!-- The rest of the document body goes here -->
</body>
```

The file **code0403.htm** generates the multiple rose image background example of Figure 4.3.

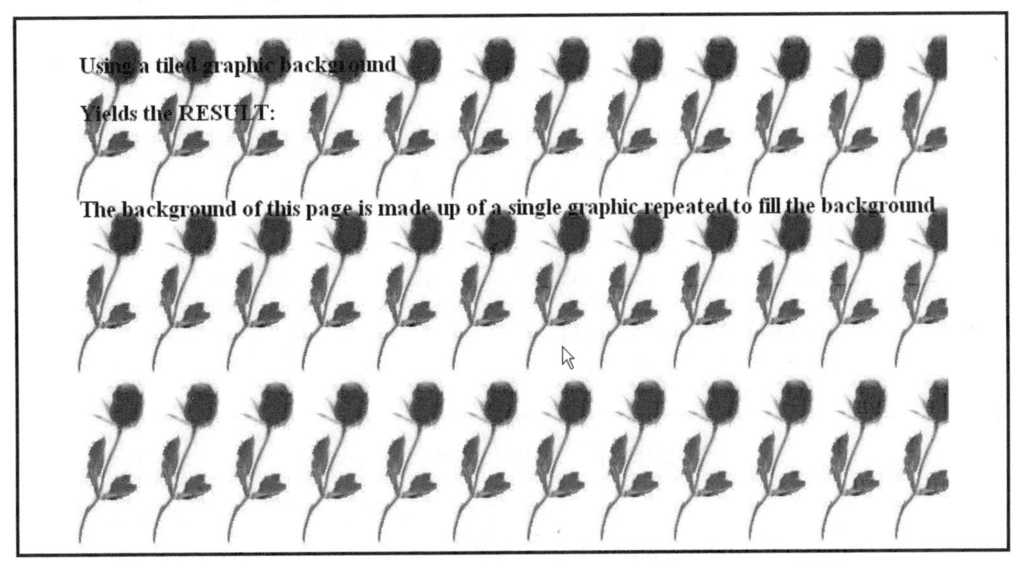

Figure 4.3. Using a Tiled Graphic Background (code0403.htm)

This figure illustrates one reason for trying out your pages before putting them online! Clearly, this particular rose image is much too powerful for a tiled background. Should you want to use this technique, how to correct it is discussed in Chapter 5, where we look at images in more depth.

The **body** tag can also include **link**, **vlink** and **alink** attributes. These are attributes used to control the default way that hyperlinks are seen on your Web page. Normally, unvisited **link** hyperlinks are colored blue and are underlined. The active **alink** hyperlinks are colored purple and are also underlined. We can also define the color for visited or **vlink** hyperlinks. These defaults are illustrated in Figure 4.4.

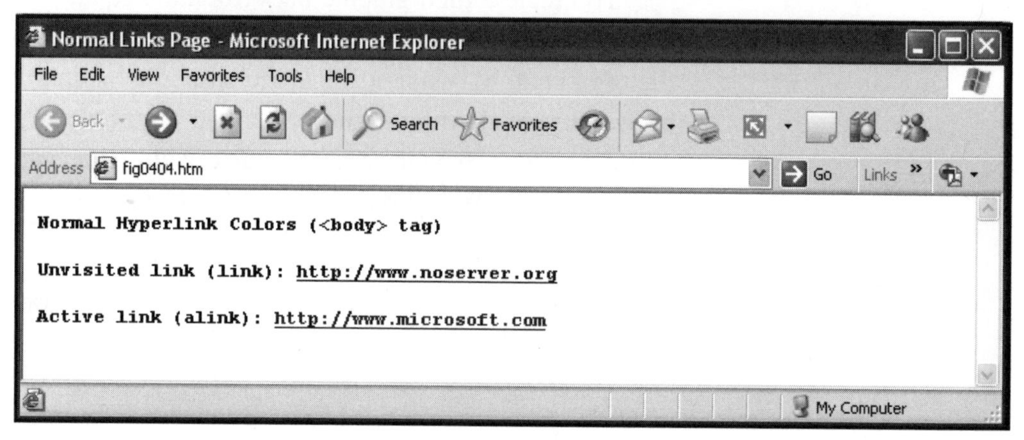

Figure 4.4. Normal Hyperlink Colors (code0404.htm)

In Figure 4.5 we see that using the **body** tag, we can change the display characteristics such that the unvisited **link** hyperlinks are colored red and the active **alink** hyperlinks are colored green. Note that once you try a link the colors may change.

Customized Hyperlink Colors (<body link="red" alink="green"> tag)

Unvisited link (link): http://www.noserver.org

Active link (alink): http://www.microsoft.com

Figure 4.5. Customized Hyperlink Colors (code0405.htm)

We'll see in Chapter 6 that we can truly define these links any way we like using **style** or style sheet concepts. For now you can change the way that hyperlinks and text are displayed using the attributes above within the **body** element tag.

Document Heading and Block Formatting Elements

Heading and block formatting elements typically apply to titles and whole blocks of text rather than individual characters. Formatting elements can modify text formats, too, but they are also useful in creating line breaks and new paragraphs and creating horizontal lines on your Web page.

Heading elements are used to create different font sizes and styles, as is typically seen in headlines in a newsletter. They include **h#** to create different sized headings, where # represents a number between **1** and **6**. This heading tag defines six distinct levels of heading, from **h1** (the most important) to **h6** (the least important). Each heading includes a paragraph (**p**) break before and after the specific heading style change. See Figure 4.6.

CODE: <**h1**>Top-level heading</**h1**>Other text	**Top-level heading** Other text
<**h2**>Second level heading</**h2**>Other text	**Second level heading** Other text
<**h3**>Third level heading</**h3**>Other text	**Third level heading** Other text
<**h4**>Fourth level heading</**h4**>Other text	**Fourth level heading** Other text
<**h5**>Fifth level heading</**h5**>Other text	**Fifth level heading** Other text
<**h6**>Sixth, lowest level heading</**h6**>Other text	**Sixth, lowest level heading** Other text

Figure 4.6. Heading Examples (code0406.htm)

The content inside of the heading tags can contain a wide variety of elements, such as the hyperlink anchor (**a**), images (**img**), line breaks (**br**), and text style elements (**b**, **em**, **strong**, **code**, **samp**, **kbd**, **cite**, **tt**, **var**, **i**, and **u**). You can place your heading tags inside the **body**, in a **blockquote**, and even inside a **form**. You can use **align**, **style**, and **class** attributes in the heading tags themselves.

An **h1** heading is the top-level heading displayed as a large boldface font. **h6** is the smallest predefined heading style. Although Figure 4.6 only shows heading elements encapsulating text, they may also include a variety of stylizations, links, and images.

It is important to note that the heading tags insert a paragraph (carriage return and line feed) on closing the heading tag. That is why the phrase “Other text” does not appear in line with the header but at the regular font size. The other way of handling headings that permits inline changes of font sizes is by using the **font** element’s **size** attribute, as shown later in this chapter in Figure 4.15.

Forcing Line Breaks

The **br** element is an empty tag that causes a line break to be inserted in the displayed text at the point of its insertion, but does not add a line space, as we will see the paragraph element (**p**) doing in the next section. The line break element is used either as **
** or more correctly as **
. The **br can be used just about anywhere in your HTML document, including when you use the preformatted text (**pre**) element. The line break can be used with **clear**, **style**, or **class** attributes.

The line break’s **clear** attribute controls how text that is aligned with images behaves when a line break tag is encountered. The default **clear** attribute causes a new line to start below the image, back to the original margin. A value of **left** tells the browser that you want to break to a clear left margin, **right** to a clear right margin, and **all** to a full clear line.

Making Text into Paragraphs

The paragraph element **p** is used to separate the text in the **body** of your HTML document, list, **table**, or **form** into paragraphs. (See Figure 4.7.) The opening and closing paragraph tags can show the end of the current paragraph and the start of a new paragraph; some browsers allow the use of an empty paragraph tag **<p />**. Either way the paragraph attributes can be used to change text display at the paragraph level. Text, line breaks, and character formatting (style tags like **b**, **u**, and **i**) as well as hyperlinks and images can exist inside paragraphs. Like the line break, the paragraph tag can be used with **clear**, **style**, or **class** attributes. Sometimes the paragraph tag is approximated by a pair of line breaks (**

**).

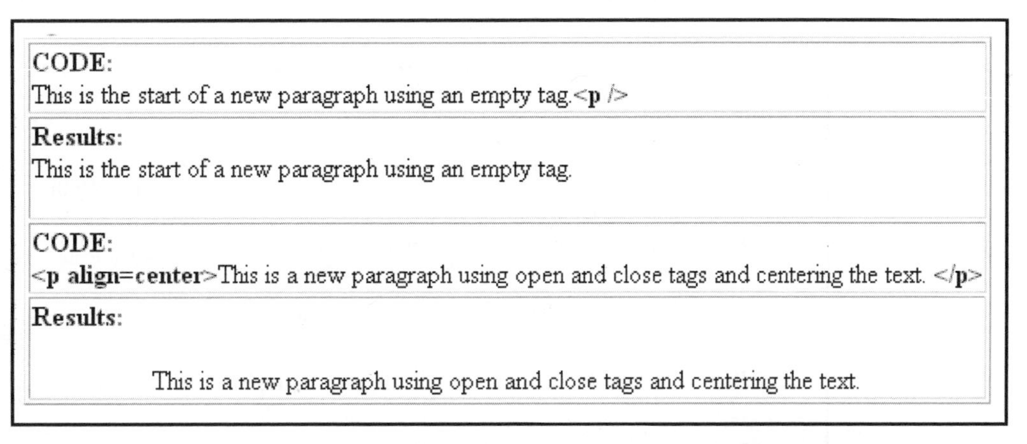

Figure 4.7. Using the Paragraph Element (code0407.htm)

Horizontal Rules

In addition to generating a line break, the horizontal rule <**hr**> element is an empty tag that causes a horizontal line to be rendered on the screen, usually at the full width of the screen. The **hr** tag, normally inside the body of your document, can also be used inside the preformat (**pre**), **blockquote**, or **form** portions of your document. It can be used with **align**, **width**, **size**, and **noshade** attributes.

The **align** attribute, which can have the value **left**, **right**, or **center**, defines how the rule will be aligned on the page. The tag **<hr align= "center">** creates a centered line.

The **width** attribute specifies the width of the horizontal rule, in pixels, or in percent of screen width, and can have the values **"###"** or **"###%"**. The tag **<hr width="450">** creates a centered line 450 pixels wide regardless of the screen window width. A better solution is **<hr width="50%">**, which creates a centered line half the width of the screen window.

The **size** attribute specifies the thickness of the rule line, in pixels. The **noshade** attribute displays horizontal rules as solid black lines rather than the default line style with a shadow or shade.

Figure 4.8 shows a variety of horizontal rules and how they are displayed.

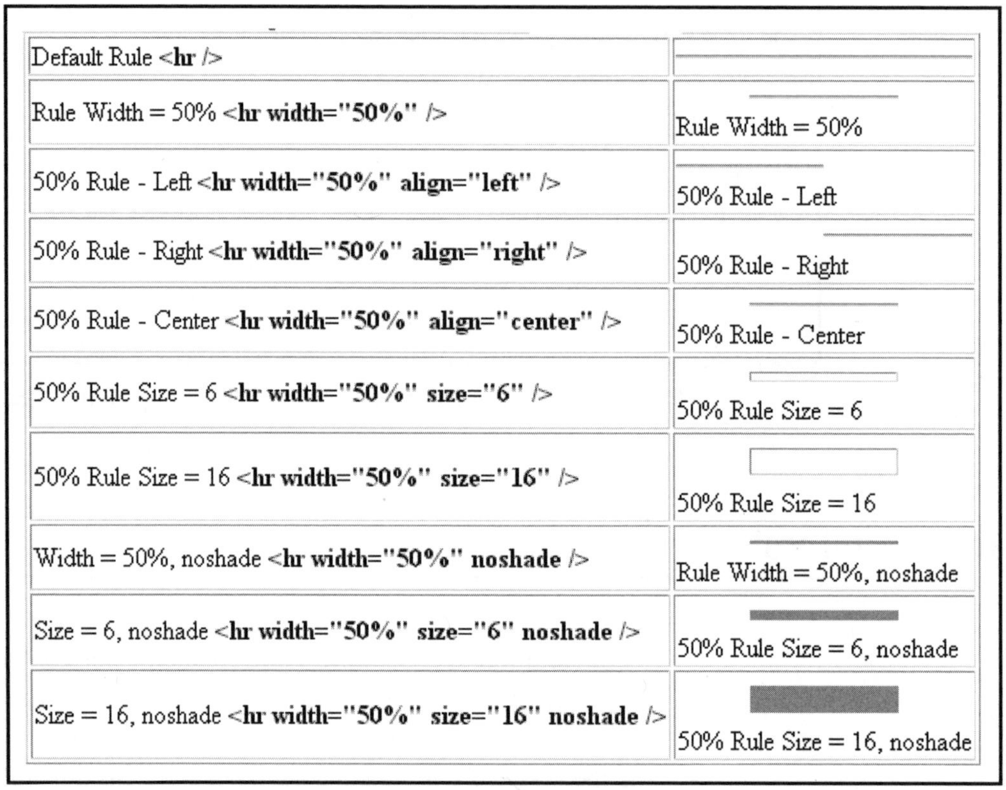

Default Rule **<hr />**	
Rule Width = 50% **<hr width="50%" />**	Rule Width = 50%
50% Rule - Left **<hr width="50%" align="left" />**	50% Rule - Left
50% Rule - Right **<hr width="50%" align="right" />**	50% Rule - Right
50% Rule - Center **<hr width="50%" align="center" />**	50% Rule - Center
50% Rule Size = 6 **<hr width="50%" size="6" />**	50% Rule Size = 6
50% Rule Size = 16 **<hr width="50%" size="16" />**	50% Rule Size = 16
Width = 50%, noshade **<hr width="50%" noshade />**	Rule Width = 50%, noshade
Size = 6, noshade **<hr width="50%" size="6" noshade />**	50% Rule Size = 6, noshade
Size = 16, noshade **<hr width="50%" size="16" noshade />**	50% Rule Size = 16, noshade

Figure 4.8. Examples of Horizontal Rules (code0408.htm)

Centering Text

The **center** element is a shorthand notation for the **<div align="center">** division tag that can be used to center a block of text and other elements, such as paragraphs, images, and headings, on a Web page. It can contain text, character formatting, hyperlink, headings, and images. It can be used inside the HTML **body**, **blockquote**, **form**, **table**, or list. The center tag includes a default paragraph tag as part of its opening and closing element set.

Although still in active use, the **center** element is a deprecated element in future HTML definitions, which means it is being replaced by the use of the **div** element with an **align** attribute. If you are worried about future browser versions not displaying your work properly, note that the two lines below are equivalent:

<center>This displays as a centered line as if in between two paragraph tags**</center>**

<div align="center"> This displays as a centered line as if in between two paragraph tags **</div>**

Using the Preformat Element for Easy Text Display

Your HTML browser usually ignores extra spaces and tabs as well as line spacing of your content. As we saw in Chapter 1, not only can the **pre** element be used to quickly display your content with a minimum of effort, but it also allows you to retain all the line breaks and character spacing you have in your HTML document. As with most of the tags in this chapter, you can use the **pre** tag inside the HTML **body**, **blockquote**, **form**, **table**, or list elements. It can contain text, character formatting, images, and hyperlinks.

Using the **pre** element instructs your browser to display blocks of text in a fixed-width font, retaining all spacing and allowing hyperlinks within the text, as shown in Figure 4.9 . As with most block formatting elements, the **pre** element automatically inserts a paragraph tag before and after the text it surrounds. You can use the **pre** tag with the class or style attributes described above, or with a width attribute.

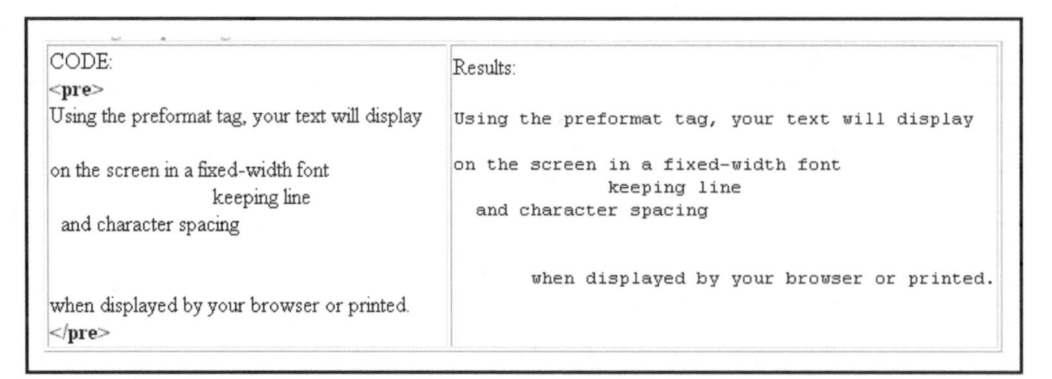

Figure 4.9. Viewing the pre Tag in a Browser (code0409.htm)

The **width** attribute has a default of eighty characters and can be used to specify the maximum number of characters in a line of text. This forces a line break once the character width is reached that has an appearance of a wrapped text.

As all text spacing is retained using the **pre** element, there is no need for paragraph and line break tags, as would be required if one of the mono-spaced fonts described later in this chapter were used. The use of preformatted text in a Web page can help you to quickly post your message, but it is not at all an elegant way to create Web pages with a word processed look and feel.

Representing Quoted Text as a Block

Although the **blockquote** element is normally used to indicate that one or more blocks of text are quotations or citations, it is often used to add a word processor style to your page without resorting to the somewhat more difficult use of tables (see Chapter 8). The **blockquote** can be nested, and it can also be used inside forms, tables, and lists to give your text a more word processed appearance. You can nest a variety of HTML elements inside a **blockquote** (including other **blockquote**s), such as headers, horizontal rules, and lists.

The **blockquote** can be used to create a single line quote, as seen in Figure 4.10, but it is more typically used to create indented paragraphs, as shown in the Red Rose Library example in Figure 4.11. It can also be used to indent lists (see Chapter 7) and other HTML elements, as noted above. As shown in the browser views of both Figures 4.10 and 4.11, the opening **blockquote** tag will insert a paragraph tag before the "quoted" text and again after the closing **blockquote** tag, to separate the quoted information from the rest of the text (etc.) on the page.

CODE:	Results:
The following text is a quote: <**blockquote**> Yada, yada, yada means yada, yada, yada. </**blockquote**> As was noted quite often on the TV series Seinfeld...	The following text is a quote: Yada, yada, yada means yada, yada, yada. As was noted quite often on the TV series Seinfeld...

Figure 4.10. Viewing a Blockquote (code0410.htm)

Any time we "force" a look onto an HTML page, we need to keep the differences in browser rendering in mind. If you are using the **blockquote** element set to create a certain word processed look, you need to make sure to view it not only in your usual browser, but also in other browsers to make sure it looks the way you want to all your patrons.

CODE:
Annual trip to the American Museum of Natural History and the Hayden Planetarium <**blockquote**> Sign up now! <**br** /> The bus to New York City will be leaving on Sunday January 15th at 6:00am. <**br** /> Trip cost is $50 which includes bus tickets, snacks on the bus, lunch at the Museum, and a souvenir. <**br** /> Be sure to make your reservation early as this is a fast sell out! </**blockquote**> The bus trip is sponsored by the Cultural Committee of the Friends of the Rose Library.
Results: Annual trip to the American Museum of Natural History and the Hayden Planetarium Sign up now! The bus to New York City will be leaving on Sunday January 15th at 6:00am. Trip cost is $50 which includes bus tickets, snacks on the bus, lunch at the Museum, and a souvenir. Be sure to make your reservation early as this is a fast sell out! The bus trip is sponsored by the Cultural Committee of the Friends of the Rose Library.

Figure 4.11. Using Blockquotes (code0411.htm)

Character Formatting

Although block formatting can be used to stylize your text, the paragraph breaks that go before and after your content provide unnecessary and unwanted line spaces that can be distracting. Like all elements, character formatting elements work like switches to turn style on and off for the specific text they surround. This allows you to display text in bold, italics, or with underline in paragraphs, sentences, or even individual characters in line.

Displaying Text in Boldface

There are two elements that display surrounded text in boldface. These are the boldface (**b**) and the **strong** elements. The more common **b** tag denotes the physical element that adds emphasis to text, whereas the **strong** tag adds emphasis to text with a semantic element name. Most common elements can modify content inside the boldface tags, and most common elements can contain boldface elements.

Encapsulating individual letters, words, and sentences with a character element allows instant, and temporary, resetting of the character display anywhere on your Web page. These elements can use either a physical name that notes their displayed look, or a semantic name that explains their typical function. The first set of these elements is used to display text in boldface.

Whereas the **b** element is clearly a physical element formatting tool used to create boldface text, the **strong** element is a semantic element that uses a name that more clearly denotes its effect on text. Figure 4.12 shows how both the **b** and **strong** elements cause the marked text to be rendered in boldface, with no difference in how the text is displayed.

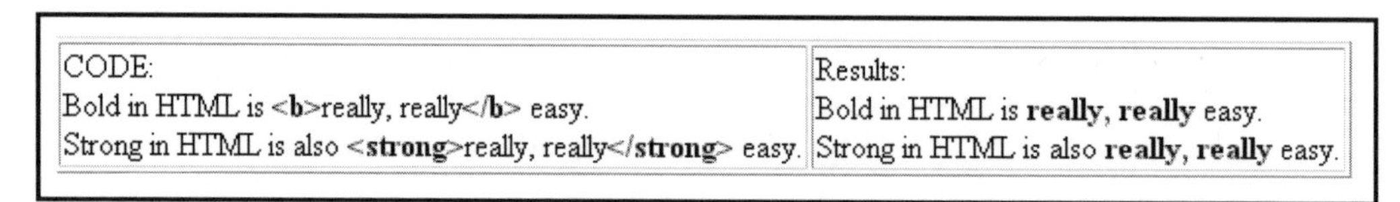

CODE:	Results:
Bold in HTML is <b>really, really</b> easy.	Bold in HTML is **really, really** easy.
Strong in HTML is also <strong>really, really</strong> easy.	Strong in HTML is also **really, really** easy.

Figure 4.12. How Boldface Characters Are Displayed (code0412.htm)

Italics

Just as there are several elements that can be used to display text in boldface, there are also several that display italicized text. The four elements are the element that denotes the physical italics change to your text (**i**) and three semantic names that are used to italicize text; emphasis (**em**); **cite**, which notes book or text citations; and **var**, which represents variable names in a program. These elements behave very much like the boldface elements and can contain or be found inside the elements listed above. The use of the four different elements (**i**, **em**, **cite,** and **var**) to display the text surrounded by them in italics is shown in Figure 4.13.

CODE:	Results:
The following text is <i> an italicized font</i> and this text is not.	The following text is *an italicized font* and this text is not.
The following text is <**em**> an emphasized font</**em**> and this text is not.	The following text is *an emphasized font* and this text is not.
The following text is <**cite**> a citation font</**cite**> and this text is not.	The following text is *a citation font* and this text is not.
The following text is <**var**> a variable name font</**var**> and this text is not.	The following text is *a variable name font* and this text is not.

Figure 4.13. How Characters Look in Italics (code0413.htm)

Changing Font Typefaces

On occasion you might want to vary, or substitute, a different typeface instead of using the default or base font's typeface. HTML tags can be easily used to display text in a fixed-width font, as we did when we used the **pre** element where we wanted to retain line and character spacing inside the tags, but this time in line, without the need to insert paragraph tags before and after the text.

The teletype (**tt**), keyboard (**kbd**), computer code fragments (**code**), and sample elements (**samp**) mark text typically displayed in a fixed-width (nonproportional) monotype typewriter style font, as shown in Figure 4.14, and can be used much like the boldface and italics elements covered above.

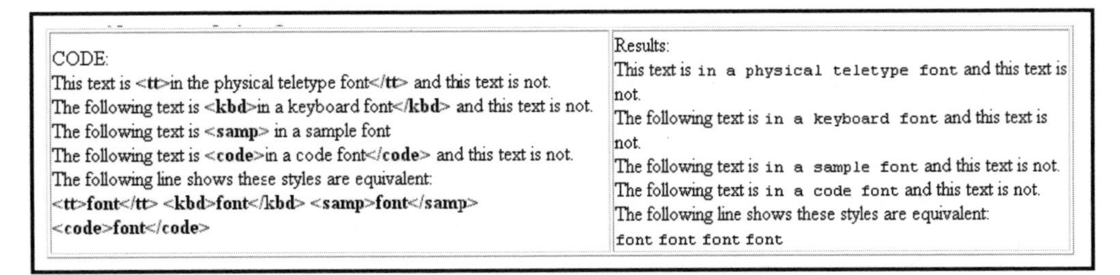

CODE:	Results:
This text is <**tt**>in the physical teletype font</**tt**> and this text is not. The following text is <**kbd**>in a keyboard font</**kbd**> and this text is not. The following text is <**samp**> in a sample font The following text is <**code**>in a code font</**code**> and this text is not. The following line shows these styles are equivalent: <**tt**>**font**</**tt**> <**kbd**>**font**</**kbd**> <**samp**>**font**</**samp**> <**code**>**font**</**code**>	This text is `in a physical teletype font` and this text is not. The following text is `in a keyboard font` and this text is not. The following text is `in a sample font` and this text is not. The following text is `in a code font` and this text is not. The following line shows these styles are equivalent: `font font font font`

Figure 4.14. Monotype Text Display (code0414.htm)

It's All About the Fonts

Speaking of fonts, perhaps the most popular and flexible of character-level elements is the **font** element. Even though the font element is expected to be discontinued in future HTML versions, it is very easy to use and much simpler than the more customizable style declarations that we will look at in Chapter 6.

The popular and versatile **font** element allows inline changes of text style, without the paragraph separation created using header (**h#**) or **blockquote** tags. Encapsulating individual letters, words, and sentences with a **font** element allows instant, and temporary, resetting of the size, typeface, and color of text anywhere on your Web page. Any included attribute changes toggle off at the appearance of the **font** closing tag **</font>**. We'll see below that several attributes can be included in a single **font** tag, or attributes can be individually, sequentially, turned on and off as needed.

In our discussion of headings, **size="#"** specified the size of the font with values ranging from 1 to 6. However, unlike heading tags, where the larger the number, the smaller the font (recall that **h#** creates different sized headings, with **h1** the most important and **h6** the least important), the **size** attribute has larger numbers, giving larger text. Including a **+** or – before the **size** value makes the size change relative to the **basefont size**, which has a default value of **"3"**. As seen in the results section of Figure 4.15, code lines b and c, **font size="1"** is the smallest font size and **font size="7"** is the largest font size. Any +/– changes are relative and limited to these maximum and minimum values. That is why the default size of the **basefont** is so important.

CODE: a. Using absolute font sizes: font size = "n" (the 0 is in default size 3)

```
0<font size="1">1</font> <font size="2">2</font> <font size="3">3</font> <font size="4">4</font>
<font size="5">5</font> <font size="6">6</font> <font size="7">7</font> <font size="6">6</font>
<font size="5">5</font> <font size="4">4</font> <font size="3">3</font> <font size="2">2</font>
<font size="1">1</font> 0
```

Results: a. Using absolute font sizes: font size = "n" (the 0 is in default size 3)

0 1 2 3 4 5 6 7 6 5 4 3 2 1 0

CODE: b. Making text relatively smaller: font sizes = "-n" (the 0 is in default size 3)

```
0<font size="-1">-1</font> <font size="-2">-2</font> <font size="-3">-3</font> <font size="-4">-4</font>
<font size="-5">-5</font> <font size="-6">-6</font> <font size="-7">-7</font> <font size="-6">-6</font>
<font size="-5">-5</font> <font size="-4">-4</font> <font size="-3">-3</font> <font size="-2">-2</font>
<font size="-1">-1</font> 0
```

Results: b. Making text relatively smaller: font sizes = "-n" (the 0 is in default size 3)

0 -1 -2 -3 -4 -5 -6 -7 -6 -5 -4 -3 -2 -1 0

CODE: c. Making text relatively larger: font sizes = "+n" (the 0 is in default size 3)

```
0 <font size="+1">+1</font> <font size="+2">+2</font> <font size="+3">+3</font> <font size="+4">+4</font>
<font size="+5">+5</font> <font size="+6">+6</font> <font size="+7">+7</font> <font size="+6">+6</font>
<font size="+5">+5</font> <font size="+4">+4</font> <font size="+3">+3</font> <font size="+2">+2</font>
<font size="+1">+1</font> 0
```

Results: c. Making text relatively larger: font sizes = "+n" (the 0 is in default size 3)

0 +1 +2 +3 +4 +5 +6 +7 +6 +5 +4 +3 +2 +1 0

Figure 4.15. Inline Font Size Changes on Your Browser (code0415.htm)

Now that we understand a bit about changing the size of our text, we can investigate how the **face** attribute can be used to select one or more typefaces or font names to stylize your text. The browser will check to see which of these typefaces, in the order you have listed them (e.g., **face="name [,name2[,name3]]"**) , is available on your computer and then display the text in the new typeface.

The generic font families have a font type as well as typical names. Figure 4.16 shows browser views of the major font face types.

CODE: **a. Using Serif font faces** (default is Serif font face)
Default font, <**font face="serif"**>Generic Serif font face,</**font**> <**font face="times new roman"**>Times New Roman font face,</**font**>
<**font face="palatino"**>Palatino font face,</**font**> Default font

Results: a. Using Serif font faces (default is Serif font face)
Default font, Generic Serif font face, Times New Roman font face, Palatino font face, Default font

CODE: **b. Using Sans-serif font faces** (default is Serif font face)
Default font, <**font face="sans-serif"**>Generic Sans-serif font face,</**font**> <**font face="arial"**>Arial font face,</**font**>
<**font face="helvetica"**>Helvetica font face,</**font**> Default font

Results: b. Using Sans-serif font faces (default is Serif font face)
Default font, Generic Sans-serif font face, Arial font face, Helvetica font face, Default font

CODE: **c. Using Cursive font faces** (default is Serif font face)
Default font, <**font face="cursive"**>Generic Cursive font face,</**font**> <**font face="script"**>Script font face,</**font**>
Default font

Results: c. Using Cursive font faces (default is Serif font face)
Default font, **Generic Cursive font face**, *Script font face*, Default font

CODE: **d. Using Fantasy font faces** (default is Serif font face)
Default font, <**font face="fantasy"**>Generic Fantasy font face,</**font**> Default font

Results: d. Using Fantasy font faces (default is Serif font face)
Default font, **Generic fantasy font face.** Default font

CODE: **e. Using Monospace font faces** (default is Serif font face)
Default, <**font face="monospace"**>Generic Monospace font face,</**font**> <**font face="courier"**>Courier font face,</**font**> Default

Results: e. Using Monospace font faces (default is Serif font face)
Default, `Generic Monospace font face, Courier font face,` Default

Figure 4.16. Inline Font Face Changes on Your Browser (code0416.htm)

The **serif** font face is most often seen in Times New Roman (Font style example) and Palatino (Font style example) styles, and it is the default browser font face. Arial (Font style example) is a common **sans-serif** font face and is typically more readable than a serif font. There are **cursive** font faces with a variety of script names as well as **fantasy** and **monospace** (Courier `Font style example`) styles. Note that **font face** is an inline tag that does not add paragraph breaks.

Caution! As with so many special element attributes, you must use the **font face** attribute carefully. If none of the typefaces you requested is installed on the user's computer, the browser's default font will be used—and that could spoil your desired effect. This effect is noted in Results 04-16 code line c, above, where the default cursive font, isn't cursive! It's a bold sans-serif font. You can get really creative results using **font faces** until you get the hang of using the style and cascading style sheet techniques discussed in Chapter 6.

The **font** element's **color** attribute is, as before, a predefined name or a triplet of hexadecimal numbers. The added magic here is that as an inline tag, **font color** can be changed at will, even changing colors for single characters one at a time—a neat trick, when added to the **font size** attribute—to keep your Children's Room patrons happy, as seen in Figure 4.17, code line results b, which are best viewed in your browser as the colorful stylization does not show up well in the black-and-white figure.

```
CODE:    a.    Changing Font Colors in line (base color is black #000000)
Black (default) #000000: <font color="black">Black</font>, Navy #000080: <font color="navy">Navy</font>,
Blue #0000ff: <font color="blue">Blue</font>, Green #008000: <font color="green">Green</font>,
Gray #808080: <font color="gray">Gray</font>, Red #ff0000: <font color="red">Red</font>,
Fuchsia #ff00ff: <font color="fuchsia">Fuchsia</font>, Yellow #ffff00: <font color="yellow">Yellow</font>,
White (it really is!) #ffffff: <font color="white">White</font>

Results:    a.    Changing Font Colors in line (base color is black #000000)
Black (default) #000000: Black, Navy #000080: Navy, Blue #0000ff: Blue, Green #008000: Green,
Gray #808080: Gray, Red #ff0000: Red, Fuchsia #ff00ff: Fuchsia, Yellow #ffff00: Yellow, White (it really is!) #ffffff:

CODE:    b.    Children's Room Example Using Size and Color:
<font color="black" size="1">W</font><font color="navy" size="2">e</font><font color="blue"
size="3">l</font><font color="green" size="4">c</font><font color="gray" size="5">o</font><font
color="red" size="6">m</font><font color="fuchsia" size="7">e</font> <font color="yellow"
size="6">2</font> <font color="black" size="5">T</font><font color="navy" size="4">h</font><font
color="blue" size="3">e</font> <font color="green" size="2">C</font><font color="gray"
size="1">h</font><font color="red" size="2">i</font><font color="fuchsia" size="3">l</font><font
color="yellow" size="4">d</font><font color="black" size="5">r</font><font color="navy"
size="6">e</font><font color="blue" size="7">n</font><font color="green" size="6">s</font> <font
color="gray" size="5">R</font><font color="red" size="4">o</font><font color="fuchsia"
size="3">o</font><font color="yellow" size="2">m</font> <font color="black" size="1">!</font>

Results:    b.    Children's Room Example Using Size and Color

Welcome 2 The Childrens Room!
```

Figure 4.17. Inline Font Color Change on Your Browser (code0417.htm)

Using Multiple Attributes in a Font Tag

Putting three **font** attributes (**color**, **size**, and **face**) together can spice up your Web page, as **font** tags can be nested for interesting effects. The example in Figure 4.18 displays your content (we'll use the term "stuff" in this example) using a single multiple attribute tag and then shows the effect of nesting **font** tags using **red**, size **+2 (="5")**, and **arial** font face values. The **font** tag turns on each and then closes all attribute changes one at a time, returning to the default basefont. Figure 4.18 shows the effect of nested **font** tags.

CODE:

```
<font color="red"> <font size="+2"> <font face="arial"> < -- color, size, face turned ON
stuff1 </font> < -- Turn off the font face change
stuff2 </font> <-- Turn off the font size change
stuff3 </font> < -- Turn off the font color change
stuff4 < -- Returns to defaults

<font color="red" size="+2" face="arial"> < -- Turns ON all three font changes
stuff5 </font> <-- Turning off all font changes, returns to default
```

Results:

< -- color, size, face turned ON
stuff1 < -- Turn off the font face change
stuff2 < -- Turn off the font size change
stuff3 < -- Turn off the font color change
stuff4 < -- Returns to defaults

< -- Turn ON all three font changes
stuff5 <-- Turning off all font changes, returns to default

Figure 4.18. Nested Font Changes on Your Browser (code0418.htm)

Note that here the attribute can change one at a time, or be nested. This set of commands result in "Stuff1" displayed as **Red**, size **+2**, and **Arial**. "Stuff2" is **Red** and size **+2**, but in the default **basefont** face style. "Stuff3" is **Red** in the default **basefont** style size and face, "Stuff4" is completely displayed in the **basefont**. "Stuff5" shows all attributes turned on and off using a single tag.

Special Characters (Entities)

Your HTML browser can display a number of special characters that could otherwise not be part of your Web page. These include the registered trademark symbol ®, the copyright symbol ©, the ampersand symbol &, and a blank space character that is used for adjusting the space between text that is normally ignored by your browser. The angle bracket characters (used in creating the tag structure) must also be generated by entity relationships, as they would otherwise be parsed (reviewed by your browser) for the element names and commands contained within them. Entity characters include

® The registered trademark symbol ®

© The copyright symbol ©

& The ampersand symbol &

** ** The blank space character (non-breaking space)

< The less than (angle bracket) symbol: <

> The greater than (angle bracket) symbol: >

Text Format Tricks Enhance Your Web Page

Using the neat tricks we have added to our repertoire in this chapter, we can enhance the Red Rose Library newsletter page we saw in the first chapter with color, size, and font face variations as well as with bold and italics, as shown in Figure 4.19.

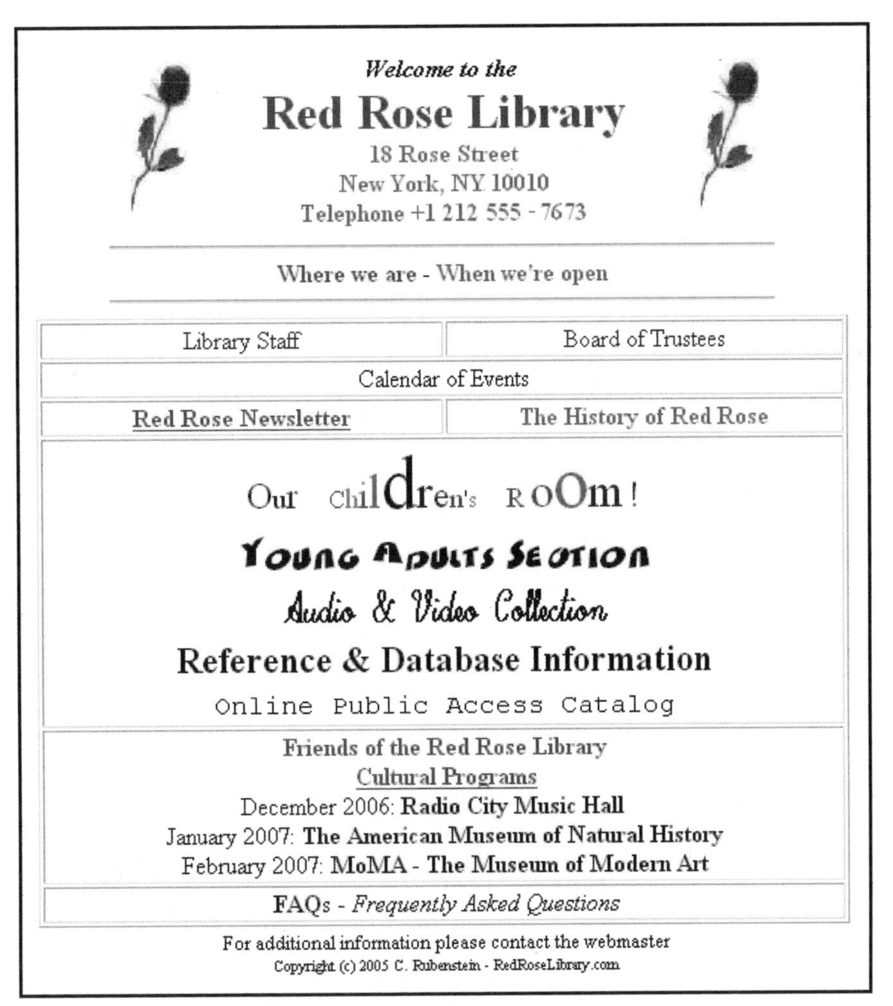

Figure 4.19. Enhancing Your Web Page with Format Tricks (code0419.htm)

What's Next?

Chapter 5 continues our quest for HTML elements and their use by giving us the tools for perhaps the most important of HTML elements—those dealing with hyperlinking and displaying images.

Chapter 5

Images and Linking to Other Web Pages

This chapter begins with using graphics you download from someone else's Web site to use on your Web pages. You will advance to helping your static HTML pages come alive with the use of inline images and hyperlinks. In this chapter you'll see how to use these techniques to insert images on your page and to create hypertext links, and you'll see how to activate images to achieve hypergraphics.

Graphics and Copyright

As noted in our first chapter, having tools such as Adobe Photoshop, Corel's Paint Shop Pro, or Microsoft's Paint program won't make you an artist, but starting from the myriad of clip art available on the Internet (use Google or Yahoo to find the treasure troves, see below) or digital photographs that you can take or find, you should be able to find several graphics that suit your needs. The challenge here is to make sure you aren't violating copyright with the images you select.

If you take the photo or create a graphic yourself, you can probably use it without restrictions. Of course, if the photo is a picture of a painting you may have some copyright issues, but in general, city scenes and photos of staff or others who have granted you permission to use their image are good to use on your Web page. In fact, they give a more personal look to the otherwise commercial-looking photos. But be very careful if you use graphics from someone's Web site without permission, as you may be guilty of copyright infringement. Also use clip art collections described in the next section carefully, as they have certain license restrictions for commercial use.

Clip Art Collections

Clip art comes in many shapes and sizes, as freely usable public domain or as subscription or royalty fee-based images. Some of the clip art collections available via the Web do allow truly free use: free of cost, free of royalty, and free of copyright restrictions. Some have a small subscription charge, and still others have a license fee for each file you download. You must read the fine print! In most cases the graphics are downloaded by right-clicking on the clip art or photo, selecting "Save as" from the pop-up menu, and then selecting the place on your computer (preferably a new folder on your desktop or the images folder in your Web site folder so you can find them later!) to save the file.

Among the over 250,000 free clip art Web sites that you can find if you do a Google search, several have thousands of high-quality, royalty-free clip art images in hundreds of categories that could be usable on your library Web pages. I am particularly grateful to Mehmet Emin Ericek, Webmaster at free-clipart-pictures.net (**http://www.free-clipart-pictures.net**) for giving me permission to use the pages and pages of free categorized clip art on his Web site in this text.

To most of us, free clip art means without any charge, BUT you may have to register and give your name and e-mail, or navigate around sponsor advertisements, or download special software to access this free material. Figure 5.1 shows just a few of these free treasure troves of clip art. Please beware! Free may be without cost, but you may receive a great many pop-up pages, because many free sites are sponsored and have pop-up pages, sponsored site ads to avoid—unless these ads offer something you might want to download.

1. FREE Clipart without major advertising distractions:

Free Clipart Pictures.Net **http://www.free-clipart-pictures.net**
Pages and pages of free categorized clipart – many used in this text!

ChristiaNet® **http://www.christianet.com**
Free clipart, cursors, photos, etc., and a large amount of Christian themed material.

Clipart Connection **http://www.clipartconnection.com**
includes Color Chooser: **http://www.clipartconnection.com/colorchooser.php**
Use the Color Chooser tool to select the defaults you want to use in your **body** tag by adjusting a set of color sliders until you get the color you like, displayed dynamically on the page. Start with red, green or blue adding their 256 color levels together to create one of the 16.7 million colors (24-bit color palette) available to make your ideal background, etc. Then copy the HTML code and place it in your web page.

Flaming Text **http://www.flamingtext.com/start.html**
In addition to clipart, buttons, arrows, bullets, dividers, etc., create logos online

GIF.com **http://www.gif.com**
Free searchable clipart, animations, photos, etc.

2. FREE Clipart with software downloading and sponsor offer selection required:

Freeze.Com **http://www.freeze.com**
No fees, 10 minute registration (be careful to select only the offers you want!)

3. FREE Clipart with major sponsor and advertising distractions:

All Free Clipart **http://www.free-clipart.net/main.html**
Animated gifs, backgrounds, clipart and icons

4. Subscription and Fee Based (Royalty Free) Clipart URLs

Animation Factory **http://www.animationfactory.com**
Animated royalty free images ands templates, etc. ($20/month to $100/year)

Broderbund **http://www.broderbund.com**
CD-ROM Clipart Collections and software (prices vary)

Clipart .Com **http://www.clipart.com**
Millions of clipart and photos, etc. ($16/week to $169/year)

iStockphoto **http://www.istockphoto.com**
Royalty free stock photos. (with $1 - $3 PER PHOTO license fees)

Figure 5.1. Web Page Clip Art URLs

Subscription and Fee-Based, Royalty-Free Clip Art

Other sites require subscriptions for access to royalty-free clip art that you can then use without continuing your subscription. The Animation Factory hosts an online subscription service for a wide variety of clip art and animated graphics, backgrounds, and PowerPoint templates. iStockphoto provides a nonsubscription service that permits you to upload and download royalty-free stock images. Each download is $1 for low resolution, $2 for medium resolution, or $3 for high resolution stock photos. Other vendors have CD-ROM clip art collections and software for using them.

Broderbund has a variety of graphics and publishing products, many with online access to additional artwork. Several of these not-so-free resources are found in Figure 5.1, Section 4. Even these fee-based services may have free samples of their contents that you should look at before paying for any services.

In addition to clip art, buttons, arrows, bullets, dividers, etc., you can also create logos online—for free! Flaming Text (see Figure 5.1, Section 1) is a really interesting site as it has an online heading-generation program that permits adding style to text without the use of a "paint" program like Adobe Photoshop. Create a vast variety of heading types using the Flaming Text fonts and styles shown in Figure 5.2 (this black-and-white figure doesn't do justice to the vibrant colors and shades you'll see on your browser or online).

Figure 5.2. Flaming Text Sample Logos (code0502.htm) (from http://www.flamingtext.com/start.html)

To show how this type of online tool can be used in enhancing your library Web site, we selected the Old Stone example at FlamingText.Com. The tool's online screen looks like Figure 5.3.

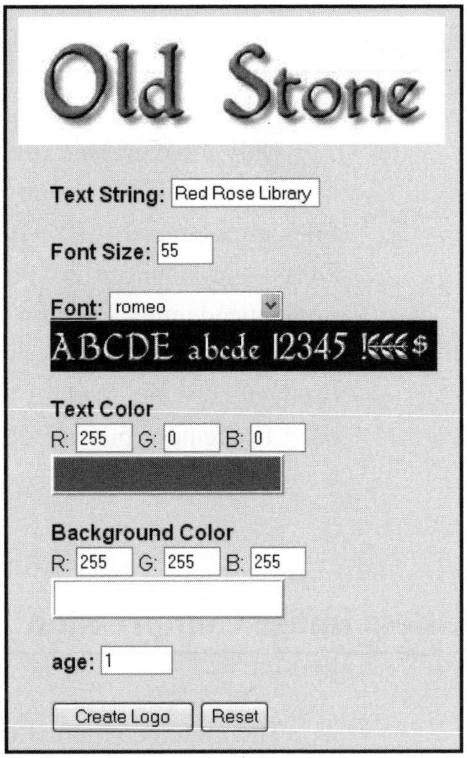

Figure 5.3. FlamingText.com "Old Stone" Logo Creator Screen (code0503.htm)

Using the parameters noted, we entered "Red Rose Library" and pressed the **Create Logo** button to create the library logo (**img002.jpg**) seen in Figure 5.4.

Figure 5.4. Flaming Text Red Rose Library Logo (Romeo Font, img002.jpg)

This is an easy way to create logos or headers (for FREE!) one at a time, but if you expect to be using this type of heading tool a lot, rather than creating them online, you can download the FlamingText GIMP logo creator software program (about $30) for use directly on your desktop.

Graphic File Types

Only three graphic file types are readily usable on most browsers. These have the extension **gif** (Compuserve's Graphics Interchange File—pronounced jiff), **jpg** or **jpeg** (Joint Photographic Editors Group—pronounced jay-peg), or **png** (Portable Network Graphics—pronounced ping). The **png** file type was created in the late 1990s to offset potential legal issues surrounding the **gif**'s use of patented LZW (Lempel, Ziv and Welch) lossless compression algorithm that threatened to create a per use charge for **gif** file images. This has not yet occurred.

Lossy and Lossless Image Compression

The more common JPEG graphic file standard analyzes an image and uses nonpatented mathematical "lossy" compression algorithms to compress a photo or complex graphic such that it faithfully represents the image but without keeping all the pixels. The lossless **gif** typically creates a larger file than a JPEG. Most images look about the same in either **gif** or **jpg** versions, but only the **gif** format can be transparent or be animated to look like a short cartoon.

For small icons and simple line graphics (or animations) the 8-bit, 256 color palette **gif** is an excellent choice. For photos you get best results with the 24-bit, 16.7 million color palette JPEG compression. Typically you will use whichever file type gives a good graphic image in the smallest file size. Even though more and more patrons are going online via a high speed connection, you should always pay attention to file size where you can.

Spicing up Your Web Page with Clip Art

Okay, so now you have some artwork, photos, or clip art with a **gif** or **jpg** file type that you want to use on your pages. Let's see how you can get these graphics to do what you want them to.

The **img** element is an empty HTML element used to insert a graphic image from a file into a Web document. This insertion is in line and does not generate line or paragraph breaks before or after the image insertion.

Images are not embedded inside of HTML documents, as they are when you see them in word processed documents or PowerPoint slide shows, but rather one or more separate files are retrieved by the browser using the **img** element's **src** (source) attribute. The image files are stored as temporary files on your hard disk and then assembled by the browser on your local computer into a Web page.

Let's look at those **img** element attributes that can be used to enhance the way your browser displays images.

Relative and Absolute File Addresses

The file location source attribute **src** is required to be present in all **img** tags. This attribute tells your browser where to look for the file of the image you want to insert on the page. If you are using a standard Web site structure for your Web site, it is most convenient to locate all of your images in an **images** folder. Then, if the image file you want is located on your Web site, the files can be addressed relative to where your HTML document is. If we presume your document is in a folder on your desktop named **library** that contains a subfolder called **images** where the red rose graphic **img004.jpg** is stored, the **img** tag's **src** attribute with a relative address

```
<img src="images/img004.jpg" />
```

could be used. *Notice that there is no mention of the outer folder **library**, as we are looking for the file relative to where the current HTML document is located.* This "relative" addressing technique permits your Web site to be developed on your desktop or on a removable drive. Your browser would look for the image files in an **images** folder within the folder or directory *wherever* your HTML document is *currently* located. If you transfer this folder structure to another medium, or folder, all the relative addresses will be valid as they are not fixed to any particular computer, location, or path.

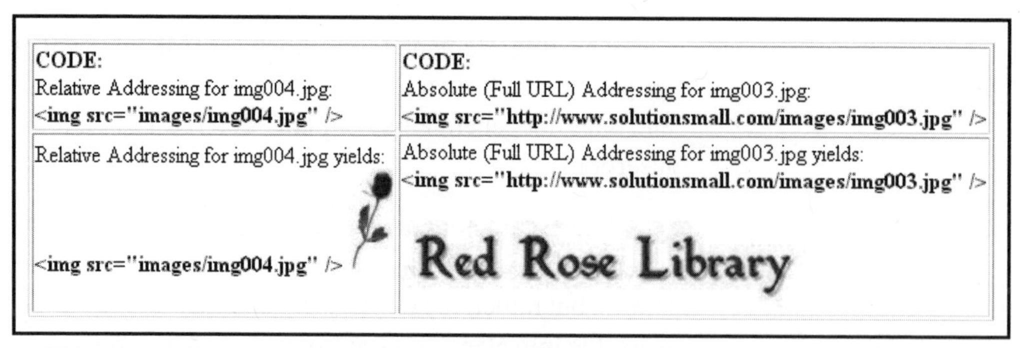

Figure 5.5. Relative and Absolute Addressing in img Tags (code0505.htm)

If we presume your document is in the root folder on a Web server that contains a subfolder called **images** where **img003.jpg** is stored, the **img** tag's **src** attribute requires the full uniform resource locator (URL) using

<img src="http://www.redroselibrary.com/images/img003.jpg" />

with an "absolute" addressing scheme to locate the file. The result, your image being displayed on your Web page, is shown on the right in Figure 5.5.

The absolute addressing method is best used when the image is NOT on your Web site, as it fully describes the file's location and path. The **img** tag using the absolute address of the **img004.jpg** file in the **images** folder in the **library** folder on your computer's desktop might be

<img src="C:\Documents and Settings\LibraryName\Desktop\library\images\ img004.jpg" />

However, if you decided to change the location of this folder, using absolute addressing you would need to use the new path or your browser would not find your files. Relative addressing doesn't much care where the folder set is located. Whenever possible you should use relative addressing to avoid future file location problems, unless the file is in a folder on someone else's Web site (say, on the Internet), where you would have to use absolute addressing with the fully described URL.

Missing Images and the alt Attribute

As shown in Figure 5.6, when you go to someone else's Web site for resources and find that the location or name of a file on that Web site described with either an absolute or a relative address has changed, your browser will show a blank rectangle space with a broken link icon where the graphic belongs.

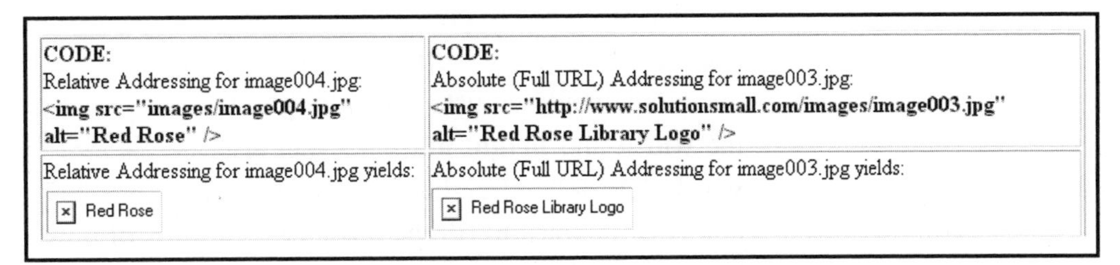

CODE: Relative Addressing for image004.jpg: **<img src="images/image004.jpg" alt="Red Rose" />**	CODE: Absolute (Full URL) Addressing for image003.jpg: **<img src="http://www.solutionsmall.com/images/image003.jpg" alt="Red Rose Library Logo" />**
Relative Addressing for image004.jpg yields: ☒ Red Rose	Absolute (Full URL) Addressing for image003.jpg yields: ☒ Red Rose Library Logo

Figure 5.6. Adding Information with the alt Attribute (code0506.htm)

Broken links happen most often when an external server's images are used and the other Web site has modified where it stored the original files, or when you make a typo or folder name error in the **img** tag **src** attribute. If you use the **alt** attribute in your **img** tag, your browser display the text information "value" associated with this attribute in the image area.

The **alt** attribute can be used to add information about the image when your mouse pointer hovers over the image. When the image is also used to hyperlink to another Web site (see "Hypertext and Hypergraphics: Linking to Images and Other Web Pages" below), it is common to add that URL in the **alt** attribute. The information appears for a few seconds in a text box near the pointer.

The **alt** also adds to your Web page's accessibility, as voice output readers or Lynx (non-graphic) browsers can use the **alt** attribute to inform their user what the image represents.

Sizing Your Images and Multiplying Them

The **img** tag's **width** and **height** attributes can be used to shrink or enlarge your graphic to fit a particular space on your page. The **img** element tag itself, as it is a true inline element, can be repeated as if it were merely a character on a line.

As shown in Figure 5.7, the **width** attribute defines the width of the displayed image in pixels, the smallest graphic element on a screen. Similarly, the **height** attribute defines the height of the displayed image in pixels. When only dimension is used, the current aspect ratio of the image is maintained. Using **img001.jpg**, with a 69x154 (width x height) pixel image and using **height="77"** the width will be automatically adjusted to give a 35x77 displayed image size. Using **height="308"** the image is stretched to give a 138x308 image size. A similar result would occur if we fixed the **width** attribute allowing the height of the image to be automatically adjusted according to the image's aspect ratio. Either the **width** and **height** attributes can also use **"###%"** values such as **width="10%"** or **height="500%"** to permit your Web page to be scalable, that is, for it to fill the browser regardless of how small or big the browser window is.

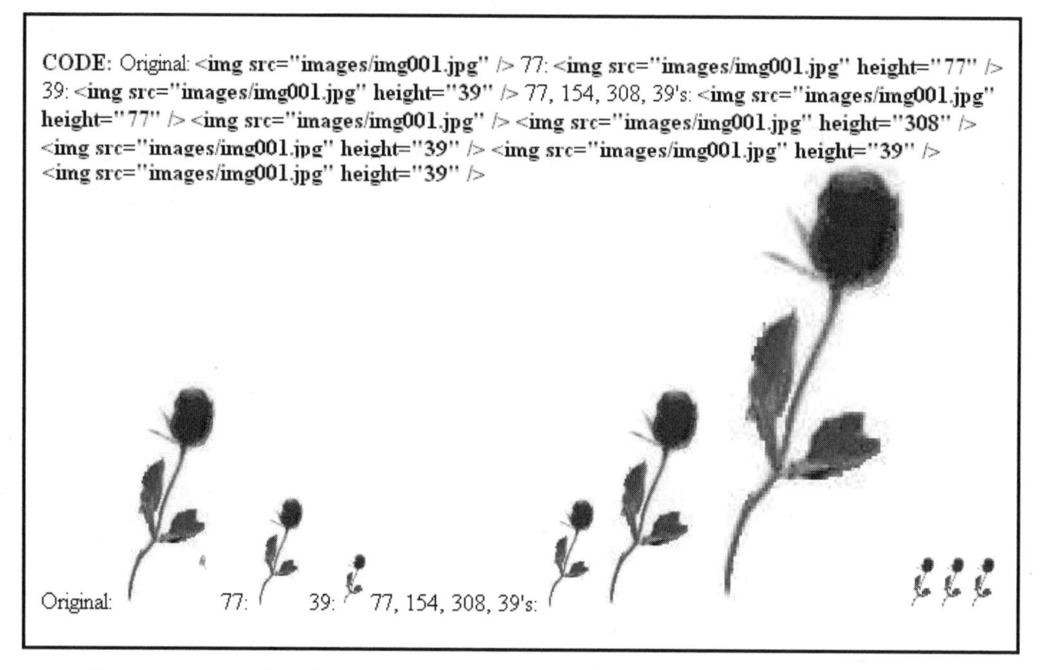

Figure 5.7. Adjusting Image Height to Fit Your Space (code0507.htm)

As you can also see in Figure 5.7, web images are not very scalable. Even when the height is doubled (308 pixels) the image starts to become "fuzzy" or pixilated. This is due to the image's pixels being merely repeated to accommodate stretching of the height and width, resulting in a very poor image quality when the browser fits the image into a much larger defined space.

In the few instances when you want a fully defined image space, both the **width** and **height** attributes can be used in a single **img** tag. The benefit of using both is that the image size is maintained while the image file is being processed by your browser. If there is a broken link to the image, an empty area the size it would have used is displayed on the browser.

Using the resize function on an art program like Paint Shop Pro or Adobe PhotoShop is the most efficient way to shrink or enlarge an image. But note that the special mathematical calculations used in resizing affect the new file size. Using the **width** and **height** attributes forces a temporary size change in your browser without any file size changes.

Our 69-pixel-wide and 154-pixel-high red rose graphic (**img001.jpg**), for example, contains well over 10,000 pixels, but is compressed into a JPEG file size of only 3 kilobytes (kb). The file size for a 32 wide by 72 high graphic (**img004.jpg**) is about 1.5 kilobytes, BUT resizing **img001.jpg** using a **width** or **height** attribute still requires that the full 3 kb file be retrieved regardless of the resulting displayed image size.

Also demonstrated in Figure 5.7 is the ability of the **img** tag to display images in line, without line breaks before and after images.

Boxing in Your Images

Notice in the figures above that there was no border around the images. The **img** element's default **border** attribute (**"0"**) can be set to **"1"** for a one-pixel border or for as thick a border (in pixels) as you want it! Figure 5.8 shows some sample border thicknesses as well as the spacing (about two pixels) that is used automatically to separate inline images. A few caveats: first, note that placing a thick, black, border around a photo can yield an "in memoriam" effect. Of course that might be what you are intending! Also, as we'll see later in this chapter, when we use hypergraphics, an image that is hyperlinked to another page or Web site, the color the border takes on would be the color scheme defined for all hyperlinks.

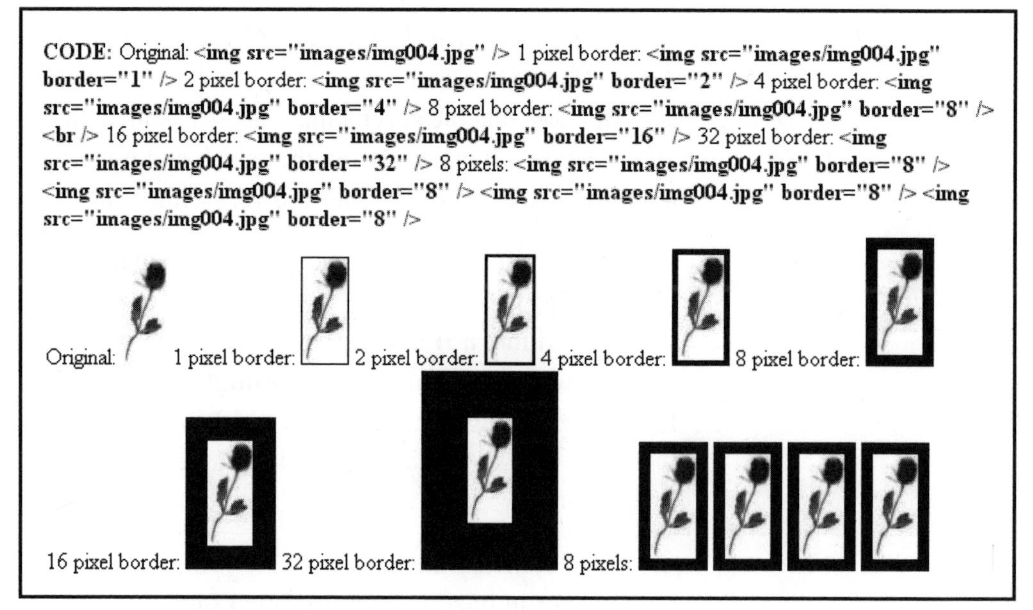

Figure 5.8. Boxing in Your Images (code0508.htm)

Adding White Space Around Your Images

Although your browser automatically includes a small border around each of your images, it may not be enough of a separation to suit your page's needs. The horizontal space **hspace** and/or vertical space **vspace** attributes can be used to position the image on the page using the value **n**, in pixels, as is seen in Figure 5.9. Now that we can position the image by defining the horizontal and/or vertical margins surrounding them, what if we didn't want our text to appear flush with the bottom of our images all the time?

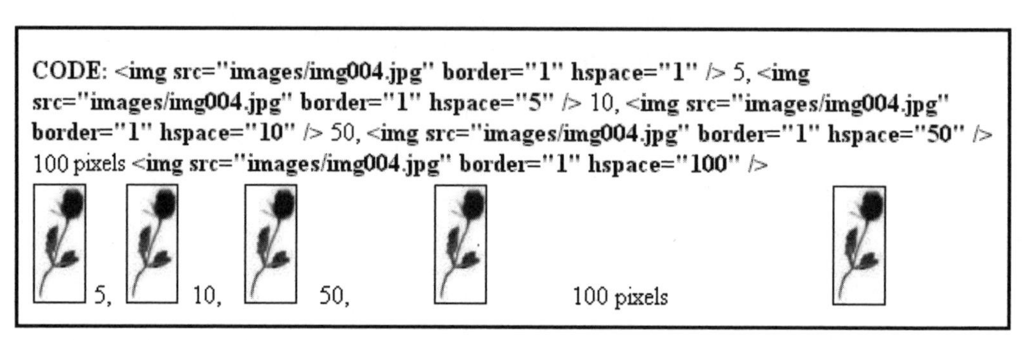

Figure 5.9. Adding Horizontal Space Between Your Images (code0509.htm)

Aligning Your Images and Text

As shown in Figure 5.10, when the image is larger than the text line, the **align** attribute defines where the image will be located relative to adjacent text. This attribute can define the location as the top (default), the middle, or bottom, right or left.

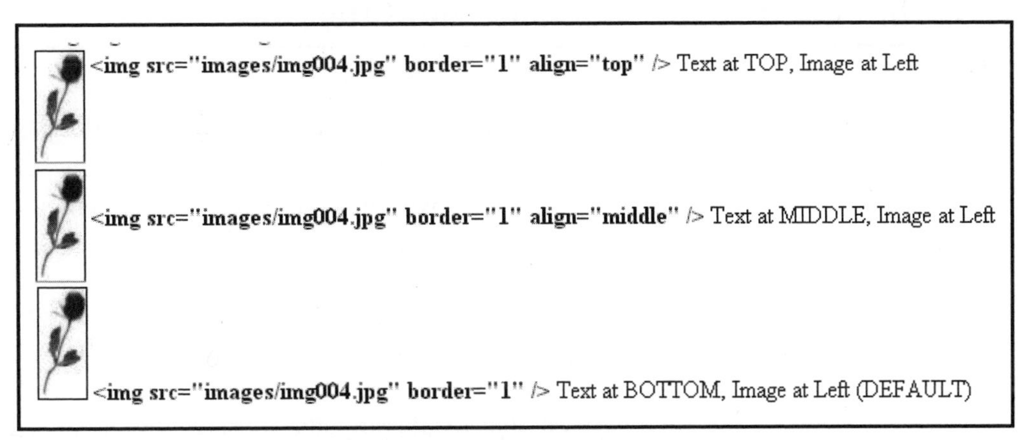

Figure 5.10. Aligning Text and Images (code0510.htm)

When the **align** attribute is used with its right and left values (**align="right"** and **align="left"**), it creates text that seems to flow around images, as in Figure 5.11.

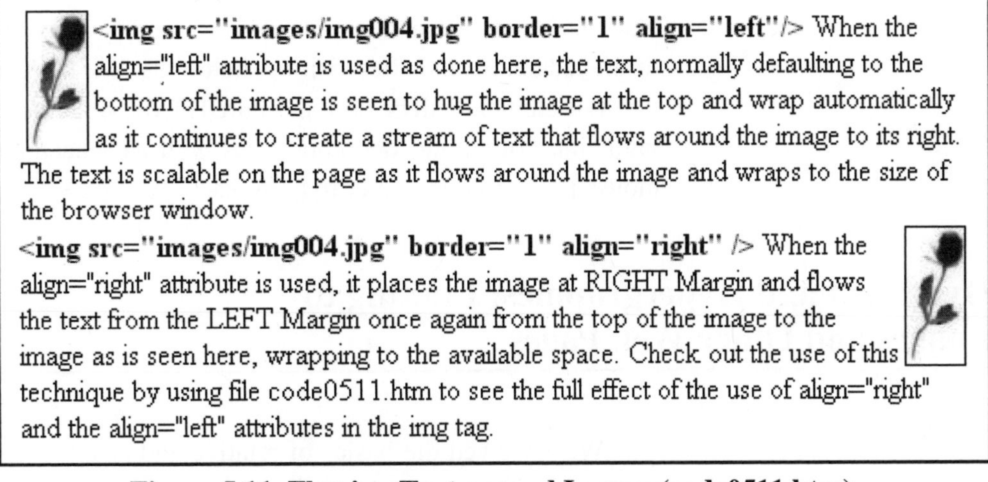

Figure 5.11. Flowing Text around Images (code0511.htm)

This technique is used quite often in the creation of newsletters. Of course the **img** attributes of **border**, **vspace**, and **hspace**, as well as **width** and **height**, can all be used with the **align** attribute (in any convenient order), giving an appearance of a word processed newsletter. Try it with your own images and text and see if you don't agree that it is a great way to simulate word processing in HTML documents without resorting to the table element that we'll review in Chapter 8. As the table element is being phased out in later HTML versions, this trick will no doubt become a standard presentation alternative.

Hyperlinking: Locally, Globally, and Internally

A book is typically read sequentially, page after page, from the beginning to the end. Sometimes textbooks are read by selecting chapters out of sequence to cover material in a class, but here, too, the pages are usually turned one by one in order.

The magic of the Web is its ability to randomly select the path and page that one wishes to go to in any order. The Web page's target or link may be internal, to a section or paragraph in the current Web page; local, to a page on your local computer or server; or global or external—anywhere on the Internet.

The HTML anchor element **a** is used when you want to redirect your Web page user to an internal, local, or external Web page using hypertext or hypergraphic links. The anchor opening tag must include either the **href** or the **name** attribute. If used to surround text, the text is highlighted to identify it as hypertext link, typically underscored and in blue. The **body** element can be used to modify the way hyperlinks are displayed before and after visiting their links. We'll see in Chapter 6 that the **style** element will be used in future HTML versions to change the default link colors and decorations as well as what happens when the mouse pointer hovers over hyperlinks.

Hypertext and Hypergraphics: Linking to Images and Other Web Pages

We reviewed the basics of relative and absolute addressing in the last section when we looked at how the **img src** attribute is used. The anchor **a** element's **href** is a hypertext transfer protocol reference link that works in much the same way as the **img src** attribute as it points the browser to either relative or absolute addresses for a Web page or graphic image file. The text between the anchor element opening and closing tags becomes hypertext, and when clicked on, your browser gets the file at the URL value of the **href** attribute. Clicking on a hyperlink signals the browser to load a new page or display an image from the same server (relative addressing), or retrieve a file from a Web location defined by a full URL (absolute addressing).

As you can see, Figure 5.12 is a full-page screen shot. I strongly recommend that you view it on your browser using the file **code0512.htm** since it is a very busy figure. This figure contains nearly all the coding we can use for hyperlinking on an HMTL page in one place. We will use it to see how to retrieve graphic files to display by themselves on your browser, how to link to other files and Web sites using both text (hypertext) and graphics (hypergraphics), as well as to navigate within the same Web page using the anchor's other attribute, the **name** attribute (Figure 5.12 code lines a, f, and g).

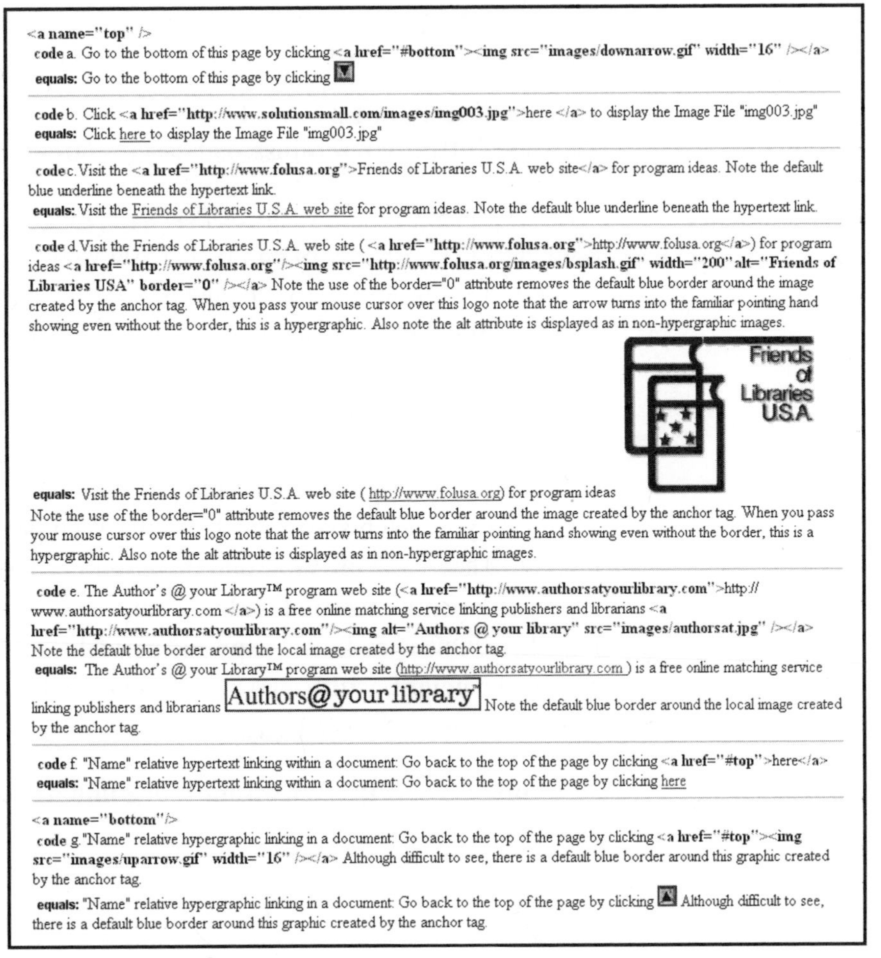

Figure 5.12. Hypertext, Hypergraphics, and the name Attribute (code0512.htm)

Just as we saw when we were loading images onto our Web page, it is always easier to hyperlink to local files using relative linking. But if we want our patron to go from the current Web page to a file on another server, we need to use absolute addressing. Let's see how we direct the browser to view an image file named **img003.jpg** that is in the subfolder called **images** in the Web server root folder on the Solutions Mall Web site. The anchor tag's **href** attribute requires absolute addressing using the full uniform resource locator (URL) that describes exactly where the file is. To suggest that your patron view that image, you might use a snippet of code (code line b) as shown in Figure 5.12 and repeated here:

Click **<a href="http://www.solutionsmall.com/images/img003.jpg">** here **</a>**

to display the Image File **"img003.jpg"**

If your patron was a volunteer on your Friends of The Red Rose Library page and you wanted that person to visit the Friends of Libraries U.S.A. Web site for information on improving the library's program, you might use Figure 5.12 code line c, repeated here:

Visit the Friends of Libraries U.S.A. Web site
<a href="http://www.folusa.org">here**</a>** for program ideas

Perhaps the most exciting aspect of linking is that you can also link graphics to Web pages. Let's say that you want to show the logo for the Friends of Libraries U.S.A. on your Web page and have the logo link to that Web site. Figure 5.12 shows the result, but how did we know where to get the logo? Clearly you could e-mail the owner of the Web site (we'll see how you can set that up for your Web pages in the next section) or Webmaster—the person responsible for the pages—for permission to save the logo on your Web site. But what if you don't want to save it on your Web site? First go to the Web page that you found the logo on. Then click on View and then Source. The source code for the page will open in **notepad** and you can search for the **img** tag for the logo there. Once you find it, copy and paste the tag information. You can change the **height**, **width**, and **alt** information, but what you really need from that page is the **src** URL:

<img src="http://www.folusa.org/images/bsplash.gif" />

We can modify the other attributes in the HTML file, add some text, and surround the new **img** tag by an anchor link to the full URL of the Web site, as in Figure 5.12 code line d, repeated here:

Visit the Friends of Libraries U.S.A. web site
(**<a href="http://www.folusa.org">http://www.folusa.org</a>**)
for program ideas **<a href="http://www.folusa.org"><img src="http://www.folusa.org/images/bsplash.gif" width="200" alt="Friends of Libraries USA" border="0" /></a>**

Note that in many HTML files **img** and other empty tags are not closed. Make sure that you add the **/>** at the end of these empty tags. In the example of Figure 5.12 code line d, we have created a hypertext link to **http://www.folusa.org**, which will not only tell your patrons what the URL is, but also bring them there if they click on that text. Similarly, by surrounding the **img** tag with a hyperlink we can click on the organization's logo to go to the Web site. It is important to note that using absolute addressing for image files, or Web pages, has a major drawback. As shown in Figure 5.6, should the folder structure or location of these links on an external Web site change, some or all of your links will be broken. Broken Web page links yield a "404" server error, which results in the browser displaying a "page not found" warning. Although the links above were all accomplished with absolute addressing, you can use relative addresses if you have permission to store these images and pages are on your local Web space. This is apparent where the logo file authorsat.jpg in your local images folder is used as the link to the Author's @ Your Library™ program Web site (**http://www.authorsatyourlibrary.com**) using the code in Figure 5.12 code line e:

The Author's @ your Library™ program web site
(**<a href="http://www.authorsatyourlibrary.com">
http://www.authorsatyourlibrary.com </a>**)

is a free online matching service linking publishers and librarians

<a href="http:// www.authorsatyourlibrary.com"><img src= "images/authorsat.jpg" alt="Authors @ your library" /></a>

Note that unlike the Friends of Libraries image, which used the **border="0"** attribute, without this attribute set to zero your anchor element automatically adds a one-pixel border, which takes on the default **link**, **vlink**, and **alink** color scheme for hyperlinks.

Relative Links Within a Web Page: The Name Attribute

Now is probably a good time to remind you how YOU did not like it when you were surfing the Web sometime in the past and clicked "print" on a paragraph you wanted to print out only to have five, ten, or even fifteen pages print out! If you are careful in designing your Web pages, they will print one physical page per Web page, but even then your page could be too long to fit in one browser screen.

When a Web page is very long, at least more than a screen window high, the anchor tag's **name** attribute can be used to navigate between the top, bottom, and other sections of your page.

The anchor opening tag in this instance uses the technique of Figure 5.12 code lines f and g to link either text or an image to a location using the **href** attribute and **name** value of the location. The anchor's location variable is preceded by the "#" sign as in **href="#location"** to link it to the empty anchor tag **<a name="location" />** (note there is no # in the **name** attribute tag), which shows the browser where to jump to in the document. Figure 5.12 code lines a and g show the **top** and **bottom** target codes respectively, with Figure 5.12 code lines a, f, and g illustrating the hyperlink codes. Figure 5.12 code lines a and g also show the use of images, in this case up and down arrows, to navigate to the top and bottom of the page using hypergraphics.

Opening a New Browser Window

When you navigate between Web pages and Web sites, the default anchor attribute tag is **target="_self"**, which opens the new page in the same browser window that the current page resides in. This requires the back arrow to be used to return to the original or calling page. The **target** attribute is often used with the value **target="_blank"** to open a new browser window when you link to a new page, as in the following example:

<a href="http:// www.authorsatyourlibrary.com" target="_ blank">Web Site**</a>**

Other values for the **target** attribute are utilized when the Web page contains frames—a technique in which smaller windows divide the browser window into sections. We will NOT be discussing frames in this text, as they are more complicated and best left to other texts.

Adding Your E-mail Address to Your Web Page

The last link type that we need to discuss is the **mailto:** protocol variation of the **href** attribute that automatically sends an e-mail to the Webmaster, etc. The e-mail address is often used with the italics text style to yield the effect shown in Figure 5.13. As always, watch your element tag nesting order.

Adding an email contact address without hyperlinking:
You can reach me at <i>c.rubenstein@ieee.org</i>
You can reach me at *c.rubenstein@ieee.org*

Adding an email contact address with hyperlinking:
You can reach me at <**a href="mailto:c.rubenstein@ieee.org"**><i>c.rubenstein@ieee.org</i></a>
You can reach me at *c.rubenstein@ieee.org*

Figure 5.13. Using the mailto: Hyperlink (code0516.htm)

In Figure 5.13 we have not only shown a typical font style for an e-mail address, but have shown the use of the anchor element **a** and **href** attribute to create an automatic call to your browser's e-mail program. This action embeds the e-mail address on your Web page into an e-mail. Please note that many libraries and other public area systems have e-mail turned off. If the **mailto:** technique is used on public computers, your patrons may find themselves unable to directly use the public computer's e-mail software. The technique should work fine on your patrons' home computers if they have been set up properly.

What's Next?

In this chapter we looked at how HTML is used to include images of various sizes on your Web page with the **img** element, how text can be aligned with respect to these images, and how to hyperlink text or graphics using the anchor element.

In Chapter 6 we look at the basics of stylizing small sections of text using the inline **style** attribute, Web page level document stylization using the internal **style** element, and the Web site wide **style** files using the technique known as cascading style sheets.

Chapter 6

div, span, Style Sheets, and Floating Images

In this chapter the **div** and **span** elements are introduced and the use of the inline **style** attribute to customize text in paragraphs and whole sections on your Web page is explained. A review is made of how **style** attributes can also be used in line and with several other HTML elements. Then style will be used as an element to redefine HTML element defaults on a page. Saving these style definitions in a separate file allows us to "call" that file when any page needs that specific styling. This method, called cascading style sheets or CSS, is a convenient way to use collections of style sheet files to create a uniform look and feel for each different page type on your Web site. Finally, the use of style techniques in line or in external Style Sheet files to modify the display of images is illustrated. This will include the illusion of floating images on a Web page. Stylization techniques will be shown in the chapters on lists, tables, and forms. Enough style is covered so that you will understand how to use it to change the display characteristics of the HTML elements already covered in previous chapters. These include adding style one page at a time, changing multiple defaults with style on a single page, anchor link styles, and defining style within elements using classes. Please note that as CSS effects are browser-specific, your browser may render some stylizations differently, or ignore them. Internet Explorer was used to create the examples shown in this chapter.

The div and span Elements

Up until this point we have dealt with text as a series of continuous characters, forming them into lines and paragraphs using **br** and/or **p** tags. We learned in Chapter 4 how to use the **font** element to stylize text and that the **font** element is being phased out in future HTML versions to be replaced by style sheets. In this chapter we cover how to use the **style** attribute in the block-level **div** element, which defines text in paragraph-like divisions as well as the **span** element, used to stylize sections of text in line without paragraph or line break effect.

The **div** element is used to format small sections or divisions of text on a Web page, treating them as a block. The **div** is surrounded by implied line breaks just like heading and paragraph tags.

The **span** element, on the other hand, can be used to style sections of text in line without line breaks. Neither the **div** nor **span** element has any default formatting. **div** is typically used with the **align** attribute.

Figure 6.1 shows some sample text surrounded by default **div** and **span** elements to demonstrate the basic differences between them.

CODE: **<font color="red">** This red text line is before the div starting tag.**</font>** **<div>** This text is surrounded by the div element. ... **</div><font color="red">** This red text line is after the div ending tag and before the span starting tag.**</font>** **<span>** This text is surrounded by the span element. ... **</span><font color="red">** This red text line is after the span ending tag.**</font>**

This red text line is before the div starting tag.
This text is surrounded by the div element. Note that although it has neither a line break before, or after it, as a block-level formatting element there is a paragraph break before and after this line.
This red text line is after the div ending tag and before the span starting tag. This text is surrounded by the span element. Note that as it does not have a line break before, or after it, the next line continues right here, at the end of this line. This line is after the span ending tag.

Figure 6.1.Comparing the div and span Elements (code0601.htm)

Although all the HTML elements within the **div** element *do* acquire its style definition, Figure 6.2 illustrates that when an **align** attribute is placed in a **span** tag, the surrounded HTML content does *not* acquire the **align** attribute.

CODE: **<font="red" >** This red text line is before the div starting tag.**</font>** **<div align="center">** This text is surrounded by the div align="center" element tag (breaks after each line). ... **</div><font color="red">** This red text line is after the div ending tag and before the span starting tag.**</font>** **<span align="right">** This text is surrounded by the span align="right" element tag (breaks after each line). ... **</span><font color="red">** This red text line is after the span ending tag.**</font>**

This red text line is before the div starting tag.

This text is surrounded by the div align="center" element tag (breaks after each line).
Note that it has neither a line break before or after it.
It is a block-level formatting element with a line break before and after this section. Also note that alignment is throughout the section.

This red text line is after the div ending tag and before the span starting tag. This text is surrounded by the span align="right" element tag (breaks after each line).
Note that it does not have a line break before or after the tag.
The next line continues right here, at the end of this line. Also note the absence of any alignment to the right... This red text line is after the span ending tag.

Figure 6.2. Acquiring div and span Styles in Line (code0602.htm)

Cascading Style Sheets (CSS)

Cascading style sheets (CSS) redefine how a browser displays audio and visual HTML elements. CSS are nearly as powerful as a new markup language and are upward compatible to XHTML and XML. The basic use of the three variations of style sheets—style attributes added in line directly to HTML elements, internal style sheets used to define properties of HTML elements on a single Web page, and external style sheets that can be used throughout a Web site—are reviewed here.

Adding Inline Style Attributes to HTML Elements

The **style** attribute can be added to HTML elements to create inline stylizations of the content the element contains. “Sub-attributes” of the style attribute include text properties (**text-align**, **text-indent**, **text-transform**, **text-decoration**), color, font characteristics (**font-weight**, **font-color**, **font-style**, **font-variant**, **font-size**, **font-family**), margins (**margin-left**, **margin-right**, **margin-top**, **margin-bottom**), borders, backgrounds, and padding. For simple stylizations, where you only need to style a few HTML elements on a page, **style** attributes are used to define how your tagged content will be displayed with inline commands.

Unfortunately, as with any nonstandard method of displaying HTML, depending on your browser, not all style sub-attribute values display properly. Be sure to check your display results on several browser types, as *many* inline **style** attributes do *not* work on all browsers or their older versions. For example, although **font size** *can* be measured in points, browsers do pretty much everything in terms of pixels, with the result that point size text is not always displayed uniformly. So don't fight with your browser, use pixels!

As noted in Chapter 4's discussion about the **font** element's **face** attribute, defining a **fontfamily** can be done with a series of font types, in the order in which you want them used. You will not be using the thousands of available fonts, and if none of your desired font faces is available on your user's computer, a default generic typeface (e.g., sans serif) will be used instead.

Using Border Attributes with Horizontal Rules

We saw in Figure 4.8 that we can modify the **hr** horizontal rule element with **height, width, noshade,** and **align** attributes to make a variety of thicker and width-controlled rule lines.

When inline style attributes are added to rule lines, we have better control of rule line height and width in pixels or points (**1pt** to **100pt**) or with words (**thin**, **medium**—the default, and **thick**). We can define line color in the standard colors (**aqua**, **black**, **blue**, **fuchsia**, **gray**, **green**, **lime**, **maroon**, **navy**, **olive**, **purple**, **red**, **silver**, **teal**, **white**, **yellow**) or using **#rrggbb** values. We can also add the border style attribute values **solid**, **dashed**, **dotted**, **groove**, **ridge**, **double**, **inset**, and **outset**.

These stylizations increase the ways you can separate sections of your Web page (recall that the horizontal rule behaves much like a heading with implied paragraph tags surrounding it). You can add many other style sheet sub-attributes inline to the **hr** element, for example, adding five-pixel-thick border sub-attributes gives more power to the simple horizontal rule, as shown in the examples in Figure 6.3, as displayed by Internet Explorer. Firefox will not properly render the border type or color commands for the horizontal rule. Some Web pages use the footnote "Best viewed with Internet Explorer, Version 6" (etc.) to advise you that their page will not render well in other browsers.

Default Rule <hr />	
50% Rule - Left <hr style="width:50%; text-align:left" />	50% Rule - Left
50% Rule - Right <hr style="width:50%; text-align:right" />	50% Rule - Right
50% Rule <hr style="width:50%" />	Rule Width = 50%
50% Rule, height = 16 <hr style="width:50%; height:16" />	50% Rule, Height = 16
50% Rule, color=red <hr style="width:50%; color:red" />	50% Rule, Color = red
50% Rule, color=red, height = 6 <hr style="width:50%; color:red; height:6" />	Color = red, Height = 6
50% Rule, Color=red, Height = 16 <hr style="width:50%; color:red; height:16" />	Color = red, Height = 16
Width = 50%, noshade <hr style="width:50%" noshade />	50% Rule, noshade
Height = 16, noshade <hr style="width:50%; height:16" noshade />	Height = 16, noshade
Inset Green Border <hr style="height:16; border:5 inset green" />	Inset Green Border
Outset Green Border <hr style="height:16; border:5 outset green" />	Outset Green Border
Solid Green Border <hr style="height:16; border:5 solid green" />	Solid Green Border
Dotted Blue Border <hr style="height:16; border:5 dotted blue" />	Dotted Blue Border
Dashed Blue Border <hr style="height:16; border:5 dashed blue" />	Dashed Blue Border
Double Red Border <hr style="height:16; border:5 double red" />	Double Red Border
Groove Red Border <hr style="height:16; border:5 groove red" />	Groove Red Border
Ridge Red Border <hr style="height:16; border:5 ridge red" />	Ridge Red Border

Figure 6.3. Inline Horizontal Line Style Examples (code0603.htm)

These same border styles and techniques could be used for creating borders around images and for creating tables.

There is no limit to the creativity you can show using inline **style** attributes. Other styling options for inline style attributes include adding spaces between text characters, changing background colors, and even adding image backgrounds behind text. Setting the background color in a single **div** block to the color **#00ff00** can be accomplished using the code:

```
<div style="background-color:#00ff00">
```

Defining the font size and adding additional space between all the letters in one paragraph of your text can be accomplished with inline **style**:

<p style="font-size:30px; letter-spacing:25px">

Setting the text size and color of a local italicized section of your text can also be accomplished with the **style** attribute:

<i style="font-size:18px; color:#00ff00">

Internal or Embedded Cascading Style Sheets

In the previous section we saw that style sheet concepts can be used, with some good results, as an inline **style** attribute for many HMTL elements. This technique makes for larger files, because each time you use an inline attribute, you need to repeat it just before the text, division, or span you want to stylize.

If you standardize the look and feel of your Web page with a style table that includes all the **style** definitions at the element level, you have internal or embedded cascading style sheets. The internal stylesheet "overwrites" the default values your browser uses for any element attributes you have redefined. That way you need not use inline style, as we saw in the last section, for each and every paragraph (etc.) to use the new stylization. The **style** element defines style characteristics at the document or page level and needs to be placed inside the **head** of an HTML document.

The **style** element in its simplest form can modify your page's text properties by aligning the text (**text-align**), indenting it (**text-indent**) and underlining it (**text-decoration**), and altering its **color** and one or more **font** characteristics (**font-weight**, **font-color**, **font-style**, **font—size**, and **font-family**). Using style you also can modify the page's **border**, **background**, **padding**, and margins (**margin-left**, **margin-right**, **margin-top**, **margin-bottom**).

In Chapter 7, where we discuss creating Web page lists, we'll see that style can be used to modify list attributes (**list-style**, **list-type**, **list-image**, **list-position**); in Chapter 8, where we discuss creating Web tables, we'll review stylizing **table** attributes; and in Chapter 9 we'll use style to define **form** attributes.

Adding Style—One Page at a Time

The internal **style** element can list the style definitions that will be used on a single Web page without requiring individual inline **style** attributes. This style listing is located just after your **title** definition in your Web page's **head** area. The **style** element opening tag must contain the **type** attribute with its value set to **"text/css"**.

In early style sheet designs, the comment tag (**<!--** and **-->**) surrounded the style definitions to address the needs of early browsers. Although you may still see the comment tags, they are unnecessary. (Although the Internet Explorer Version 6 browser ignores comment tags around style definitions, the Firefox browser does not allow them at all.) All you need is the opening **style** tag followed by each styled element's name, with its attribute value(s) definitions separated by semicolons between a pair of curly brackets (**{ ... }**). After all definitions are made, the closing **style** tag completes the page's internal set of style definitions. You will also need to close the **head** (**</head>**) of your document. This style structure, with the element name and curly braces typed in line for Internet Explorer, is simply

<style type="text/css">

element { property1:value; property2:value(s)} ← new default(s)
</style>

(The Firefox browser does not use quotes around property values. As noted previously, it also fails to recognize some of the properties that Internet Explorer uses.)

The internal style sheet requires a different set of comment tags than those we have already used (**<!--** and **-->**) for general comments in your HTML or style sheet document. The comment in a style sheet consists of a forward slash followed immediately by an asterisk (**/***) opening style comment tag, and a closing style comment tag, which reverses the opening tag (***/**):

/* this is a style sheet comment */

As stated previously, your browser ignores extra spaces and tabs. Style definitions can be written to more clearly show the individual element definitions by adding these ignored spaces and line breaks. Notice that there are no additional characters between each element redefinition in the following example of an internal generic two-element (element1 and element2) style definition set:

```
<style type="text/css">
/* element1 is described in this code */
element1 {
property1: value;
property2: value(s)}
/* element2 is described in this code */
element2      {
property1:value;
   property2:value(s)
}
</style>
```

Style changes can be made for any HTML element. If you want to change the way that the **h1** headline tag is treated, for example, from merely changing its color default to red and font family default to **arial,** the style codes, written as single lines, look like:

```
<style type="text/css"> h1 { color: red; font-family: arial} </style>
```

and the resulting displayed change in **h1** defaults would look like Figure 6.4. To obtain this same effect using a Firefox browser, do not use quotes around the property values unless the value is a multiple word (e.g., **"sans serif"**) , as noted in the following code:

```
< style type="text/css" > h1 { color: red; font-family: arial}
</style>
```

CODE:

```
<html><head><title>Changing h1 style Definitions</title> <style type="text/css">
 h1 { color:"red"; font-family:"arial"; } </style> </head><body>
<h1>New H1 Default: Red Color, Arial Font </h1> </body></html>
```

New H1 Default: Red Color, Arial Font

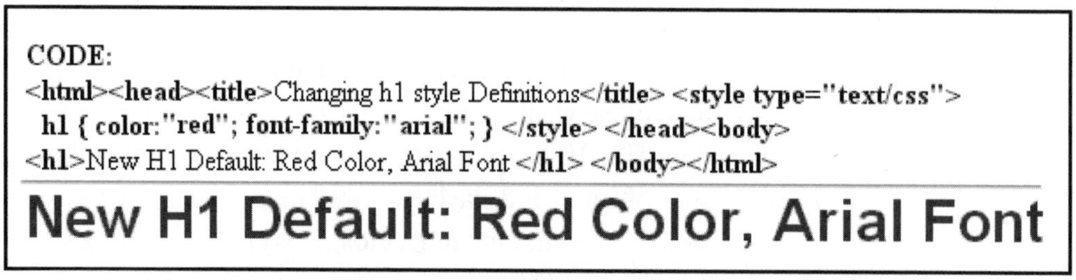

Figure 6.4. Changing h1 Style Definitions (code0604.htm)

Changing Multiple Defaults with Style on a Single Page

Of course more than one element can be defined at a time to create a specific look and feel on a single Web page using this internal style sheet method. And you can add as many element definitions to the internal style sheet list as you would like using the structure above.

Adding more attributes to the element's style definition requires each attribute and its value to be separated by semicolons, as shown in Figure 6.4. If you would like to stylize several elements with the same definition rather than rekey the same definition several times, once for each element, here is a solution. You can actually stylize more than one element with the same new default definition by merely separating the element names with commas before the curly bracket definitions:

```
h1, h3, h5 { color:aqua; font-family:serif }
h2, h4, h6 { color:green; font-family:sans-serif}
b, strong { color:red; font-size:20}
```

Figure 6.5 shows that even when using internal or embedded style sheets, the inline **font color="blue"** coding overrides the internal style sheet **h3 red** color redefinition, just as it would override the **black** default color for **h3** in HTML documents that didn't use style sheets.

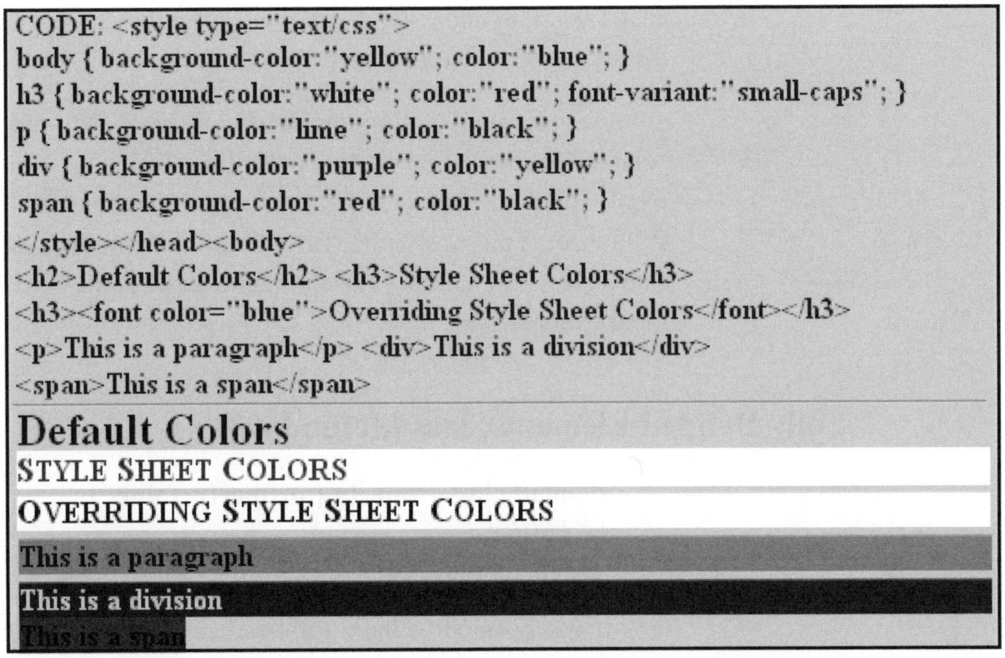

```
CODE: <style type="text/css">
body { background-color:"yellow"; color:"blue"; }
h3 { background-color:"white"; color:"red"; font-variant:"small-caps"; }
p { background-color:"lime"; color:"black"; }
div { background-color:"purple"; color:"yellow"; }
span { background-color:"red"; color:"black"; }
</style></head><body>
<h2>Default Colors</h2> <h3>Style Sheet Colors</h3>
<h3><font color="blue">Overriding Style Sheet Colors</font></h3>
<p>This is a paragraph</p> <div>This is a division</div>
<span>This is a span</span>
```

Default Colors

STYLE SHEET COLORS

OVERRIDING STYLE SHEET COLORS

This is a paragraph

This is a division

This is a span

Figure 6.5. Using an Internal Style Sheet (code0605.htm)

Defining Style Within Elements Using Classes

If you want to have several variations available to you to select a particular heading or a distinct heading for different areas of the library, using a single style for **h4** would probably require you to remember to add inline styling each time you wanted a different typeface or color. That's when your style sheets need **class**.

Class is an element selector name used in cascading style sheets that provides for a secondary level of **style** descriptions for elements. Using **class** techniques permits you to define more than one type of **style** (**class**) for a given element and then select that particular style in your document at the element level. You can consider classes as nothing more than names given to an element you want to define with more than one set of attributes. Try to make class names semantic, for example, use the "comic sans" font for your children's page, calling it the "children" class, while using a more formal serif font like "new times roman" for your Board's Web pages, calling it the "board class." This will make it easy for you to understand rather than spending time trying to figure out the style effect you wanted.

Any element within the **body** of an HTML document can be "classed" in the listing of style definitions inside the **head** of your document. There are two ways to structure the elements and their classes in a style sheet. You can use the "**fully defined element class**" method to define a class that includes the element's name and a class identifier separated by a period.

Fully Defined Element Class Method

element.classproperty { property:value; }
EXAMPLE:
h4.red { color:red}

If you wanted to have the headers all look the same (e.g., same **font-family**) except for their **color,** you could completely code each tag:

h1.red { color:red; font-family:Arial}
h1.green { color:green; font-family:Arial}

Similarly, you can use the "**generic class**" method for those classes that only contain the attribute or other name, preceded by a period.

Generic Class Method

.classproperty { property:value; }
EXAMPLE:
.green { color:green; font-family:arial}

For finer HTML tag control, you could code the headline **font-family** as one style definition and define text different colors as separate classes, giving greater flexibility by defining **red** and **green** as additional classes. Once defined, the color styles can be declared as separate classes in the style sheet set, and they can be used in other elements that require added colorization. Note that if you want to stylize more than one element with the same default, for example declaring all the header elements as **Arial**, you merely string them one after the other separated by commas and then define the group:

```
h1, h2, h3, h4, h5, h6 { font-family:Arial}
.red { color:red
.green { color:green}
```

Notice that although the **fully defined element class** can *only* be used for that particular element, the **generic class** definition can be used to stylize *any* element in the document. Bear in mind that we have only *defined* the **class** in the style sheet. You must "call" it as a **class** attribute by its name within the element surrounding the information you wish to stylize with it on your Web page.

With the generic class method you can use the **red** or **green** color classes in any element of your document as if that element had that added attribute. Whenever you want to use one of these colors you merely "call" them by adding the class statement inside of your normal HTML element's opening tag, as shown in Figure 6.6:

<h1 class="red"> or **<h3 class="green">**

or even elements you have not included in the style set:

<p class="green"> or **<span class="red">**

In our next example, the **h3.red** and the **.green** classes in your style sheet are defined:

```
<style>
    h3.red { color:red; }
    .green { color:green; font-family:Arial}
</style>
```

Once defined, the **h3.red** and the **.green** classes can be used as simply as adding the **class** attribute to an element's code. You must also drop the element's name and class period, as appropriate:

```
<h3 class="red">Stylized h3 heading</h3>
<h3 class="green"> Stylized h3 heading</h3>
```

The **h3** element has not been defined with a green class (**h3.green**) in the style sheet. It acquires the **color** and **font-family** definitions from the generic class **green**, resulting in Figure 6.6.

```
CODE: <html><head> <title> Fully Defined Element and Generic Class Definitions</title>
<style type="text/css"> h3.red { color:"red"; } .green { color:"green"; font-family:"arial"; } </style> </head><body>
<h3> Default h3 Heading</h3> <h3 class="red">h3.red Stylized h3 Heading</h3>
<h3 class="green">.green Stylized h3 Heading</h3>
</body></html>
```

Default h3 Heading
h3.red Stylized h3 Heading
.green Stylized h3 Heading

Figure 6.6. Fully Defined Element and Generic Class Definitions (code0606.htm)

Other Class Acts

Classes have only been used with one or two definitions in these examples. Any or all of the styles listed at the beginning of the "Internal or Embedded Cascading Style Sheets" section can be used to stylize your elements as well as your classes. The **div** element, for example, can be stylized defining not only how the text will look in terms of **font-size** and **color** but also its alignment. In the following code line the top margin is defined showing where on the Web page the **div** section of your document will be placed using the **margin** styles.

```
div { font-size:12px; color:maroon; text-align:center;
margin-top:100px; }
```

The **margin** attribute can be used in any element in style sheets to place items exactly where you would like them to be.

Using External Style Sheet Files

Should you want a series of pages or even your whole Web site to have the same style sheet coding, this is possible. Suppose you wanted to use the set of style definitions of Figure 6.5, as they added just the color style you were looking for. Just save the page's **style** components in a plain text file (created with Notepad or another text editor) with the extension "**css**" (e.g., **colors.css**) and store it in the **images** folder on the Web server. Place the following code in a plain text file called **colors.css**:

```
body { background-color:yellow; color: blue; }
h3 { background-color:white; color: red; }
p { background-color:lime; color: black; }
div { background-color:purple; color: yellow; }
span { background-color:red; color: black; }
```

Do not include the style element opening or closing tags in the file, as they are not needed.

To use the **colors.css** style sheet definitions on a particular Web page, merely use the **link** element in the HTML document's **head** instead of the internal **style** sheet element definition list used in the past few pages.

```
<html><head><title>Using External Style Sheets </title>
<link rel="stylesheet" type="text/css" href="images/colors.css" />
</head>
```

The result would be the same as if you had an internal style sheet definition set with all of those styles. If at any time you want to update all the styles on that set of pages, merely revise the **colors.css** file in the **images** folder, and all pages that refer to it will immediately acquire these changes on viewing the page. Please note that although the page is displayed by your browser as if the style sheet was an internal or embedded style sheet, it actually calls the CSS file(s) and overlays the internal HTML stylings before it renders the page. You can see this by looking at the source code on your browser. (Open the file in the browser, click on View in the taskbar and then Source from the pull down menu.) This is called a client-side technique even though the actual files need to be on the server.

If the CSS file has moved or cannot be found, the normal browser defaults will still be there to use. If more than one CSS file is linked to your Web page, your browser will try to cascade or write over the element changes one on top of the other as appropriate.

Of course you might decide, as your Web server is on the Web anyway, to use one of the standard template style sheets from an online resource. You can review and test several core W3C Web page style templates at **http://www.w3.org/StyleSheets/Core/preview**

As external style sheets are often made for the use of more than one person, it is important that style comments (**/* style comments */**) be included and liberally used for the information of others using them. You might also want to consider making a style sheet test page for each of the cascading style sheets you plan on using so you'll know which handles the styles you want for any particular page display.

Updating Our Red Rose Library Home Page

To apply some cascading style sheet concepts to a sample for the Red Rose Library Home Page, as in Figure 6.7, the first step is to decide which styles to incorporate on the page.

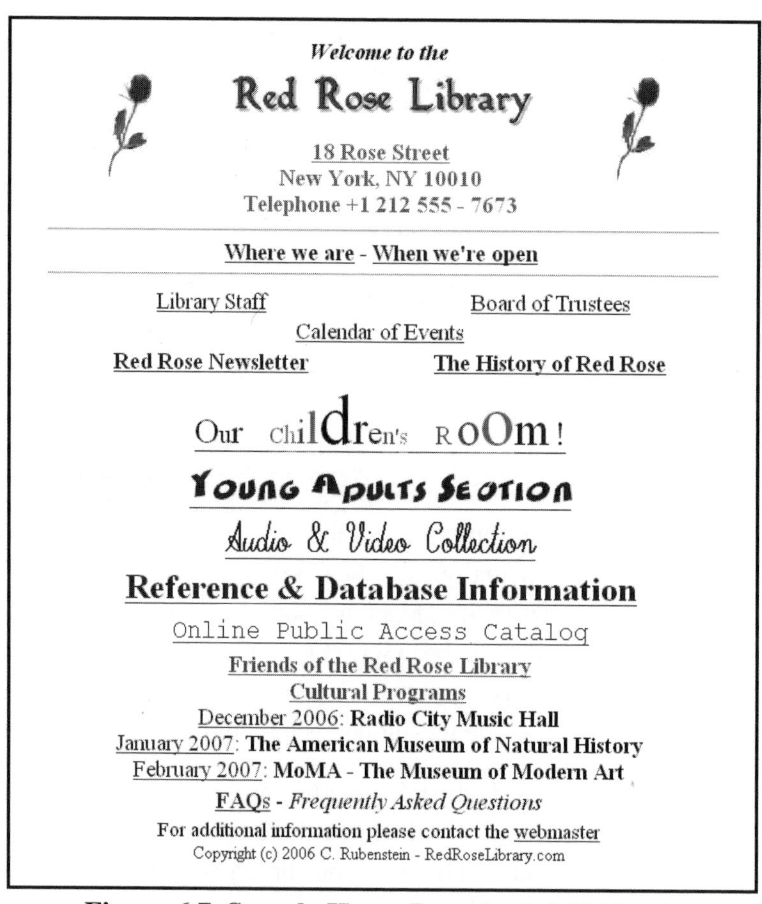

Figure 6.7. Sample Home Page (code0607.htm)

This sample home page has nearly every text phrase hyperlinked to another page on the Web site; therefore, it makes good sense to remove all hyperlink underlining. Using CSS pseudo-classes we can define each possible anchor option. The **text-decoration: none** attribute with the various hyperlink elements becomes

```
a:link, a:visited, a:active { text-decoration: none}
```

Once the underlining is removed, the only way to distinguish between text and hypertext is by carefully watching to see if the mouse cursor changes into a hyperlink hand. (Although many Webmasters use these style techniques to remove the obvious underlining and blue coloring of hypertext, it is not always wise to do so. We all know what happens with the default hypertext. Would your new technique be obvious enough for those not looking for your "hidden" hyperlinks? Usability experts suggest that making it obvious what is a hyperlink will make it easier for your Web page users and more likely that they will return to your site.) The actual control for changing the way the text looks when the mouse pointer is over it is called a mouseover, and it is changed by defining the anchor elements "hover" subelement characteristics (**a:hover**). To make sure that your user sees that a hyperlink is available after removing the underlining, you can stylize the hypertext area mouseover with a bold, red text that is 25 percent larger than the surrounding text, using the styling attributes **font-weight: bold**, **color: red** and **font-size: 125%**:

```
a:hover { font-weight: bold; color: red; font-size: 125% }
```

In those browsers where the order in which the anchor pseudo-classes must be described matters, the order is: **a:link**, **a:visited**, **a:hoover**, **a:active**.

If these are the only default changes we are interested in (at this time), and remembering that elements with the same style definition can be stylized in one code line when their names are comma separated, we can easily set up an internal style sheet with the following styles:

```
    <style>
a:link, a:visited { text-decoration: none }
a:hover { font-weight: bold; color: red; font-size: 125%}
a:active { text-decoration: none }
</style>
```

That same code can be saved as a plain text style sheet file and a link provided to the external style sheet file in your HTML document. The coding for the internal style sheet implementation of Figure 6.8 is **code0608int.htm**, with the file set for the external style sheet version being **code0608ext.htm** and **0608style.css** (it is a required style sheet file that is located in the **image**s folder). The result of removing the hypertext underlining and enhancing the mouseover links is demonstrated by hovering over the "History of Red Rose" hyperlink in Figure 6.8.

Figure 6.8. Internal and External CSS Techniques (code0608.htm)

Please note that hyperlinks that have inline attributes override the style sheet styles (yes, this is a form of cascading!). Thus the fancy font styles and colors of the Children's Room, Young Adults Section, 18 Rose Street, and Cultural Program phrases are all enlarged, but their font face and color is styled by the local, inline, attributes.

Also note that although this technique will change the response to hypertext when moused over, hypergraphics (images with anchor tags surrounding them) are unable to display the text changes in the **a:hover** stylization. They will display and link with a border (unless **border="0"**) regardless of the **a:hover** style changes.

Please be comforted that should you make an error in the coding, all that would happen is that your page wouldn't display properly. What you will need to do is troubleshoot the coding to correct your error.

Styling Paragraph Indents and Margins

There are lots of other tricks you can do with CSS. Examples can be found on the W3Schools Web site **http://www.w3schools.com/css/** Among these, the styling of paragraphs is made easy with style sheets, as the margin and indentation can be set for whatever style you like, with one or more paragraph styles. Assigning a paragraph style that has the first letter of the paragraph indented by thirty-five pixels (about five to six character widths) with a twenty-pixel margin on the left and a ninety-pixel margin on the right would look like:

p.one { text-indent:35px; margin-left:20px; margin- right:90px}

To add a few more classes to your document to see how best to structure your page, you could add the following style code class snippets:

p.two { text-indent:35px; margin-left:90px; margin- right:20px}
p.three { text-indent:35px; margin-left:55px; margin- right:55px}
p.four { text-indent:35px; margin-left:30px; margin- right:60px}
p.five { text-indent:35px; margin-left:60px; margin- right:30px}

Using the appropriate paragraph opening tags (e.g., **<p class="four">**) around your paragraphs of text will give results something like the first chapter of Genesis from **http://www.sacred-texts.com/bib/kjv/gen001.htm**, shown in Figure 6.9.

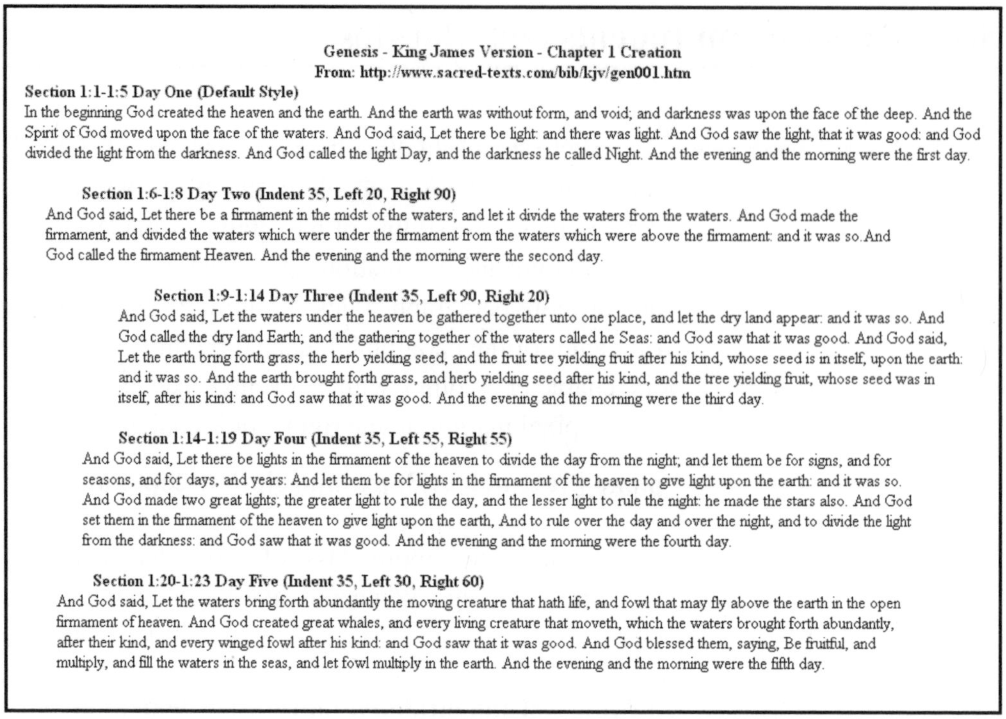

Genesis - King James Version - Chapter 1 Creation
From: http://www.sacred-texts.com/bib/kjv/gen001.htm

Section 1:1-1:5 Day One (Default Style)
In the beginning God created the heaven and the earth. And the earth was without form, and void; and darkness was upon the face of the deep. And the Spirit of God moved upon the face of the waters. And God said, Let there be light: and there was light. And God saw the light, that it was good: and God divided the light from the darkness. And God called the light Day, and the darkness he called Night. And the evening and the morning were the first day.

Section 1:6-1:8 Day Two (Indent 35, Left 20, Right 90)
And God said, Let there be a firmament in the midst of the waters, and let it divide the waters from the waters. And God made the firmament, and divided the waters which were under the firmament from the waters which were above the firmament: and it was so.And God called the firmament Heaven. And the evening and the morning were the second day.

Section 1:9-1:14 Day Three (Indent 35, Left 90, Right 20)
And God said, Let the waters under the heaven be gathered together unto one place, and let the dry land appear: and it was so. And God called the dry land Earth; and the gathering together of the waters called he Seas: and God saw that it was good. And God said, Let the earth bring forth grass, the herb yielding seed, and the fruit tree yielding fruit after his kind, whose seed is in itself, upon the earth: and it was so. And the earth brought forth grass, and herb yielding seed after his kind, and the tree yielding fruit, whose seed was in itself, after his kind: and God saw that it was good. And the evening and the morning were the third day.

Section 1:14-1:19 Day Four (Indent 35, Left 55, Right 55)
And God said, Let there be lights in the firmament of the heaven to divide the day from the night; and let them be for signs, and for seasons, and for days, and years: And let them be for lights in the firmament of the heaven to give light upon the earth: and it was so. And God made two great lights; the greater light to rule the day, and the lesser light to rule the night: he made the stars also. And God set them in the firmament of the heaven to give light upon the earth, And to rule over the day and over the night, and to divide the light from the darkness: and God saw that it was good. And the evening and the morning were the fourth day.

Section 1:20-1:23 Day Five (Indent 35, Left 30, Right 60)
And God said, Let the waters bring forth abundantly the moving creature that hath life, and fowl that may fly above the earth in the open firmament of heaven. And God created great whales, and every living creature that moveth, which the waters brought forth abundantly, after their kind, and every winged fowl after his kind: and God saw that it was good. And God blessed them, saying, Be fruitful, and multiply, and fill the waters in the seas, and let fowl multiply in the earth. And the evening and the morning were the fifth day.

Figure 6.9. Defining Paragraph Classes (code0609.htm)

Background Images

Background images can also be enhanced by using cascading style sheets. By looking at examples that use the internal style sheet, you can use what you have learned to create more useful external style sheet files with all the styles you want to use on your Web pages. In the first chapter, images were inserted on the Web page, and in Chapter 4, a tiled image background was added using the **body** element opening tag:

```
<body background:"images/img001.jpg">
```

Create a suitably soft image like the one of Figure 6.10 using Adobe Photoshop or Corel's Paint Shop Pro, or the image might have the effect of making your page unreadable (as was shown in the rose-tiled background of Figure 4.3).

Figure 6.10. Softened Logo for Watermarking Your Page (img005.jpg)

Using cascading style sheets can create the same effect by styling the body element, but using style values you can style the page to show a background image that won't tile or a single background image centered on the page, and even add a background color in case the image can't be found, or for those who can't see the image. Some sample codes for these styles are

Non-tiled Background image:

body { background:"url(images/img005.jpg) no-repeat"}

Centered background image displayed once with yellow background color:

body { background:"#ffff00 url(images/img005.jpg) no-repeat center"}

Centered background image displayed once—no background color (Figure 6.10):

body { background:"url(images/img005.jpg) no-repeat center"}

The centered, nonrepeating image method can be used with the first three paragraphs of the Genesis page (Figure 6.9) and the **img005.jpg** watermark graphic to create the style sheet watermarking Figure 6.11. You will find that as you change the size of your browser window, the "centered" image repositions as it is positioned relative to the window, not the content.

Genesis - King James Version - Chapter 1 Creation
From: http://www.sacred-texts.com/bib/kjv/gen001.htm

Section 1:1-1:5 Day One (Default Style)
King James Version: Genesis Chapter 1 In the beginning God created the heaven and the earth. And the earth was without form, and void; and darkness was upon the face of the deep. And the Spirit of God moved upon the face of the waters. And God said, Let there be light: and there was light. And God saw the light, that it was good: and God divided the light from the darkness. And God called the light Day, and the darkness he called Night. And the evening and the morning were the first day.

Section 1:6-1:8 Day Two (Indent 35, Left 20, Right 90)
And God said, Let there be a firmament in the midst of the waters, and let it divide the waters from the waters. And God made the firmament, and divided the waters which were under the firmament from the waters which were above the firmament: and it was so.And God called the firmament Heaven. And the evening and the morning were the second day.

Red Rose Library

Section 1:9-1:14 Day Three (Indent 35, Left 90, Right 20)
And God said, Let the waters under the heaven be gathered together unto one place, and let the dry land appear: and it was so. And God called the dry land Earth; and the gathering together of the waters called he Seas: and God saw that it was good. And God said, Let the earth bring forth grass, the herb yielding seed, and the fruit tree yielding fruit after his kind, whose seed is in itself, upon the earth: and it was so. And the earth brought forth grass, and herb yielding seed after his kind, and the tree yielding fruit, whose seed was in itself, after his kind: and God saw that it was good. And the evening and the morning were the third day.

Figure 6.11. Style Sheet Watermarking (code0611.htm)

Image Borders

As shown previously, simple borders can be placed around your images because **img** is also an HTML element. We can use style sheets to stylize that border using the border values we saw in Figure 6.6 (**solid**, **dashed**, **dotted**, **groove**, **ridge**, **double**, **inset**, **outset**) either as inline style attributes or as style sheet codes. In each of the code sets below the **border** default is changed to a **five-pixel** thick, **silver** colored, **dotted** border:

```
<img src="images/img004.jpg" width="120" height="83"
alt="logo" style="border:5px dotted silver" />
```

Style Sheet Code to stylize *all* image borders (quotes used for multiword value):

```
img { border:"5px dotted silver"}
```

We can use this technique to define how a picture is stylized and use it on a staff Web page for each of our library staff. The first step would be to have someone with a digital camera take your picture. Once it is transferred into your computer, you can use the **img** element to bring the picture into your Web page. You don't need to resize, as your browser can do the resizing automatically, but if your digital photo is typically 2600 x 2000 pixels, your JPEG photo file would be about 1.5 megabytes in size. Your patron's browser window might be only 640 pixels wide and 480 pixels long. Your original photo would fill about sixteen windows! But even worse is that your patron will need to wait until 1.5 megabytes of data have been received by his or her computer each time your picture is sent to it. Some digital cameras take 5 mega pixel and larger photos. That's a lot of waste. Web pages typically use 72 pixels-per-inch displays. So if we were to crop and reduce the size of the photo to 175–200 pixels on a side, it would become a 6–10 kilobyte file and yield a photo about 2.5 inches square—just enough to make you look great!

Figure 6.12 shows a possible template you can use for your library Web pages.

Name: Dr. Charles Rubenstein
Department/Title: Web Page Creator
email: c.rubenstein@ieee.org
Phone Number: +1 516 598-4619

Bio:
Charles P. Rubenstein is a professor in the graduate School of Information and Library Science at Pratt Institute and a visiting professor of engineering in the Institute for Research and Technology Transfer at Farmingdale State University, in New York. He has an engineering doctorate from New York's Polytechnic University and a masters degree in library and information science from Pratt Institute. He has developed web sites for professional societies and educational entities and was creator of the Institute of Electrical and Electronic Engineers, Inc. (IEEE) Region 1 web site and its webmaster for more than a decade. Dr. Rubenstein has been a distinguished lecturer for the IEEE Computer Society and IEEE Engineering Management Society presenting dozens of workshops and tutorials on HTML Web Page Design and Construction in Canada, India, Puerto Rico, and the United States since 1996.

Figure 6.12. Images with Fancy Borders (code0612.htm = bio.htm)

Text Boxes and Borders

As shown in Figure 6.3, an inline **style** attribute can be added to horizontal rules that will stylize their type, thickness, and/or color. Style and style sheets can be used to adjust the thickness of any style border around an image. In previous sections a colored background was created behind text and margins and indents were established. In the next section border stylization is added to your text as well as your images. Please remember that although these techniques work well for Internet Explorer browser users, they will not be rendered properly, if at all, for Firefox browser users.

First create an internal style sheet body definition for the page margins and dotted and dashed border style class (**.dot** and **.dash**). Use the same color scheme for the set of border colors—red (top) lime (right side), blue (bottom), and black (left side) respectively. Add twenty pixels of padding between the text, or image, and the ten-pixel borders. The watermark class style adds a background image behind text in the second paragraph. The styling that will be used to create a History of the Red Rose Library Web page shown in Figure 6.13 is:

```
body { margin-left:100px; margin-right:100px}
.dash { padding:20px; border-color:red lime blue black;
        border-style:dashed; border-width:10px}
.dot { padding:20px; border-color:red lime blue black;
        border-style:dotted; border-width:10px}
.watermark { background-image:url(images/img005.jpg);
        font-weight:bold}
```

Figure 6.13. Styling Text and Image Borders (code0613.htm = history.htm)

Dropped Caps

As people of the book, library folks are often enamored by the effect that the use of dropped caps has on an opening paragraph of a chapter. To do this, you must convince the first letter of a paragraph to act as if it were an inline image located at the left side of the text. You can quadruple the size of this first letter, color it **navy**, and possibly change its **font-family** or other characteristics.

There are several ways to implement this style. We could set the style as a paragraph, **div**, **span**, or other text element attribute in a style sheet. In Figure 6.14 the **span** element surrounds the text "Section 1:1" that we want to make into dropped caps. The generic class **.dropcap** is used to stylize "Section 1:6" and **p.cap:first-letter** is used in Section 1:9. (The **p.cap:first-letter** command is a cascading style sheet pseudo-element that defines the styling for only the first letter of text.) Pseudo-elements (**first-letter**, **first-line**, **before** and **after**) are structured like the anchor pseudo-classes we have already used (e.g., **a:hover**) in this chapter.

After isolating the letter(s) to style the trick is to use the float attribute **float:left** in the style definition. Then each of the techniques will result in a dropped cap, with all other text in the paragraph retaining "normal" styling.

```
span { float:left; width:0.7em; font-size:400%;
        font-family:serif,courier; line-height:80%}
.dropcap { float:left; font-size:400%; color:navy}
p.dropcap:first-letter { float:left; font-size:400%; color:navy}
```

When you want to style a paragraph with a dropped cap, call the **dropcap** class as an attribute for either the paragraph opening tag, or the text line, respectively:

```
<p class="dropcap">Your paragraph of text goes here ...</p> or
<b class="dropcap">Y</b>our text line goes here ...
```

Figure 6.14 shows a variety of different ways to define and use dropped caps.

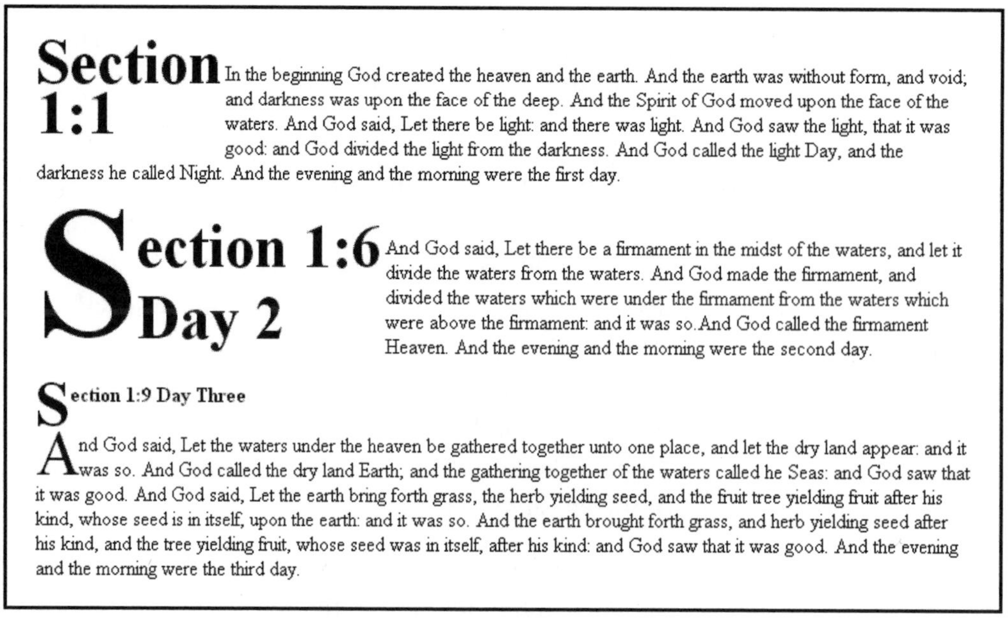

Section 1:1 In the beginning God created the heaven and the earth. And the earth was without form, and void; and darkness was upon the face of the deep. And the Spirit of God moved upon the face of the waters. And God said, Let there be light: and there was light. And God saw the light, that it was good: and God divided the light from the darkness. And God called the light Day, and the darkness he called Night. And the evening and the morning were the first day.

Section 1:6 Day 2 And God said, Let there be a firmament in the midst of the waters, and let it divide the waters from the waters. And God made the firmament, and divided the waters which were under the firmament from the waters which were above the firmament: and it was so. And God called the firmament Heaven. And the evening and the morning were the second day.

Section 1:9 Day Three

And God said, Let the waters under the heaven be gathered together unto one place, and let the dry land appear: and it was so. And God called the dry land Earth; and the gathering together of the waters called he Seas: and God saw that it was good. And God said, Let the earth bring forth grass, the herb yielding seed, and the fruit tree yielding fruit after his kind, whose seed is in itself, upon the earth: and it was so. And the earth brought forth grass, and herb yielding seed after his kind, and the tree yielding fruit, whose seed was in itself, after his kind: and God saw that it was good. And the evening and the morning were the third day.

Figure 6.14. Dropped Caps (code0614.htm)

Floating Images for Newsletter Designs

The last cascading style sheet trick reviewed in this chapter will show you how to create a newsletter with images that can be paced on the page using the **float** attribute.

Positioning images to the left or to the right of your text is as easy as defining a style with the **float** attribute. The value **float:right** displays an image to the right of our text. Add some space between the image and the text by using the **padding-left** attribute. Similarly, to have your image displayed to the left of your text, use the padding on the right of it:

```
img.left { float:left; padding-right:50}
img.right { float:right; padding-left:50}
```

You already know how to add border styles and colors and to display text with dropped caps. In Figure 6.15 we have used these techniques and the Genesis text with a few rose images to illustrate how images float around the text. We floated a rose image to the right of Section 1:1, floated a second rose image to left of Section 1:6, and a third rose image to the right of Section 1:9. To appreciate the power of the floating image, expand the HTML file **code0615.htm** to fill the page.

Note where the images are positioned with respect to the text. Now reduce the browser window width and see that as the width of the window changes, the relative position of the images and special dropped caps characters stays "fixed" and the text flows around the images.

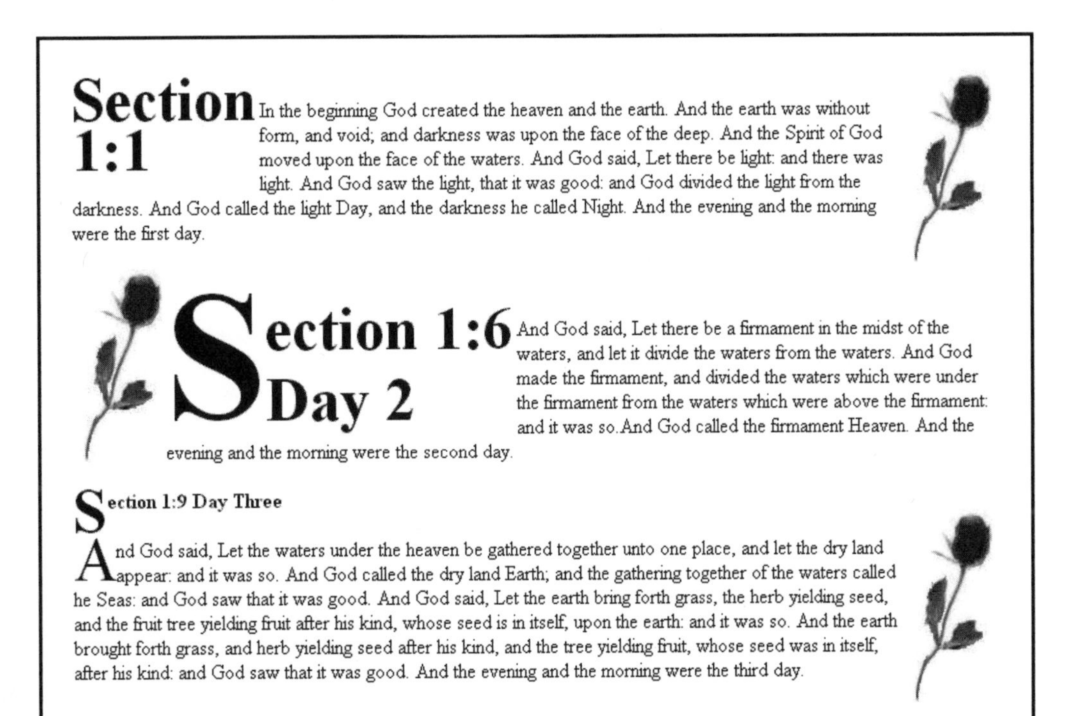

Figure 6.15. Floating Images (code0615.htm)

Additional CSS Resources

In this chapter we have introduced many cascading style sheet ideas. Among the dozen CSS Web sites where you can find additional help in understanding the power of this powerful tool are:

The CSS Reference Sheet
http://www.w3schools.com/css/css_reference.asp
http://www.w3schools.com/css/default.asp
http://www.w3schools.com/html/html_fonts.asp
The W3C Web site
http://www.w3.org/Style/CSS
http://www.webstyleguide.com/type/face.html
http://www.webstyleguide.com/index.html?/pages/font_face.html
Building a Web Page with CSS
http://www.draac.com/css/css1.html

What's Next?

Chapter 7 reviews the basic **list** generating HTML elements and then presents how to use cascading style sheets to stylize them.

Chapter 7

Lists, Lists, and More Lists

Lists are often used instead of long strings of items in a sentence separated by commas. The list format is more readable than the same information in a sentence. Lists come in a wide variety, from simple lists with one idea or item on a line to those with numbered, lettered, or "bulleted" sets of items. In this chapter HTML elements will be used to make items appear in list form on your Web page. Then cascading style sheets will be added to enhance the style of your Web list.

Three Basic Lists

Three HTML list elements—unordered list, ordered list, and definition list—are expected to be used in future HTML versions. Both ordered and unordered list elements require the list item (**li**) for correct list displays, can be nested to give your Web page a traditional outline look and feel, and are block-level elements that create paragraph separations between them and your other text. They are both easy to use. The definition list works a bit differently and will be described in the section following ordered lists.

Any of the list types can be located within the body of your document, inside a list item (**li**) or a blockquote (**blockquote**) or a **form**, or other list elements. We will review how to change the **type** (**circle** (default), **disc**, or **square** bullet) and style list attributes later in this chapter.

Unordered Lists

The **ul**, **dir**, and **menu** elements are all unordered list elements with nearly the same characteristics in that they all must contain list item elements and can be nested to accomplish a variety of different stylings. The **dir** and **menu** elements yield displays more or less equivalent to that of the unordered lists and have been deprecated. They should not be used, as they won't be used in XHTML or in later versions of HTML.

The unordered list element (**ul**) defines an unordered list, with each list item (**li**) marked by a bullet symbol, rather than the alphanumeric character of the ordered list we will discuss in the next section. The text in list items automatically wraps and indents when displayed by your browser.

The List Item

Both unordered and ordered list elements require the use of list item elements (**li**) to properly display lists. The **li** can be inside any list type, and can contain characters and their formatting (**b**, **i**, **u**), list elements, hyperlinks (**a**), line and paragraph breaks (**br**, **p**) images (**img**), blockquotes (**blockquote**), preformatted text (**pre**), and even forms. List items can be stylized and changed as necessary using bullet **type** and inline **style** attributes as well as using cascading style sheet techniques, as will be seen later in this chapter. For unordered lists the bullet types are the **disc**, **circle**, and **square** where the default bullet is a **disc**.

Although you may see the **li** used alone to force a bullet in front of text, and the **ul** or **ol** used without the **li** elements to position indented text, these are unreliable solutions and not proper ways to accomplish text styling. Full sets of list elements and items should be used at all times. Figure 7.1 shows the three types of unordered lists (**ul**, **dir**, and **menu**) side by side for easy comparison.

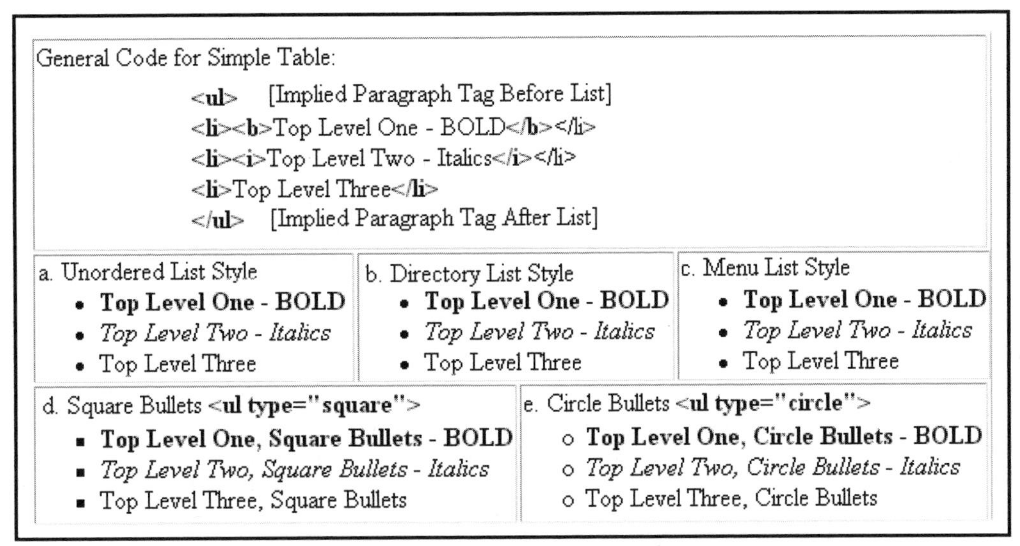

Figure 7.1. Unordered List Elements (code0701.htm)

Depending on your browser, it may only be necessary to learn the **ul** element with list items if you are constructing unordered lists. Also demonstrated in the figure is the use of the **type** attribute in changing the list item bullet shape from **disc** (a filled circle) to a filled **square** or an open **circle**.

Ordered Lists

The unordered list element (**ul**) can be used when there are only a few list items, but it does not lend itself well to longer listings or outlines, as we'll see in the section on nesting. To deal with these longer lists, we will need a bullet that has more content to it, like a letter or number. This is where the ordered list comes into play.

The HTML ordered list element (**ol**) is used just like the unordered list element (**ul**) above, except that it creates numbered lists of items. Just like the unordered list, an ordered list can be used inside of the **body** of the HTML document, blockquotes, tables, forms, list items, and other lists. Your browser assigns ascending numbers or letters to list items (**li**) in an ordered list based on the list's bullet **type** attribute (**1**, **A**, **a**, **I**, or **i**), with the Arabic numbering system (**1**) used as a default. The ordered list can also be forced to start at a particular value (**start="5"**) or have a particular **style**.

As can be seen in Figure 7.2, letters and roman numerals, either in upper- or lowercase, can be set as the default for all the items in a list using the **type** attribute in the **ol** opening tag.

General Code for Simple Table: <**ol**> <**li**><**b**>Top Level One - BOLD</**b**></**li**> <**li**><**i**>Top Level Two - Italics</**i**></**li**> <**li**>Top Level Three</**li**> </**ol**>	a. Default Arabic Numbers Ordered List <**ol type="1"**> 1. **Top Level One - BOLD** 2. *Top Level Two - Italics* 3. Top Level Three
b. Capital Letter Ordered List <**ol type="A"**> A. **Top Level One - BOLD** B. *Top Level Two - Italics* C. Top Level Three	c. Lowercase Letter Ordered List <**ol type="a"**> a. **Top Level One - BOLD** b. *Top Level Two - Italics* c. Top Level Three
d. Capital Roman Numerals Ordered List <**ol type="I"**> I. **Top Level One - BOLD** II. *Top Level Two - Italics* III. Top Level Three	e. Lowercase Roman Numerals Ordered List <**ol type="i"**> i. **Top Level One - BOLD** ii. *Top Level Two - Italics* iii. Top Level Three

Figure 7.2. Ordered Lists (code0702.htm)

Note that list items are automatically sequenced by your browser. The **start** attribute can be used to force the starting character of the series, with the remaining items sequencing in an ascending order from that point. In the next section we will see how the ordered and unordered lists nest inside themselves.

Nesting Lists

In Figures 7.1 and 7.2 we saw how to display single levels of list items using the ordered and unordered list elements. In Figure 7.3 we see how adding additional levels is accomplished using another **ol** element set to nest another list underneath any list item.

CODE:

```
<ol>
<li><b>Top Level - BOLD</b></li>
  <ol>
<li><i>Second Level - Italics</i></li>
    <ol>
<li>Third Level </li>
    </ol>
  </ol>
<li><b>Top Level - BOLD</b></li>
</ol>
```

Table Outline Example:

1. **Top Level - BOLD**
    1. *Second Level - Italics*
        1. Third Level
2. **Top Level - BOLD**

Figure 7.3. Nesting Ordered Lists (code0703.htm)

Figure 7.4 shows the nesting results for ordered and unordered lists.

a. Two Level Ordered Lists

1. **Top Level One - BOLD**
2. *Top Level Two - Italics*
    1. **Second Level One - BOLD**
    2. *Second Level Two - Italics*
3. Top Level Three

b. Two Level Unordered Lists

- **Top Level One - BOLD**
- *Top Level Two - Italics*
    - o **Second Level One - BOLD**
    - o *Second Level Two - Italics*
- Top Level Three

c. Three Level Ordered Lists

1. **Top Level One - BOLD**
2. *Top Level Two - Italics*
    1. **Second Level One - BOLD**
        1. **Third Level One - BOLD**
        2. *Third Level Two - Italics*
    2. *Second Level Two - Italics*
3. Top Level Three

d. Three Level Unordered Lists

- **Top Level One - BOLD**
- *Top Level Two - Italics*
    - o **Second Level One - BOLD**
        - ▪ **Third Level One - BOLD**
        - ▪ *Third Level Two - Italics*
    - o *Second Level Two - Italics*
- Top Level Three

e. Four Level Ordered Lists

1. **Top Level One - BOLD**
2. *Top Level Two - Italics*
    1. **Second Level One - BOLD**
        1. **Third Level One - BOLD**
            1. **Fourth Level One - BOLD**
            2. *Fourth Level Two - Italics*
        2. *Third Level Two - Italics*
    2. *Second Level Two - Italics*
3. Top Level Three

f. Four Level Unordered Lists

- **Top Level One - BOLD**
- *Top Level Two - Italics*
    - o **Second Level One - BOLD**
        - ▪ **Third Level One - BOLD**
            - ▪ **Fourth Level One - BOLD**
            - ▪ *Fourth Level Two - Italics*
        - ▪ *Third Level Two - Italics*
    - o *Second Level Two - Italics*
- Top Level Three

Figure 7.4. Nesting Ordered and Unordered Lists (code0704.htm)

Although the unordered list automatically changes the nested items from disc to circle to square, the ordered list keeps the same styles. The **type** attribute can reset the style of bullet as necessary to create more pleasing displays.

It is important to remember that a variety of styling techniques for lists can be used. These can be overall list changes, which are typically attributes inside the opening tag for the **ol** or **ul** elements. Any style changes made affect the entire list. The styling of list items themselves can also be used. Figure 7.4 shows adding color attributes in addition to the bold and italics rendering used in Figure 7.3.

Changing the list bullet type defaults is another way to improve your displays. It is easy to see the difference between the various bullet styles in unordered list examples. This is not so easy when looking at the ordered list with default numbering. In the default, all first level items start with the Arabic number 1.

In outlining long lists on your Web page, you would certainly start with Arabic numbers, but the next level down might use lowercase letters, and we might use Roman numerals, etc., to indicate successively lower levels. Varying the ordered list bullet types will go far in helping your patrons understand the outline and sublevels that are not always obvious on a list.

As an image can be inside a list item, you can have graphical list items! Hypertext might make for a great quiz tool on Children's Room pages. A simple one is shown in Figure 7.5. The answers point to files named **correct.htm** and **wrong.htm** but could be coded to point to more subtle, random page numbers if you wanted them to. When you check the **code0705.htm** file you will find that the sample here uses tables and the **start** attribute, as the second question is actually a new listing. If the two questions were in a single column, you would not need to use the **start** attribute. On the other hand, let's say that the intent was to number the question by the page on which the answer could be found. You might then use a start attribute even with the questions in a single listing.

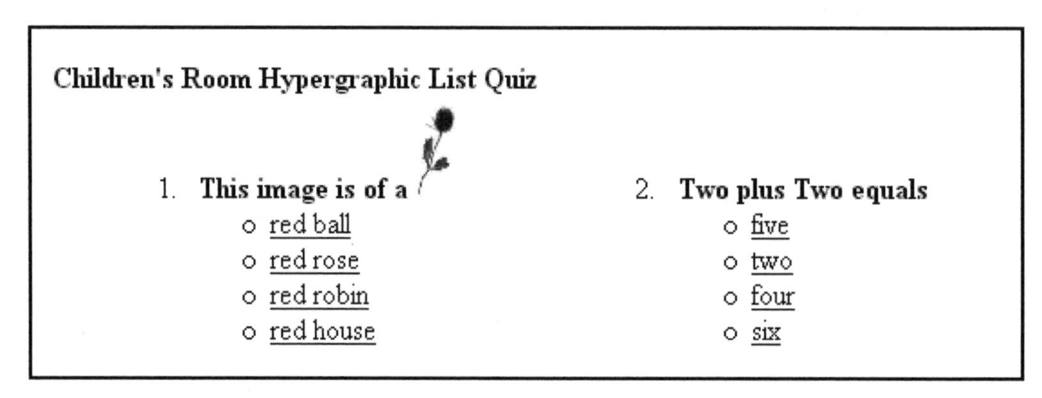

Figure 7.5. Children's Room Hypergraphic List Quiz (code0705.htm = quiz.htm)

The last list type discussed in this chapter is the definition list. Often used to render glossary listings, unlike the ordered and unordered lists, the definition list does not exhibit block-level formatting. Ordered and unordered lists (like headings) force a paragraph break before and after their use. They also indent their list items automatically, neither of which the definition does.

Definition Lists

The definition list does not utilize the list item (**li**) but rather uses the definition term (**dt**) and the definition description (**dd**) elements to style list items.

The definition list element (**dl**) can be used to create lists such as those that would be used for glossaries that contained terms and accompanying descriptions. The definition list can have nonindented (**dt**) or indented (**dd**) portions and can be found inside the **body** of an HTML document or inside block quotes (**blockquote**), other definition lists (**dd**), list items (**li**), and forms. Definition lists can use the **style** attribute for display stylization.

The nonindented part of a definition list is the definition term element (**dt**). Text in definition terms typically consists of only few words.

The indented portion of a definition list is the definition description element (**dd**).

Like the definition list itself, text in both definition terms (**dt**) and definition descriptions (**dd**) can use formatting (**b**, **i,** **u**, **pre**), use hyperlinking (**a**), contain line breaks (**br**), and contain images (**img**).They can contain blockquotes (**blockquote**), paragraphs (**p**), other lists, and forms.

A definition description (**dd**) can have any number of indented sentences and/or paragraphs in it. One use you may find for the definition list is in listing and describing your library's monthly activities, as shown in Figure 7.6.

CODE:	
<dl>	
<dt><b>Activities Calendar</b></dt>	**Activities Calendar**
<dt><i>December 2006 - February 2007</i></dt>	*December 2006 - February 2007*
<dt>December 2006</dt>	December 2006
<dd>Description of event goes here with cost and contact information.</dd>	Description of event goes here with cost and contact information.
<dt>January 2007</dt>	January 2007
<dd>Description of event goes here with cost and contact information.</dd>	Description of event goes here with cost and contact information.
<dt>February 2007</dt>	February 2007
<dd>Description of event goes here with cost and contact information.</dd>	Description of event goes here with cost and contact information.
</dl>	

Figure 7.6. Definition List (code0706.htm)

As you might have additional information for each of these activities, you may want to use anchor elements to hyperlink the months to full-page descriptions of the activities and/or forms to fill out to register for them. As noted with ordered and unordered lists, definition lists can also include images. Figure 7.7 shows an "improved" design with hyperlinks to the full description of the event in Figure 7.8 (**0612prog.htm**).

Your Red Rose Library Activities Calendar

December 2006 - February 2007

December 2006 Program
Radio City Music Hall Stage Door Tour
1260 Avenue of the Americas
New York, New York 10020

> *The Radio City Stage Door Tour is a one hour, walking tour of the interior of Radio City Music Hall that gives an insider's view of the inner-workings of this legendary showplace.*
> Click on the Red Rose above for reservations and contact information.

January 2007 Program
American Museum of Natural History
Central Park West at 79th Street
New York, NY 10024-5192

> *The world of Dinosaurs awaits you at the American Museum of Natural History! As you'll want to spend a relaxing time visiting with these prehistoric earth dwellers, we will meet at the museum for lunch but you are on your own before and after lunch. (The museum is open from 10:00 a.m.–5:45 p.m. and parking is quite expensive - take the bus or train!) Your $30 (Children are only $20) includes admission to the Museum and the Rose Center, a timed entry to the Dinosaurs exhibit, and of course our lunch together.*
> Click on the Red Rose above for reservations and contact information.

February 2007 Program
The Museum of Modern Art
11 West 53 Street
New York, NY 10019-5497

> *Your $20 (Children are only $10) includes admission to the Museum and bus transportation.*
> Click on the Red Rose above for reservations and contact information.

Figure 7.7. Program Page Template (code0707.htm = programs.htm)

Notice in Figure 7.8 that hypertext has been used for the Radio City Music Hall home page and tours page, but an unordered list of stage door highlights has been embedded inside a definition list structure. You could use a standard page template for each activity, or you might want to vary the look and feel depending on the subject or patron type you are targeting. A visit to the zoo, for example, might be less wordy and have several animal graphics to appeal to children. We'll review the use of Web forms in Chapter 9 and show a template you might want to use as an online registration system, assuming you have appropriate Web server software.

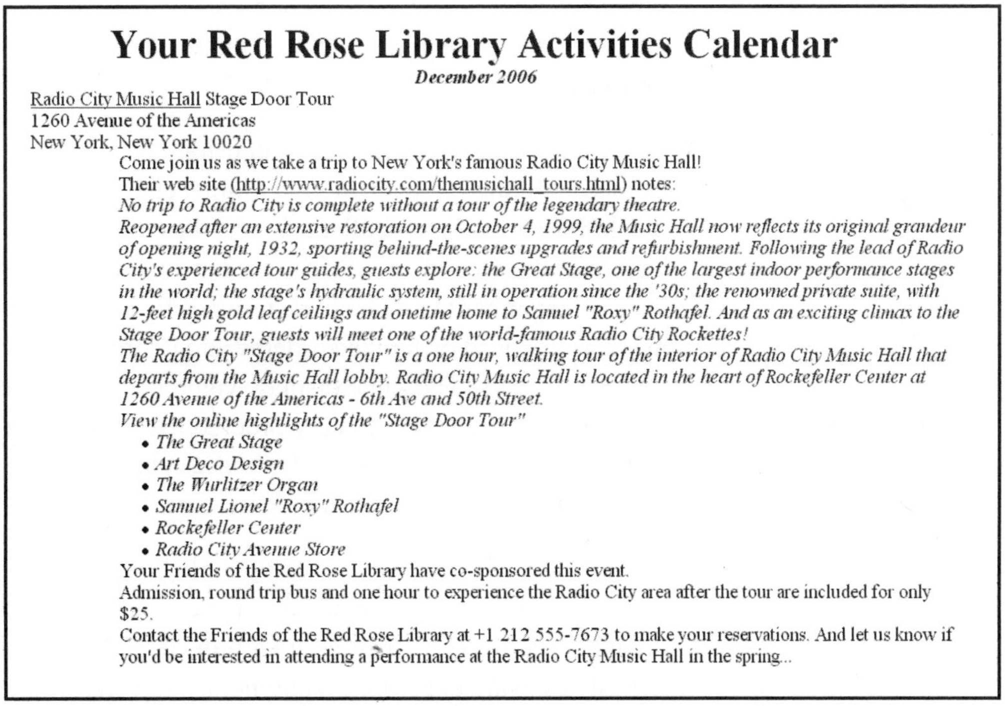

Your Red Rose Library Activities Calendar

December 2006

Radio City Music Hall Stage Door Tour
1260 Avenue of the Americas
New York, New York 10020

Come join us as we take a trip to New York's famous Radio City Music Hall!
Their web site (http://www.radiocity.com/themusichall_tours.html) notes:
No trip to Radio City is complete without a tour of the legendary theatre.
Reopened after an extensive restoration on October 4, 1999, the Music Hall now reflects its original grandeur of opening night, 1932, sporting behind-the-scenes upgrades and refurbishment. Following the lead of Radio City's experienced tour guides, guests explore: the Great Stage, one of the largest indoor performance stages in the world; the stage's hydraulic system, still in operation since the '30s; the renowned private suite, with 12-feet high gold leaf ceilings and onetime home to Samuel "Roxy" Rothafel. And as an exciting climax to the Stage Door Tour, guests will meet one of the world-famous Radio City Rockettes!
The Radio City "Stage Door Tour" is a one hour, walking tour of the interior of Radio City Music Hall that departs from the Music Hall lobby. Radio City Music Hall is located in the heart of Rockefeller Center at 1260 Avenue of the Americas - 6th Ave and 50th Street.
View the online highlights of the "Stage Door Tour"

- *The Great Stage*
- *Art Deco Design*
- *The Wurlitzer Organ*
- *Samuel Lionel "Roxy" Rothafel*
- *Rockefeller Center*
- *Radio City Avenue Store*

Your Friends of the Red Rose Library have co-sponsored this event.
Admission, round trip bus and one hour to experience the Radio City area after the tour are included for only $25.
Contact the Friends of the Red Rose Library at +1 212 555-7673 to make your reservations. And let us know if you'd be interested in attending a performance at the Radio City Music Hall in the spring...

Figure 7.8. Template for an Event (code0708.htm = 0612prog.htm)

Creating Lists with Style

The list attributes for styling lists are found in the previous chapter's discussion of cascading style sheets. To extend these possibilities, there are several internal and external style sheet properties. As seen previously, **style** redefines the inline, on page, or external style characteristics using attributes such as **list-style**, **list-style-type**, **list-style-image**, and **list-style-position**.

These style sheet properties can describe which bullet you can use, but more important, style can be used to create and use your own bullet images. Clearly the list style images need to be relatively small with respect to your text, but nonetheless, you can use **style** to create custom image bullets in a list.

The **list-style** property, if your browser supports it, is the easiest to use. With it you can describe the style for your list item's bullet on a line-by-line basis. The types of bullets supported in unordered lists are **disc** (default), **circle**, **square**, or **none**. The ordered list values are **decimal** (default), **lower-roman**, **upper-roman**, **lower-alpha**, **upper-alpha**, or **none**. But now the idea of bulleted unordered lists can be kicked up a notch by adding images using the format **url (local or web image and location)**.

You'll need to be careful about using image list item styles. As you can see in Figure 7.9, even though a bullet change was requested from an image class to a roman bullet class (at the cursor), the image bullet can be seen in the second line. This is not unusual with nesting complex bullets, as they inherit certain characteristics from earlier stylizations. You may have noticed that mixed ordered and unordered list bullets are in an ordered list here. The same display would occur if the list had been defined as unordered. You can use ordered list values in an unordered list, and when you use style sheets the bullet values are incremented in subsequent items, just as with an ordered list.

Of course if you want some of your lists to have one style and others to exhibit another, you can always use cascading style sheet classes to define several styles, such as **li.roman**, **li.lowalpha**, or **li.red** for list item styles using upper Roman numerals, lowercase letters, or a red dot image all on the same page.

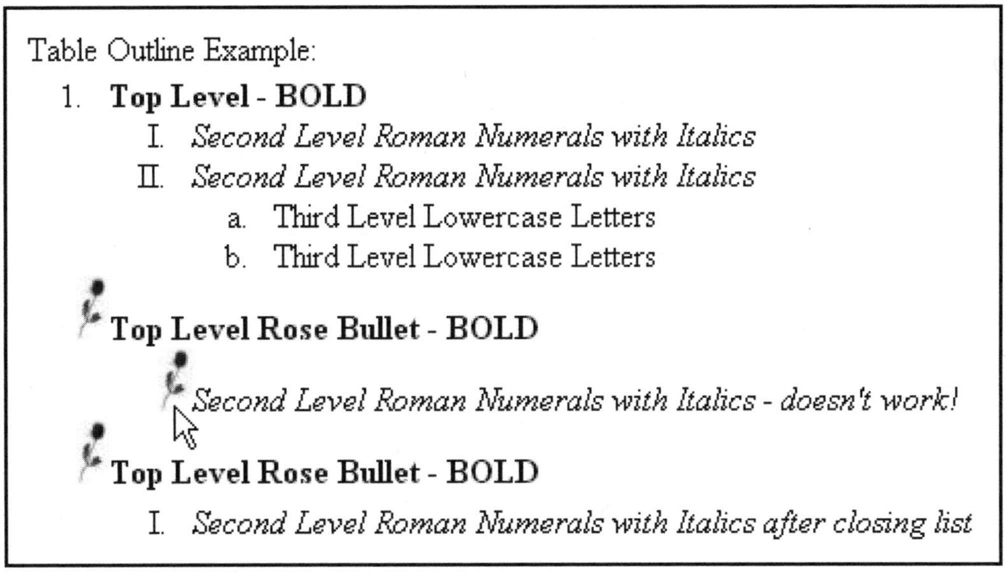

Table Outline Example:

1. **Top Level - BOLD**
    I. *Second Level Roman Numerals with Italics*
    II. *Second Level Roman Numerals with Italics*
        a. Third Level Lowercase Letters
        b. Third Level Lowercase Letters

Top Level Rose Bullet - BOLD

Second Level Roman Numerals with Italics - doesn't work!

Top Level Rose Bullet - BOLD

I. *Second Level Roman Numerals with Italics after closing list*

Figure 7.9. Lists with Style and Class (code0709.htm)

Although Internet Explorer accepts the simple **list-style** property as well as inline style:

li.roman { list-style:"upper-roman"; } or
li.roman { list-style-type:"upper-roman"; } and
li.red { list-style:"url(images/img006.jpg)"; } or
li.red { list-style-image:"url(images/img006.jpg)"; }

the Mozilla Firefox browser does not seem to like the style sheet method. Using these style sheets in Firefox merely shows the default Arabic number list bullets. Firefox seems to prefer the use of inline style coding:

<li style="list-style-type:upper-roman"; }
<li style="list-style-image:url(images/img006.jpg)"; }

As both major browsers seem to like inline styling, you might want to consider using the **style** element's **list-style-type, list-style-image**, or **list-style-position** properties *inline* instead. You have a nice set of list tools that you can try on your Web pages; keep them simple at first and then add some complexity as you get comfortable with the list elements and their attributes.

What's Next?

Some of the ins and outs of creating Web page tables are covered in Chapter 8. You will also learn to use cascading style sheets to style HTML Web pages without using **table** elements.

Chapter 8

Tables and Their Creative Uses

At the very beginning of any discussion about Web pages that compares them to word processed pages, the reader is told that HTML does NOT display like a word processed page. That challenge was not lost on Web designers, who found that many of the display modes they used trying to make a Web page look better were available if they could create rows and columns of information and position that information by using table construction techniques. We already know that tables can be designed to show, or not show, their borders, and thus you are aware that tables can be used to position content to mimic the effect of word processing. Now let's see how to work that bit of magic.

Building a Table

The HTML **table** element is used for displaying information in a table. It can also be used to force text into looking like the output of a word processor. As some of the table's features and attributes are not supported by all browsers, one way to accomplish table effects is to use cascading style sheet techniques to position text and graphics on a Web page without using one or more of the five table elements. Of course we must note that CSS effects are also browser-specific. Although most code has been adjusted for proper rendering in the Firefox browser, the Internet Explorer browser was used in designing the figures displayed in this chapter.

The HTML **table** element creates the table container. It can be located inside the HTML document's **body**, quotes (**blockquote**), list items (**li**), and forms. It can be stylized using any of these attributes: **background**, **bgcolor**, **border**, **bordercolor**, **bordercolorlight**, **bordercolordark**, **cellspacing**, **cellpadding**, or **width**, and typically contains one or more of the table elements captions (**caption**), headings (**th**), table rows (**tr**), and table data (**td**).

The **caption** element creates table captions. Captions are used inside of the **table**, can be stylized with **align** and **valign** attributes, and contain text characters and formatting, hyperlinks (**a**), line breaks (**br**), and/or images (**img**).

All tables are defined by their rows and columns. The table row (**tr**) element is used inside the **table** to define a row. It can be stylized with **background**, **bgcolor**, **border**, **bordercolor**, **bordercolorlight**, **bordercolordark**, **width**, **align**, and **valign** attributes, and can contain table data (**td**).

The table heading (**th**) and table data (**td**) elements are both used inside the **table** container and can be stylized with the attributes **background**, **bgcolor**, **border**, **bordercolor**, **align**, **valign**, **bordercolorlight**, **bordercolordark**, **colspan**, **rowspan**, and **nowrap**. Table headings and data are used inside of the **table** and can be stylized with **align** and **valign** attributes, and can contain text characters and formatting, hyperlinks (**a**), line breaks (**br**), images (**img**), and even tables. Table data (**td**) must exist inside table rows (**tr**).

The basic **table** element surrounds the **caption**, **heading**, **row**, and **data** (column) elements to define the construction of a table framework in which text and/or image content can be placed. The **table** element can be inserted anywhere as long as you remember it acts like other block-level formatting elements inserting line breaks around the table itself. The **table** element must have both an opening and a closing tag or else it is possible that the table, and all its content, will "disappear" or become distorted when displayed on your browser, and it begins with a single cell.

A simple single-cell table is constructed using just three elements to create a table with one row and one column. Nesting these **table**, **tr**, and **td** elements results in a block or cell in which the text or image content resides. The cell structure itself cannot be seen (Figure 8.1 code a) without turning the **table** element's **border** attribute "on" by setting it to a non-zero value, which is what makes it an acceptable means for managing text by simulating word-processed output displays. As shown in Figure 8.1, the **color** and thickness of the cell's **border**, as well as the cell's background **color**, can be defined using attributes within the opening tags of these three elements.

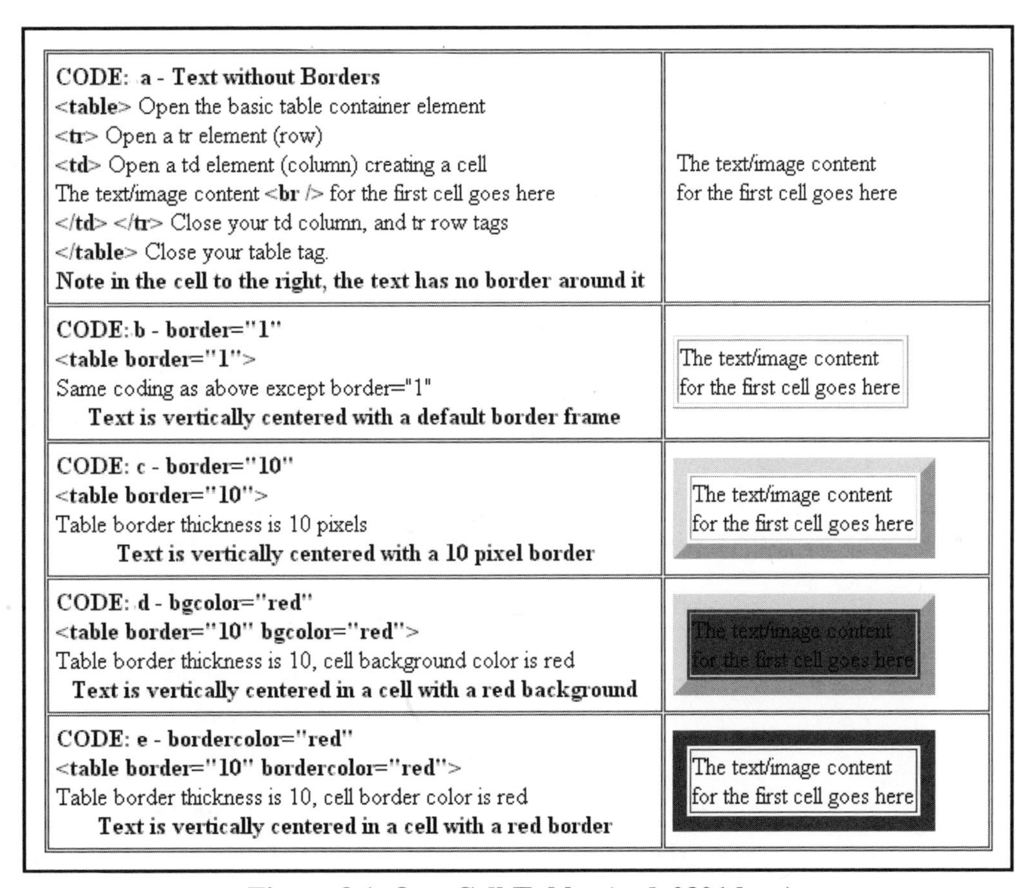

CODE: a - **Text without Borders** <**table**> Open the basic table container element <**tr**> Open a tr element (row) <**td**> Open a td element (column) creating a cell The text/image content <**br** /> for the first cell goes here </**td**> </**tr**> Close your td column, and tr row tags </**table**> Close your table tag. **Note in the cell to the right, the text has no border around it**	The text/image content for the first cell goes here
CODE: **b - border="1"** **<table border="1">** Same coding as above except border="1" **Text is vertically centered with a default border frame**	The text/image content for the first cell goes here
CODE: **c - border="10"** **<table border="10">** Table border thickness is 10 pixels **Text is vertically centered with a 10 pixel border**	The text/image content for the first cell goes here
CODE: **d - bgcolor="red"** **<table border="10" bgcolor="red">** Table border thickness is 10, cell background color is red **Text is vertically centered in a cell with a red background**	The text/image content for the first cell goes here
CODE: **e - bordercolor="red"** **<table border="10" bordercolor="red">** Table border thickness is 10, cell border color is red **Text is vertically centered in a cell with a red border**	The text/image content for the first cell goes here

Figure 8.1. One-Cell Tables (code0801.htm)

If you review how you stylized horizontal rules in Figure 6.3, and text blocks in Figure 6.13, you may now utilize a variety of inline style commands to modify the outside borders of a table or cell using border values. Figure 8.2 illustrates a few of the possible single-color table border stylizations using Internet Explorer.

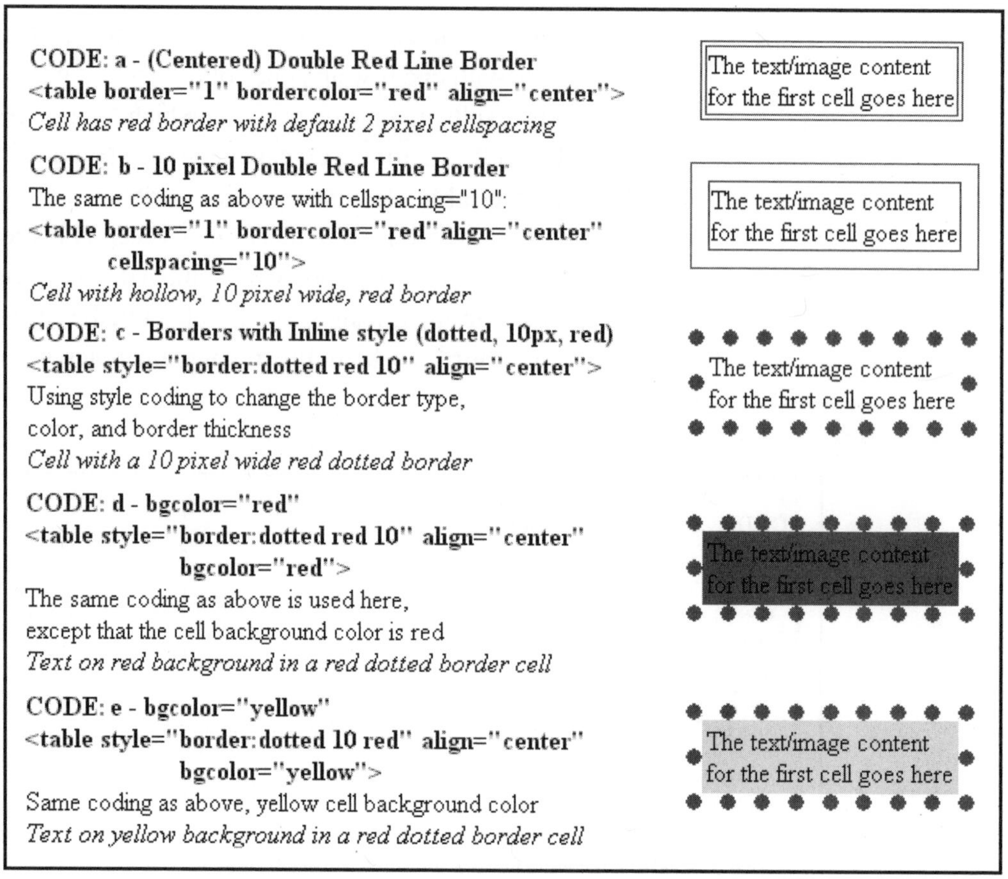

CODE: a - (Centered) Double Red Line Border
<table border="1" bordercolor="red" align="center">
Cell has red border with default 2 pixel cellspacing

The text/image content for the first cell goes here

CODE: b - 10 pixel Double Red Line Border
The same coding as above with cellspacing="10":
<table border="1" bordercolor="red" align="center" cellspacing="10">
Cell with hollow, 10 pixel wide, red border

The text/image content for the first cell goes here

CODE: c - Borders with Inline style (dotted, 10px, red)
<table style="border: dotted red 10" align="center">
Using style coding to change the border type, color, and border thickness
Cell with a 10 pixel wide red dotted border

The text/image content for the first cell goes here

CODE: d - bgcolor="red"
<table style="border: dotted red 10" align="center" bgcolor="red">
The same coding as above is used here, except that the cell background color is red
Text on red background in a red dotted border cell

The text/image content for the first cell goes here

CODE: e - bgcolor="yellow"
<table style="border: dotted 10 red" align="center" bgcolor="yellow">
Same coding as above, yellow cell background color
Text on yellow background in a red dotted border cell

The text/image content for the first cell goes here

Figure 8.2. Red-Bordered Tables (code0802.htm)

The simple two-pixel **cellspacing** default for colored table borders (Figure 8.2, code a) creates the effect of a double line border. As shown in Figure 8.2, code b, the distance between the two colored border lines can be increased by increasing this **cellspacing** value. You may also change the border style from **dotted** to **solid** or **dashed** or another style from Chapter 6 and Figure 6.3. As noted previously, these techniques are not supported by the Firefox browser.

Using only three core elements, **table**, **tr**, and **td**, turn on the border (**border="1"**), and the resulting side-by-side cells will create a single-row table with two columns.

Open a table (**<table border="1">**). Then open the row and open a column (**<tr><td>**). Insert content in this first cell. For this, you will insert "**Row One Cell One**" and then close the column and open a second column (**</td><td>**). Again insert the content, this time "**Row One Cell Two**", and close the column, close the row, and, finally, close the table (**</td></tr></table>**).

This is the code on the left of code a in Figure 8.3, and results in the output on the left side of code a.

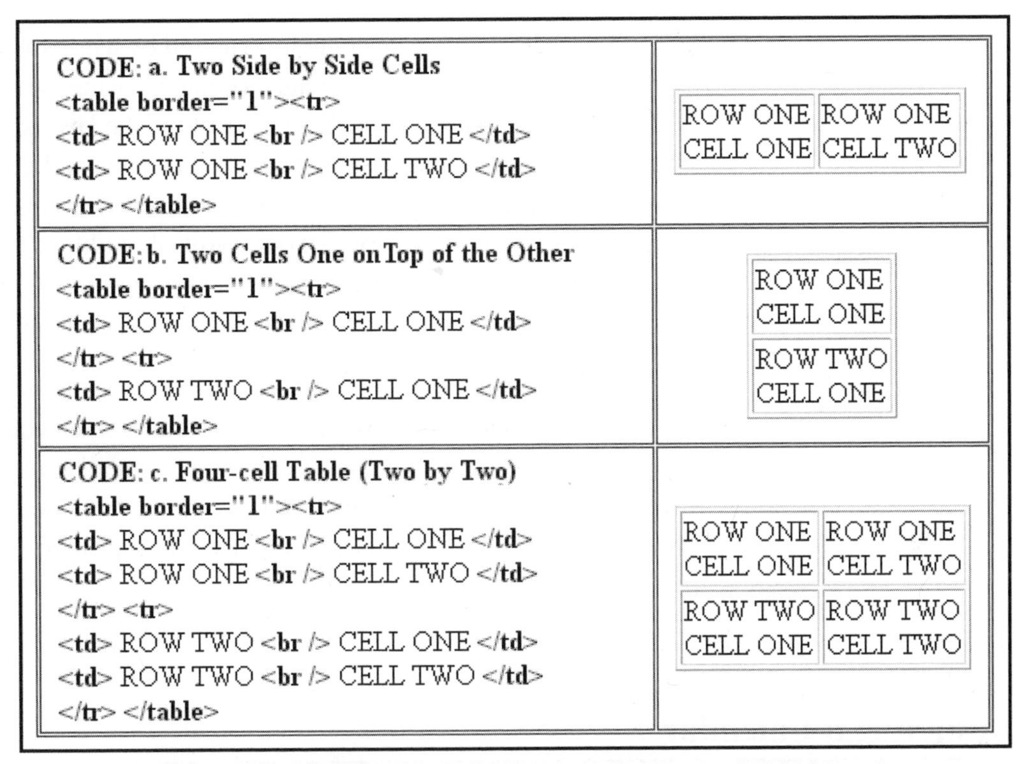

```
CODE: a. Two Side by Side Cells
<table border="1"><tr>
<td> ROW ONE <br /> CELL ONE </td>
<td> ROW ONE <br /> CELL TWO </td>
</tr> </table>
```

ROW ONE CELL ONE	ROW ONE CELL TWO

```
CODE: b. Two Cells One on Top of the Other
<table border="1"><tr>
<td> ROW ONE <br /> CELL ONE </td>
</tr> <tr>
<td> ROW TWO <br /> CELL ONE </td>
</tr> </table>
```

ROW ONE CELL ONE
ROW TWO CELL ONE

```
CODE: c. Four-cell Table (Two by Two)
<table border="1"><tr>
<td> ROW ONE <br /> CELL ONE </td>
<td> ROW ONE <br /> CELL TWO </td>
</tr> <tr>
<td> ROW TWO <br /> CELL ONE </td>
<td> ROW TWO <br /> CELL TWO </td>
</tr> </table>
```

ROW ONE CELL ONE	ROW ONE CELL TWO
ROW TWO CELL ONE	ROW TWO CELL TWO

Figure 8.3. Two-Cell and Four-Cell Tables (code0803.htm)

To create a pair of rows each having a single column, you will need to code one cell on top of another. To do this, open a table (**<table border="1">**), then open the row and open a column (**<tr><td>**). Insert content in this first cell, as shown in code b of Figure 8.3. Close the column and the row (**</td></tr>**). Open a second row and a column (**<tr><td>**), and insert content. Then close the column, close the row, and close the table (**</td></tr></table>**).

To create a four-cell table, first create a row with two side-by-side cells, see code a of Figure 8.3. Instead of closing the table, repeat the row design renaming the row contents to achieve the results of code c in Figure 8.3.

Although only text was used in these examples, you can include images and stylize the text and backgrounds of each individual cell in a table.

One thing to remember is that unless you use style sheets to define a special style for the **table**, **tr**, or **td** elements or classes for them, cells *do* *not* inherit properties from each other. A cell colored with a red background and green text, when closed, does not pass these styles on to the next cell in its row.

Any cell can have its contents centered by using the **align** attribute and can have blank space surround its contents using the **cellpadding** attribute. Like cell spacing, padding is accomplished by using pixels to enlarge the cell more than usual. The size of tables and cells can also be modified using the **width** attribute. Good practice suggests that Web page tables not normally exceed 640 pixels in width so that they will fit on your patron's screen regardless of their monitor type. Two other factors to be considered are **screen resolution** and **color quality**.

Please remember that not all screens are the same size. You will use the 640 pixel table size (**width="640"**) and center your table on the page so that the table's contents can be seen on all screens in the same size and shape. An added benefit comes when someone tries to print out the table. A width of 640 pixels is about all most printers can print in portrait mode.

Designing a Calendar

Most librarians like to put a monthly calendar on their Web pages. This begins with the simple side-by-side table process described above. To build a one-week calendar. To design anything larger than a one-week calendar takes several pages of code, and you may not wish to spend the time this takes. You will also need to use other core table elements, captions, and table headings. The use of **form** elements to create simple calendar displays will be shown in the next chapter. Note that a one-week calendar is nothing more than a one-row, seven-cell table with two more rows if you add day name and headings.

A monthly calendar is a table that has six or seven rows of seven cells each. In Chapter 9 we will see that it can be easier to construct a full-year calendar using **form** elements, but for now, we'll keep the calendars simple. Don't forget that backgrounds, text styles, and borders can have whatever style scheme you can design to accent each cell (date), and that images and hyperlinking can be used inside cells.

Figure 8.4 shows a basic design for a one-row, seven-cell table. In the next section, you'll add a second table heading row and a caption to it.

```
CODE: Simple One Row, Seven Cell Table
<table border="1"><tr>
<td> ROW ONE <br /> CELL ONE </td> <td> ROW ONE <br /> CELL TWO </td>
<td> ROW ONE <br /> CELL THREE </td> <td> ROW ONE <br /> CELL FOUR </td>
<td> ROW ONE <br /> CELL FIVE </td> <td> ROW ONE <br /> CELL SIX </td>
<td> ROW ONE <br /> CELL SEVEN </td>
</tr> </table>
```

ROW ONE CELL ONE	ROW ONE CELL TWO	ROW ONE CELL THREE	ROW ONE CELL FOUR	ROW ONE CELL FIVE	ROW ONE CELL SIX	ROW ONE CELL SEVEN

Figure 8.4. Simple One-Row, Seven-Cell Table (code0804.htm)

Adding Table Captions and Headings

To identify the one-row, seven-cell structure of Figure 8.4 as a calendar, we can add a title to the table noting the month and year, or a note that these events occur weekly. To do this, the **caption** element creates a caption or title for our table. It is placed inside the **table** element, after the optional table body element (**tbody**) and before the first row element (**tr**). When your table is displayed in the browser, the **caption** will be centered in its own row. Use the **align** attribute with the **caption** to specify its location. Using no alignment or **align="top"** (the default) will have the caption appear above the table like a title. Using **align="bottom"**, the caption will display like a photo caption, below the table. As with most table elements, you must surround the caption with opening and closing tags such that it will extend across the whole table. The **caption** can use a variety of nested elements and attributes, and contain hyperlinks. For your example, use:

```
<caption><font size="+2" color="blue"><b>Children's Room Weekly Activities </b></font> </caption>
```

As you can see in Figure 8.5, the caption line does not display with a border. To add day headings to your simple calendar table to identify the days of the week, the table heading element (**th**) is used inside the **table** element, before the first row element (**tr**). This defines the table's header information. Similar to the **tr** and **td** elements, **th** allows for background and border styling as well as hyperlinking.

The table heading element (**th**), unlike the caption, has a border around each of its heading cells like a regular **td** cell within a row. Unlike the normal table cell (**td**), the table heading element (**th**) displays its heading information in a bold typeface.

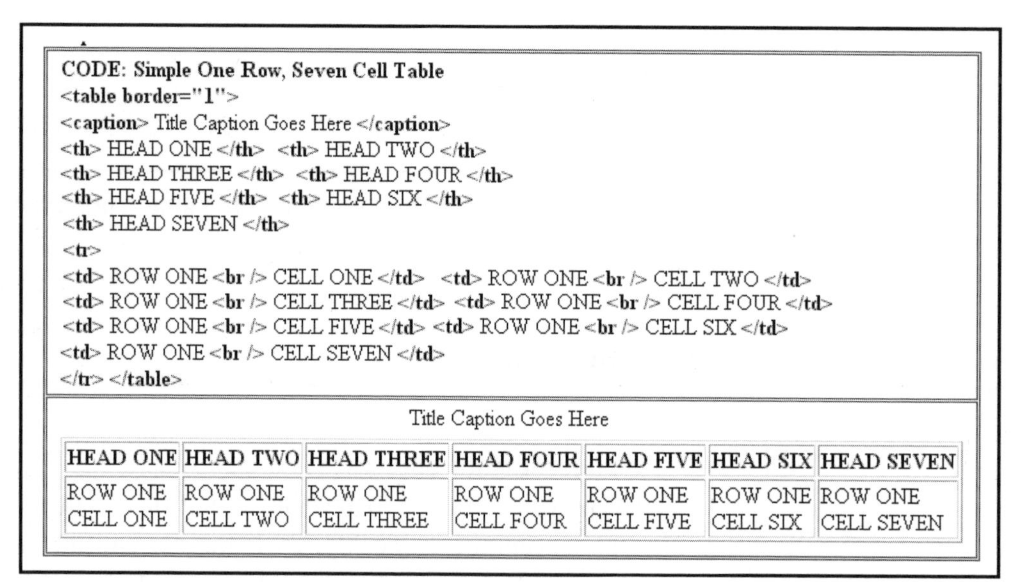

```
CODE: Simple One Row, Seven Cell Table
<table border="1">
<caption> Title Caption Goes Here </caption>
<th> HEAD ONE </th>  <th> HEAD TWO </th>
<th> HEAD THREE </th>  <th> HEAD FOUR </th>
<th> HEAD FIVE </th>  <th> HEAD SIX </th>
<th> HEAD SEVEN </th>
<tr>
<td> ROW ONE <br /> CELL ONE </td>  <td> ROW ONE <br /> CELL TWO </td>
<td> ROW ONE <br /> CELL THREE </td>  <td> ROW ONE <br /> CELL FOUR </td>
<td> ROW ONE <br /> CELL FIVE </td>  <td> ROW ONE <br /> CELL SIX </td>
<td> ROW ONE <br /> CELL SEVEN </td>
</tr> </table>
```

Title Caption Goes Here

HEAD ONE	HEAD TWO	HEAD THREE	HEAD FOUR	HEAD FIVE	HEAD SIX	HEAD SEVEN
ROW ONE CELL ONE	ROW ONE CELL TWO	ROW ONE CELL THREE	ROW ONE CELL FOUR	ROW ONE CELL FIVE	ROW ONE CELL SIX	ROW ONE CELL SEVEN

Figure 8.5. Simple One-Week Calendar Table (code0805.htm)

With captions and headings included, the code of Figure 8.5 becomes a one-week calendar template. You should be capable of using copy and paste to extract the table elements from the file **code0805.htm** and place it in your own Web page without too much difficulty. Merely substitute your text and images in each cell, as appropriate.

This calendar will be used as the basis for a scheduling page for the sample Red Rose Library Children's Room shown in Figure 8.6. The seven head cell names have been replaced with the names of the days of the week. This can be extended to a monthly calendar by merely repeating the number of rows to account for the days in the month and indicating the date in each cell.

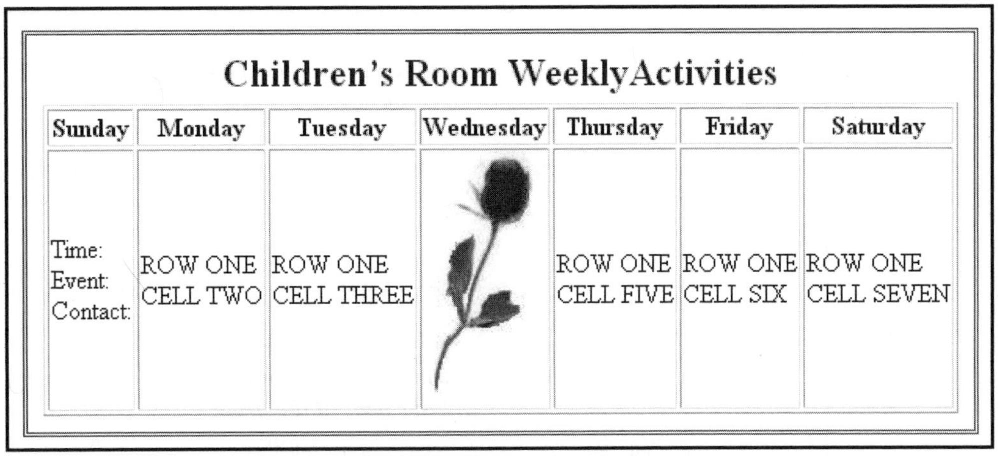

Children's Room WeeklyActivities

Sunday	Monday	Tuesday	Wednesday	Thursday	Friday	Saturday
Time: Event: Contact:	ROW ONE CELL TWO	ROW ONE CELL THREE		ROW ONE CELL FIVE	ROW ONE CELL SIX	ROW ONE CELL SEVEN

Figure 8.6. One-Week Children's Room Activity Calendar (code0806.htm)

A simple monthly calendar table for the month of May 2006 is strated in Figure 8.7.

May 2006

Sunday	Monday	Tuesday	Wednesday	Thursday	Friday	Saturday
	1	2	3	4	5	6
7	8	9	10	11	12	13
14	15	16	17	18	19	20
21	22	23	24	25	26	27
28	29	30	31			

Figure 8.7. Simple Calendar for May 2006 (code0807.htm)

Spanning Table Rows and Columns

Perhaps the two most interesting table row and column attributes are **rowspan** and **colspan**. As they imply, if you would like to have a particular table cell be two rows high, use the **<tr rowspan="2">** attribute. To use more than one column for a particular display of information, perhaps a four-day event, the tag **<td colspan="4">** can be used. The uppermost table in Figure 8.8 looks like a two-row table with one three-column row on top of a two-column row.

a. Three Columns on top of Two Columns ***An optical illusion!***		
Row One, Cell One	Row One, Cell Two	Row One, Cell Three
Row Two, Cell One	Row Two, Cell Two	

b. Three Columns on Two Columns on Four Columns ***What's behind the 'trick'***			
Row One, Cell One Uses **<td>**	Row One, Cell Two Uses **<td colspan="2">**		Row One, Cell Three Uses **<td>**
Row Two, Cell One Uses **<td colspan="2">**		Row Two, Cell Two Uses **<td colspan="2">**	
Row Three, Cell One Uses **<td>**	Row Three, Cell Two Uses **<td>**	Row Three, Cell Three Uses **<td>**	Row Three, Cell Four Uses **<td>**

Figure 8.8. Using colspan for Odd and Even Column Rows (code0808.htm)

The code file (**code0808.htm**) shows both rows styled using the **colspan** attribute. Each row is actually four columns wide, with the first row columns coded **<td>**, **<td colspan="2">** and **<td>**, and with the second row coded **<td colspan="2">** and **<td colspan="2">** to give the effect of three columns on top of two columns. The use of advanced table techniques, including spanning, can be seen in the 12 row by 19 column periodical table of the elements from the Web site (used by permission) at **http://www.webelements.com/** (see Figure 8.9).

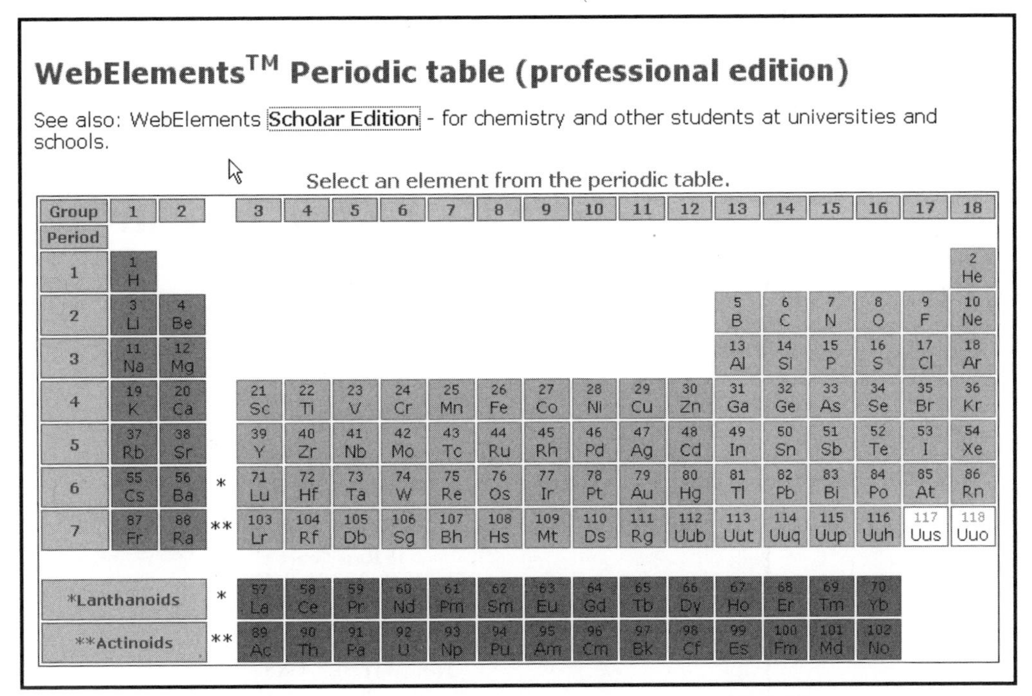

Figure 8.9. Web Page Periodical Table. From WebElements.

In addition to the coloring and table cell sizing codes, if you go online to this periodic table Web site you'll find that most table cells hyperlink to individual page descriptions. This is just one example of the level of complexity that you can design in a table display. As these are sites about chemistry, it is not unexpected that the **sub** (subscript) element is used extensively here to write chemical reactions. Water, for example, is written as **H₂O** and rendered H_2O.

Once content is in table rows and columns, it can be aligned horizontally using the **align** attribute with the values **left**, **right**, or **center**; or vertically using the **valign** attribute with the values **top**, **middle**, **bottom**, or **baseline**.

Applying Tables to Red Rose Library Web Pages

To put your knowledge of creating a table to work, you will create a Web page based on some location information your patrons need to find out how to get to your library. For this example it is assumed that you can draw or obtain a simple line drawing map of the local area, such as **img007.gif**, and that you have used it to create the simple HTML Web page of Figure 8.10. (Note, too, that like most Web pages, this one uses a navigation area. It is at the bottom of the page. We will see how to create navigation areas in Chapter 10.)

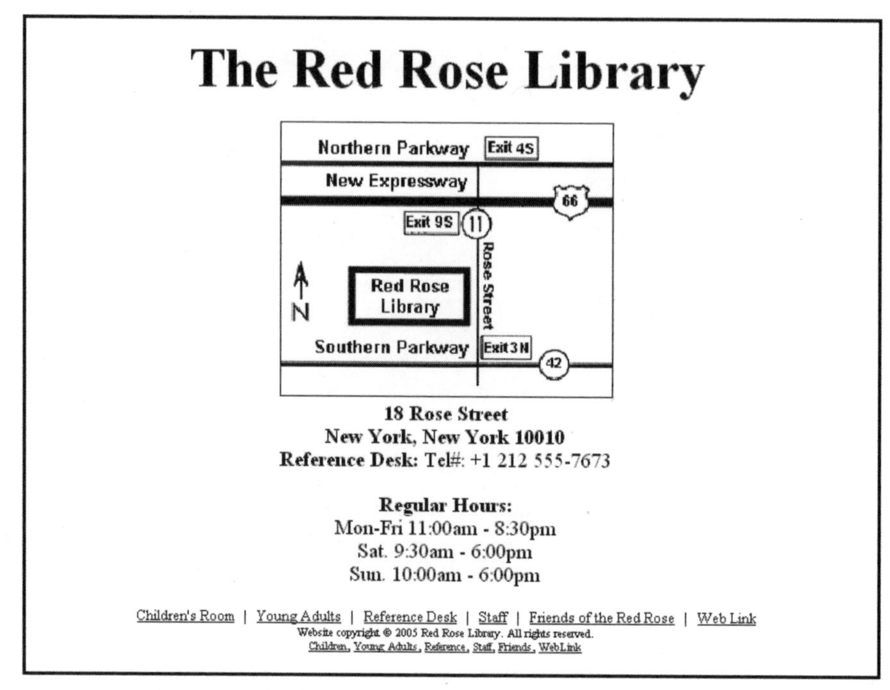

Figure 8.10. Basic Directions Page (code0810.htm)

The information is all there, but using table elements you can create the more elegant look of Figure 8.11, in which all the borders are turned on to see what spacing options are available. Note the wide, ten-pixel border around the first table (**cellpadding="10"**) and the fact that the widths of the two tables are different.

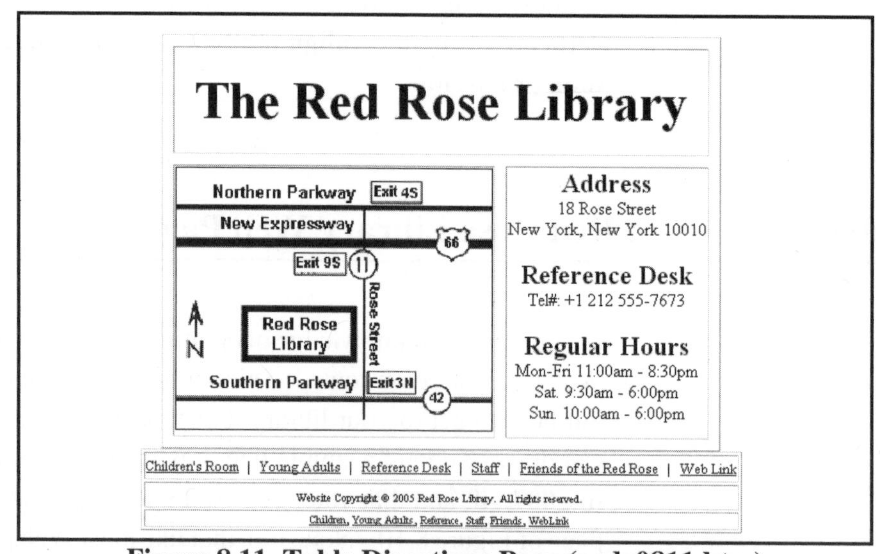

Figure 8.11. Table Directions Page (code0811.htm)

As shown in Figure 8.12, when you remove all borders and spice the page up with the Red Rose Library Logo (**img008.jpg**), the page becomes the **where.htm** file that you will use on the Red Rose Web site.

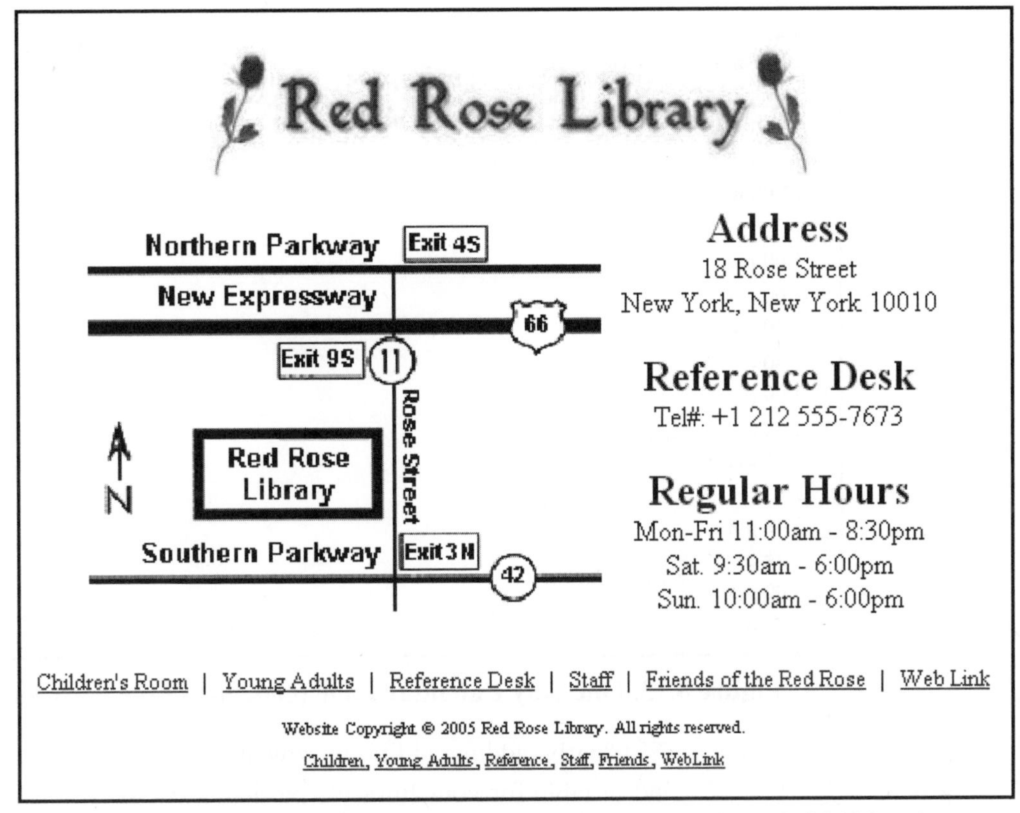

Figure 8.12. Table Directions Page with Border=0 (code0812.htm)

Earlier you created a single-row, seven-column (one week) calendar display to illustrate your Children's Room schedule of activities (Figure 8.6). You could also create a multiple-row, double-column table construction, a one-day event calendar. The first column defines the time of day and the second column tells the activity scheduled. On a very actively updated Web site this could be used for a daily activity page. In a more realistic situation, it could be the program for a one-day workshop, as seen in Figure 8.13.

One Day Workshop

Time	Activity
8:00 - 8:45 am	Welcome and Opening Session
8:45 - 10:15 am	Session 1
10:15 - 10:30 am	Coffee Break
10:30 - 12:00 noon	Session 2
12:00 - 1:00 pm	LUNCH
1:00 - 2:30 pm	Session 3
2:30 - 4:00 pm	Session 4
4:00 - 4:15 pm	Coffee Break
4:15 - 5:45 pm	Session 5
5:45 - 6:00 pm	Closing Ceremony

Figure 8.13. One-Day Calendar Page (code0813.htm = workshop.htm)

Clearly, adding additional row and column elements can yield any kind of table for your library's particular needs. For your young adult patrons, for example, you might want to prepare a Web page that can be used as a school planner with several rows, a time column, and seven blank columns, as in Figure 8.14.

In fact, for the young adult area, you might want to link to the WebElement's site for student access to the periodic table we saw in Figure 8.9 for their chemistry homework, or even request permission to "mirror" (copy) the table and other files for the periodic table onto your local server.

Weekly Planner

Time	Monday	Tuesday	Wednesday	Thursday	Friday	Saturday	Sunday
8:00 - 8:45 am							
8:45 - 10:15 am							
10:15 - 10:30 am							
10:30 - 12:00noon							
12:00 - 1:00 pm							
1:00 - 2:30 pm							
2:30 - 4:00 pm							
4:00 - 4:15 pm							
4:15 - 5:45 pm							
5:45 - 6:00 pm							

Figure 8.14. Weekly School Program Planner (code0814.htm = program.htm)

Using Cascading Style Sheets to Create Tables

You can use cascading style sheets, internal or external, to add interesting style to your tables as they have done for other HTML elements. Style sheets can be used to create division classes (**div.something**) to control text and image content in a nontable element environment. The **div** element classes can be created with style sheets for containers, headers, columns, and footers to match the **table**, **th**, **tr**, and **td** elements seen earlier in this chapter. It cannot be stressed too much that CSS effects are browser specific. Using CSS to create table structures can be tricky. If you are the least bit squeamish about "computer programming" you might wish to skip the rest of this chapter.

Style Sheet Table Element Equivalents

```
/* table equivalent (1 pixel solid blue border) */
div.container
{ width:100%; margin:0px; border:"1px solid blue"; line-height:100% }
/* table header equivalent (blue colored background) */
div.header
{ color:white; background-color:blue; text-align:center; padding:10 }
/* table data equivalent (red left side border, 200 pixel margin) */
div.column
{ margin-left:200px; border-left:"1px solid red"; padding:10 }
/* table footer equivalent (blue colored background) */
div.footer
{ color:white; background-color:blue; text-align:center; text-size:20; padding:5 }
/* Other common style definitions */
div.left
{ float:left; width:195px; margin:0; padding:10 }
h1.header
{ padding:0; margin:0 }
a:link, a:alink, a:vlink
{ text-decoration:none; color:red }
```

The style definitions above can be used to construct the table examples of Figures 8.3, 8.5, and 8.6. The internal style coding should be set for the column margins in division class statements as shown above rather than by merely adding **tr** and **td** table elements. Using these stylings you can construct the borderless, three row by two column table, shown in Figure 8.15.

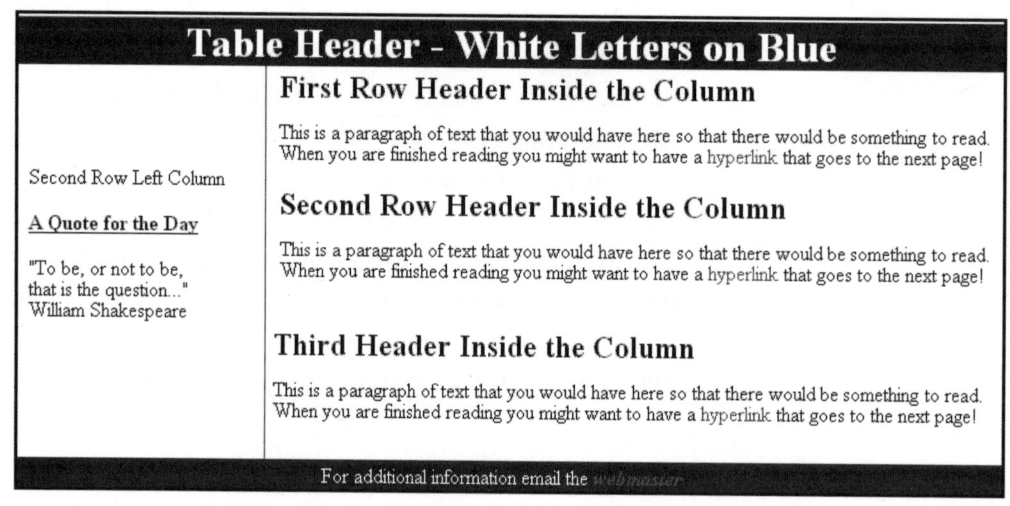

Figure 8.15. Style Sheet Table Based on W3 Example (code0815.htm)

Using **table** elements all that is needed is to stack table rows and add table columns to create a table. The first step in designing a cascading style sheet table is to decide on the actual width of each cell in the table and what styling is needed in your design. A maximum screen width of 640 pixels will be used. Because room is needed for at least seven columns for a one-week table, you must design each cell to be 90 pixels wide for an overall 630-pixel table width. Your 90-pixel columns will start at 0, 90, 180, 270, 360, 450, and 540. The cells would have to be smaller if you want padding around your content or needed thicker cell borders.

If you want to have a border around the whole table, you can add a one-pixel, red-colored, border to the left of every cell, except your first cell, and a gray border at the bottom of every cell in all rows except your last row. A borderless design might include column definitions such as:

div.col2 { margin-left:90px; padding:5px}

Alternatively, a fully bordered design could look like:

div.col2
{ margin-left:90px; margin-top: 5px; margin-bottom: 5px; border-left:"1px solid red"; border-bottom:"1px solid gray"; padding:5px}

Constructing this style sheet "shell," you need only add content to the **div** classes to create one-week or one- month table displays without using any **table** elements. Although these style sheet definition structures could be defined internally on a given page, it is more likely that you would have them as an external style sheet file. The file could be named **tables.css** and saved in your **images** folder for ease of use all over your Web site. Extend style sheet principles here on the page of Figure 8.6 to create the two-row, seven-column, one-week template demonstrated in Figure 8.16.

Seven Day Event Table						
Sun	**Mon**	**Tues**	**Wed**	**Thurs**	**Fri**	**Sat**
This is a paragraph of text that you would have here so that there would be something to read.	When you are finished reading you might want to have a hyperlink that goes to the next page!	This is a paragraph of text that you would have here so that there would be something to read.	When you are finished reading you might want to have a hyperlink that goes to the next page!	This is a paragraph of text that you would have here so that there would be something to read.	When you are finished reading you might want to have a hyperlink that goes to the next page!	This is a paragraph of text that you would have here so that there would be something to read.
For additional information email the webmaster						

Figure 8.16. Seven-Column CSS Table (code0816.htm)

In much the same way, Figure 8.17 shows a generic one- week calendar using style sheets concepts.

May 2006						
Sun	**Mon**	**Tues**	**Wed**	**Thurs**	**Fri**	**Sat**
	1	2	3	4	5	6
For additional information email the webmaster						

Figure 8.17. CSS One-Week Table Template (code0817.htm)

Figure 8.18 extends the style sheet concept into the design of a one-month calendar. Continuing with these style sheet concepts, any table can be generated on a Web page without using any **table** elements.

Tables, either written with native HTML table elements or constructed using cascading style sheet techniques, give a rigid structure to your Web pages. This structure can be used to create tabular displays, or with their borders turned off, mimic word-processed documents. Style sheet concepts can also be used to display simulated word-processed documents on a Web page.

May 2006						
Sun	Mon	Tues	Wed	Thurs	Fri	Sat
	1	2	3	4	5	6
7	8	9	10	11	12	13
14	15	16	17	18	19	20
21	22	23	24	25	26	27
28	29	30	31			
For additional information email the webmaster						

Figure 8.18. CSS One-Month Table Template (code0818.htm)

What's Next?

In Chapter 9 HTML **form** elements will be added to enhance the way your Web pages look, as well as the way your patrons can interact with your Web pages.

Chapter 9

Forms for Patron Interactivity

Not every library needs to use forms on its Web site. You may not feel you want to create forms or perhaps don't need the forms' functionality. You might have the option of leaving forms page design to the computer professionals in your community. Also, not all Web servers will permit forms usage. Forms typically require special software and configurations, and you may not have the technology to create complex forms. This chapter reviews some simple techniques with which you can create forms and use them. If you should want to create forms, what uses might your library have for them? They might include online requests to reserve a book a patron found on your OPAC or for an interlibrary book loan, an "Ask a Librarian" reference service, or to register to attend a library event. After your patrons fill out the online form, they click on a submit button that will send forms data to an e-mail address or database file on a Web server. Someone in the library needs to regularly review or retrieve these requests or your patrons will stop making them!

Forms can be used for interrogating your online public access catalog (OPAC) through your integrated library system software and server, but this interface is best left to computer professionals.

Up until now everything displayed in your browser window was assembled with your browser obtaining additional image files for display but without user input, other than hyperlinking to other Web pages or Web sites. The **form** element creates a container for data input from your patron. Forms can contain buttons (boxes (squares), radios (circles), and text), drop down lists, and text input fields. In most cases your patron's browser is used solely to collect information for the form, which sends the data to a program residing on a Web server for further processing. Some simple forms depend on the use of special software programming that may not require software to be installed on your Web server.

Creating Web Forms

In this section we begin our design and building of a form. Forms and **form** elements can be used on your Web page in much the same way as images. They can be the only coding on a page, they can exist within blocks of text, or in tables, or can be surrounded by hyperlinks. The section in the **body** of your HTML document that deals with each form's processing creates a form container that is between the opening and closing **form** element tags. Much as we can have several lists or tables on a Web page, there can be several form sections on a Web page, each forwarding the data to a specific Common Gateway Interface (CGI) software program. All active forms contain within them hidden variable names and values that must match the variables in the computer script or program that processes the information your patron's browser sends to the server for processing.

Even if you do not need to use interactive forms, there are several neat displays that form-type button graphic elements create on our Web pages. In this chapter you will see how to use **form** elements to create simple forms, use online vendor products to create small survey forms, and use button graphics to create a simple calendar.

The Form Element

Even if you do not need to use interactive forms, there are several neat displays that form-type. The various **form** elements and their attributes are listed below, although it is well beyond the scope of this text to cover all aspects of form creation and usage:

form—Fill-In Forms
Attributes: **method, action, enctype, name**
Can contain: **input, select, textarea, hn, p, hr, dir, dl, menu, ol, ul, address**
Can be inside: **blockquote, body, dd, li, td**
input—Form Field Type
Attributes: **type, name, size, maxlength, value, align, checked, src**
Can be inside: **form, any nonempty element**
textarea—Text Block Input
Attributes: **rows, cols, name**
Can contain: **characters only** Can be inside: **form**
select—Multiple Options
Attributes: **size, multiple, name**
Can contain: **option** Can be inside: **form**
option—Options for 'select' Element
Attributes: **value, selected**
Can contain: **characters only** Can be inside: **select**

The Input Element

The **input** element is an empty element whose **field-type** attributes specify the type of form field that your patron will see and be able to interact with. The basic HTML code to create a form button is:

<input type="type1" name="name1" value="value1" />

Where the **type** values for "type1" can be **checkbox** (square), **radio** (circle), **text**, **password**, **hidden**, **image**, **submit**, or **reset**. The **name** attribute values for "name1" must be consistent with those variables described in the Web server's software form processing program so that the **value** can be properly used to process your patron data. Figure 9.1 shows these field-type attributes as graphic elements, without the **form** element surrounding them.

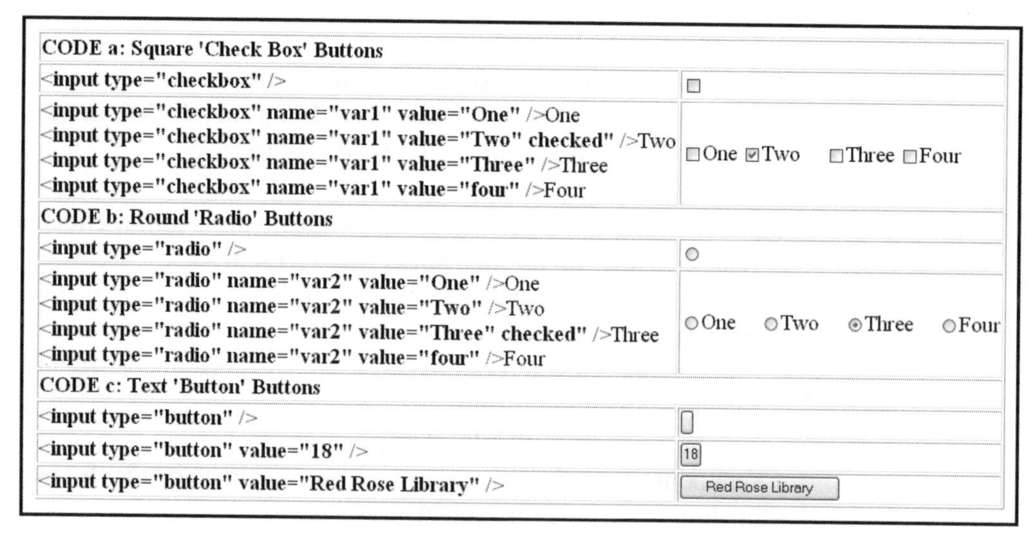

CODE a: Square 'Check Box' Buttons	
<input type="checkbox" />	
<input type="checkbox" name="var1" value="One" />One <input type="checkbox" name="var1" value="Two" checked" />Two <input type="checkbox" name="var1" value="Three" />Three <input type="checkbox" name="var1" value="four" />Four	One Two Three Four
CODE b: Round 'Radio' Buttons	
<input type="radio" />	
<input type="radio" name="var2" value="One" />One <input type="radio" name="var2" value="Two" />Two <input type="radio" name="var2" value="Three" checked" />Three <input type="radio" name="var2" value="four" />Four	One Two Three Four
CODE c: Text 'Button' Buttons	
<input type="button" />	
<input type="button" value="18" />	18
<input type="button" value="Red Rose Library" />	Red Rose Library

Figure 9.1. Check Box, Radio, and Text Buttons (code0901.htm)

By now you know that the default element styles are not always what we need for our Web pages. Figure 9.2 shows the result of adding cascading style sheet stylization to enhance the look of your buttons once again without the need to create a form or use a **form** element.

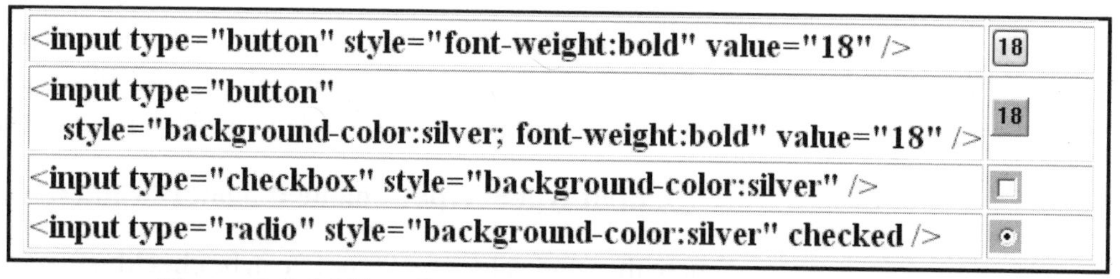

<input type="button" style="font-weight:bold" value="18" />	18
<input type="button" style="background-color:silver; font-weight:bold" value="18" />	18
<input type="checkbox" style="background-color:silver" />	
<input type="radio" style="background-color:silver" checked />	

Figure 9.2 Adding Style to Form Buttons (code0902.htm)

The Select Element

The **select** element can be used to create a menu or drop down list of items from which your patron can choose. As with all forms elements, the **select**'s variable information, used by the form processing script when it is submitted to the server, is contained in its **name="variablename"** attribute. Other **select** attributes determine the way your choices are displayed. The **size="n"** attribute specifies the length of the list or menu in displayed lines. The default value for the "exposed" list is **size="1"**, and most users have this topmost entry as a note that there is a selection possible, as shown in Figure 9.3.

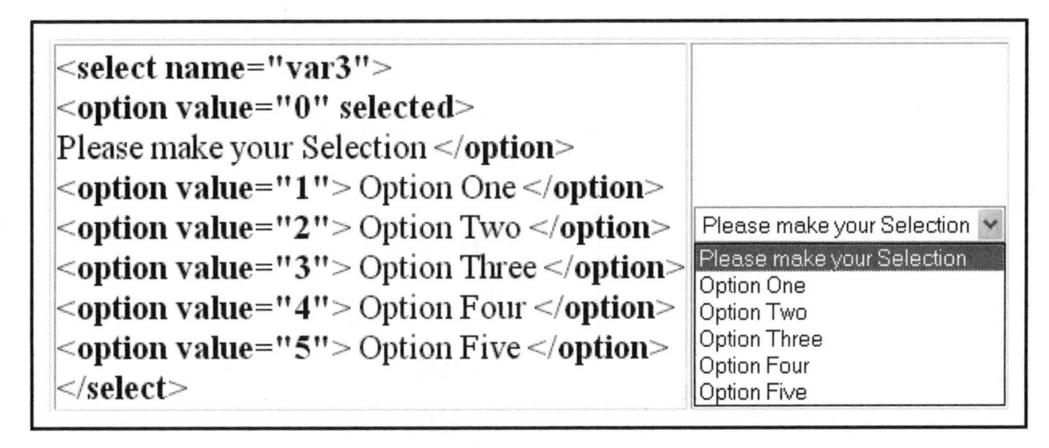

Figure 9.3 Adding Dropdown (select) Lists to Your Form (code0903.htm)

The **value="value"** attribute indicates the value to be shown on the form and sent for processing if the particular **option** is selected. In the example, we have given the options a value matching its option number. An **option** may be preselected for display on the form by adding the optional **selected** attribute, as was done for option **"0"** in Figure 9.3. The **option selected** attribute specifies which entry will be the visible or default selection on the list. Your server's processing program can be designed to check for any **value="0"** selections and respond to a **submit** command with an error message that states all form fields have to be selected, etc. Be sure to add the closing **</option>** tags, which are optional in HTML but required in XHTML and XML, for upward compatibility of your Web form. You may already have figured out that this type of selection technique could be used for surveys. Later in this chapter you'll see how to use a line of software code to have the selection of a variable from a drop down list just like this one send your patron to another Web page or even a Web site.

The **select** element is widely used in forms that have address cities and states, days, dates, and years, or other common preselectable responses where multiple choices from a set of entries are appropriate. Figure 9.4 shows a portion of a typical online hotel reservation form.

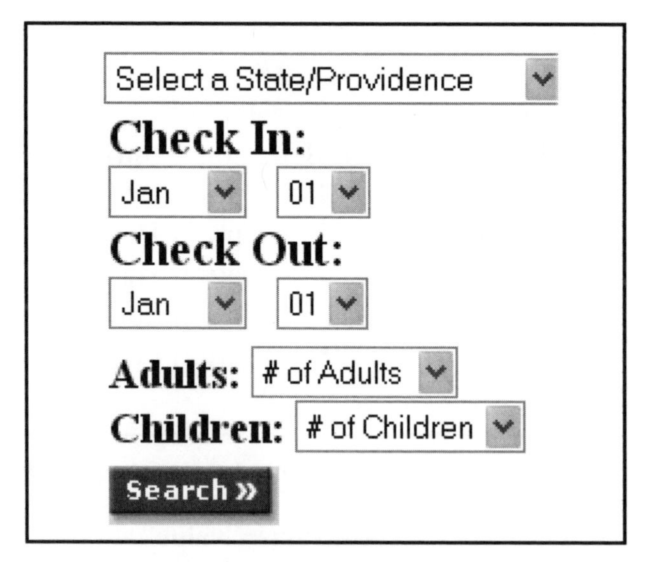

Figure 9.4 Drop Down Form for Hotel Reservations (code0904.htm)

If used in a book search, the title, author, or subject might be selectable and when processed, a new drop down list that includes the various authors or a thesaurus of search terms might be forwarded to the patron. Sometimes you want to allow more than one response for a given question; in that case, use the optional **multiple** attribute in the select command to specify that the user can select one or more items from the drop down list.

The Textarea Element

The **textarea** element is a text block input element that extends the **input** element's **text field-type** to allow the creation of multiline text input fields. It uses three required attributes to identify and provide the size of the text area. The text area's variable information, which is used by form processing script when it is submitted to the server, is contained in its **name="variablename"** attribute, and the **rows="n"** and **cols="n"** attributes that specify the height and the width of the text area in characters. See Figure 9.5.

CODE:	
Text Line 1: **<input type="text" name="text_line_1" value="" size="40" />**	Text Line 1:
Text Line 2: **<input type="text" name="text_line_2" value="30 Characters here" size="30" />**	Text Line 2: 30 Characters here
Text Area Comment Box (4 rows, 50 cols) **<textarea name="Comment" rows="5" cols="50"> </textarea>**	Text Area Comment Box (4 rows, 50 cols)

Figure 9.5. Adding Text to Your Form (code0905.htm)

Adding Color to a Textarea Box Form

You can add **color** to the **background** and text of a **textarea** box. Changing the default colors to suit your needs or match your Web page colors is a technique sure to spice up your **textarea** boxes.

Here is the inline style code for a colored **textarea** box with colored text included as a default:

```
<textarea cols="48" rows="3" style="background-color: #e6e6fa;
color: #9400d3; font-weight: bold; font-size: 12;">
Change the text box colors to suit your needs and/or match your Web
page to spice up the text area boxes on your forms.
</textarea>
```

You can also color the scrollbar in a specific **textarea** box. If you have a scrollbar on your Web page, this will not affect that scrollbar, only the scrollbar in the **textarea** box. CSS codes can add a lot to your Web pages. You can also add this colored scrollbar to the **textarea** box with just the colored background. Please be sure to close the **textarea** element, otherwise the remainder of your Web page will end up in your **textarea** box as scrollable content. Here is the code you can use to stylize a **textarea** box with a red-colored background, black text, and a multicolored text area scrollbar:

```
<textarea cols="48" rows="3" style="background-color: #ff0000;
color: #ffffff;
font-weight: bold; font-size: 12; scrollbar-highlight-color: red;
scrollbar-3dlight-color: blue; scrollbar-darkshadow-color: green;
scrollbar-track-color: pink; scrollbar-face-color: tan;
scrollbar-arrow-color: yellow">
Style sheet codes add a lot to your Web page forms. As with every-
thing that is good, over using this technique will not be well-received
by your patrons. Just because you can use it doesn't mean it will look
good when you do! You can change the colors on the scrollbar, back-
ground or text, but make sure they look good before you expect your
patron to use them.
</textarea>
```

Action Button Types

When used with the attribute **type="submit"** (or **type="reset"**) , the **input** element can become an action button that will either submit the data on your form to your e-mail or server for processing, or reset the form back to its original defaults (e.g., if an error is made). Figure 9.6 shows several examples of the code needed to add action buttons inside your form.

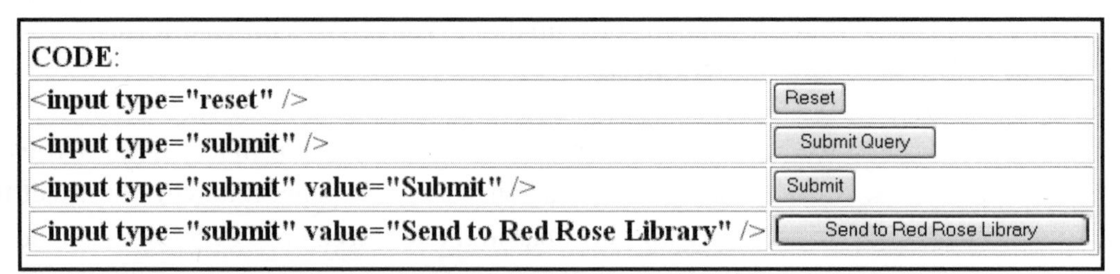

CODE:	
<input type="reset" />	Reset
<input type="submit" />	Submit Query
<input type="submit" value="Submit" />	Submit
<input type="submit" value="Send to Red Rose Library" />	Send to Red Rose Library

Figure 9.6. Adding Action Buttons to Your Form (code0906.htm)

As in the examples shown earlier in this chapter, you can use style to create colored action buttons by adding a style attribute for **back-ground-color** and **color** in a **submit** button, which you've named "Select Me", as shown in the following code line:

```
<input style="background-color: #8b008b; color: #ffff00;
font-weight: bold; font-size: 10;" type="submit" value="Select Me">
```

As you can see, depending on your application, **submit** and **reset** action buttons do not have to be literal; they can be labeled with any text value or colored without text.

Server-Side Processing: Making Forms Work with CGI

Most forms rely on a Web server to process your input. This "server-side processing" uses computer programs or scripts in a special **cgi-bin** directory (**cgi-bin** is the abbreviation of Common Gateway Interface binaries). CGI is a standard for interfacing your computer with information or database Web servers using external or gateway programs to control data requests. The CGI standard may be reviewed at **http://hoohoo.ncsa.uiuc.edu/cgi**

Stored in the server's **cgi-bin** directory are short programs written in C/C++, Fortran, Perl, etc., programming and/or scripting languages that are, you guessed it: beyond the scope of our simple text! Forms designed in this chapter show one of the simplest of **form** applications, an e-mail response generator. But all is not lost even if you can't program, or even if you can't access your Web server's **cgi-bin**! Although without a properly working **cgi-bin** script a form is just another "static" Web page, we can get around the **cgi-bin** requirement for some simple examples using internal JavaScript, so please don't skip this section if you do not have **cgi-bin** access.

How the CGI Can Work for You

If you are comfortable in any programming language, there are many textbooks that can guide you step by step through "canned" CGI code for forms handling (e.g., CGI/Perl Cookbook by Patchett and Wright; Wiley Computer Publishing). But if you just want one or two simple forms codes, they may be available for downloading from Web resources that make it possible for you to use, rather than write, processing applications; two of these resources are **http://www.cgiconnection.com/** and **http://cgi.resourceindex.com/**

The CGI Resource Index Web site also has links to hundreds of "hosted" CGI form applications. Several of these offer a "free" hosting service. These provide you with the tools to create an interactive form to use with their **cgi-bin** program on their server. You won't have to either write the forms handling code or have your own Web server set up to support CGI applications. Bear in mind that merely creating a directory on your Web site called cgi-bin and saving script files in that directory does not give you the ability to run scripts on your server. The server must be configured by the systems operator to have the software and server linkages that will make a cgi directory work. If the solution is using someone else's server, perhaps one of these will suit your needs:

http://www.response-o-matic.com/

http://www.surveymonkey.com/

http://www.formbuddy.com/

http://www.bfndevelopment.com/

http://freedback.com/

The script on most free sites will send the form information to you by e-mail. Embedded in your Web page form code will be a link to that service's **cgi-bin** code that makes it all happen. The code line that goes to the Response-O-Matic service **cgi-bin**, for example, would look like:

```
<form action="http://www.response-o-matic.com/cgi-bin/rom.pl"
method="post">
```

where the Perl script that manages your form is in the file **rom.pl** on their server. When sent to this file, your forms information would be processed and then e-mailed to the address "hidden" in your Web page coding. For example, the code

```
<input type="hidden" name="your_email_address"
value="your.email@server.com">
```

will send the processed response to your e-mail address: **your.email@server.com**. Code lines using the **type="hidden"** attribute value are hidden from the Web page user but must be inside the **form** code section of your HTML document. The important thing to understand here is that you do not control the cgi-bin script. Response-O-Matic offers this free service for any individual or organization that wants to add forms to its Web pages. But you don't get to play with their **cgi-bin** scripts, only use them.

That's good, as there are no copyright issues, but you should still check out their "terms of use" Web page if you use their service. If you want to use another **cgi-bin** program, you will need to find another hosting service. The downside of the service is that you will need to use their template coding to get any results, and when your patron submits a form, they will get a response from the server which, unless you pay a registration fee for the service, includes major advertising. After all, somebody has to pay for the server! Also note that you must use the same variable names (e.g., **name="your_email_address"**) in your form coding that are expected by the script; otherwise your form will not be processed properly.

Online Surveys

If you expect fewer than 100 patrons will respond to a particular survey, SurveyMonkey's resources (**http://www.surveymonkey.com**) can be used to create ten-question online surveys for free and without annoying banner ads. They have an online creation tool that is filled with options to create surveys of the following types:

Choice—One Answer: Vertical, Horizontal and Menu

Choice—Multiple Answers: Vertical and Horizontal

Matrix—One Answer per Row (Rating Scale)

Matrix—Multiple Answers per Row (and with Menus)

Open Ended—One or More Lines w/Prompt, Essay, Constant Sum, Date and/or Time

Presentation—Descriptive Text, Image, Spacer

If your surveys are larger, you might consider their fee plan. Using the templates or specifications from their hosting service, it takes as little as half an hour to design, create, and test your forms. Bear in mind that although these services are free, they may not provide you with XML-compliant HTML pages. Some still generate HTML code with uppercase rather than lowercase element and attribute names. You may want to revise the pages to the higher standard. Once that has been done, you can move the files to your Web site and have your patrons fill them out.

Figure 9.7 was created with only one **form** container and eight different **input** types. This shows some of the power that the **form** element has. Note that the **form** element that created this figure (see **code0907.htm**) does not include a **method** or **action** attribute that links the code to a **cgi-bin** file. Thus, although this form seems interactive, pressing either its **submit** or **reset** buttons only results in the **form** page being refreshed and reset to the built-in defaults. No messages will be sent.

a. Text Line 1:
b. Text Line 2: 30 Characters here

c. Text Area Comment Box (4 rows x 50 cols visible)

d. Vertical Radio Buttons with Button 'Three' Checked
One
Two
Three
Four

e. Horizontal Radio Buttons with Button 'One' Checked
One Two Three Four
f. Horizontal Checkbox Buttons with Button 'Dee' Checked
Aye Bee Cee Dee

g. Selection Drop Down Box Please make your Selection

h. Select an Action Button: Submit Reset

Figure 9.7. E-mail Form Elements (code0907.htm)

Forms Processing Using Simple E-mail Techniques

The "trick" of creating forms that e-mail their results to you doesn't work well with all browsers. As with all your pages, test them first on all the browsers you expect your patrons to use, before they use them and find your solutions don't work! If you include the code line

<form action="mailto:your.email@server.com?subject=Email Response" method=post enctype="text/plain">

in your HTML **form** document you are asking your browser, when you click on the **submit** button, to send an e-mail message to **your.email@server.com**, which includes the forms data encoded as plain text (**enctype="text/plain"**) .

Pressing the **submit** button on the page results in the form data being packaged in an e-mail, either as a string of text with the name of each **input** element response, followed by an equals (=) sign and then the actual content inserted with plus (+) signs separating any text inputs with the **input** element responses separated by the ampersand sign (**&**), or as a series of data lines with underscores (_) between names and an equals (=) sign before the response.

When I used Internet Explorer as the browser, it gave me a warning:
"This form was being submitted using email.
Submitting this form will reveal your e-mail address to the recipient, and will send the form data without encrypting it for privacy.
You may continue or cancel this submission."

Clicking "OK" automatically opened Microsoft's Outlook Express e-mail program with the e-mail address and "Email Response" in their correct places; however, the data were not transferred to the e-mail. When sent, the e-mail received was also empty. The same form of Figure 9.7, but with e-mail form coding, **code0907e.htm = email.htm**, opened in Mozilla's Firefox browser was able to correctly send the form information as an e-mail using Microsoft's Outlook Express. (Your patrons must have their e-mail program properly configured to send outgoing mail, or this method won't work.) The screen shot of the e-mail window, edited so you can see all the content in the message, showing all of the selected information data, is shown in Figure 9.8.

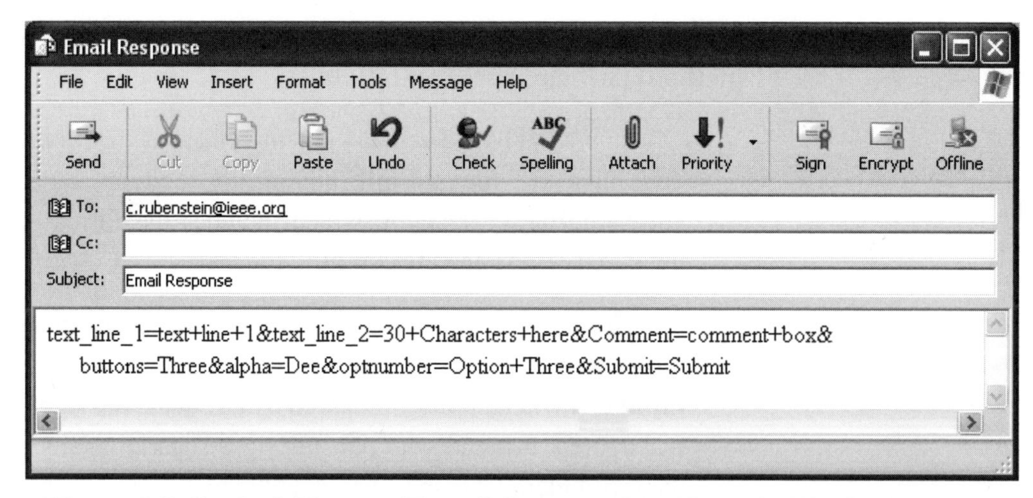

Figure 9.8. Outlook Express E-mail Generated by Form in Firefox Browser

The e-mail sending program, Outlook Express, and Netscape's e-mail receiving program all actually had the forms data text as a single long line rather than the reproductions here, which show the text wrapped so you can see it all.

The Netscape e-mail message, received seconds after clicking "send," looked like:

-------- Original Message --------
Subject: Email Response
From: Charles Rubenstein <c.rubenstein@ieee.org>
To: c.rubenstein@ieee.org
text_line_1=text+line+1&text_line_2=30+Characters+here&
Comment=comment+box&buttons=Three&al-
pha=Dee&optnumber=Option+Three&Submit=Submit

Not an elegant solution, but enough to do the job. The downside is you will have to figure out how to save the e-mails and separate the individual data information from the continuous stream of characters. Some browsers send these same data with the data received as single line entries:

text_line_1=
text_line_2=30 Characters here
Comment=
buttons=Three
radiob=One
alpha=Dee
optnumber=Please make your Selection
Submit=Submit

Experimenting a bit with the code may achieve the output set you need. One major problem with simple e-mail-creating form responses is that Outlook Express (etc.) opens up and shows your patron the e-mail address and the content of the e-mail it is about to send. If your patrons decide to get clever, they may change the contents before they press send to e-mail it to you.

Making It Work with JavaScript: Client-Side Processing

Alas, not all servers have the software needed to run server-side processing of Web forms, or they will not permit your site to access them. What do we do then? There are ways to have some forms processed directly on your computer (client-side processing) through the use of programming scripts. In this section we review a few simple workarounds for the **cgi-bin** challenge using JavaScript, a scripting language that can be used inside your Web page document—just like we did with internal style sheets. We'll see that using JavaScript techniques (covered very briefly here and well beyond the scope of this text), we can create forms that are client-side enabled. That is, when we JavaScript-enable our form Web pages, we may not need to use inelegant e-mail methods nor require a Web server to process our requests.

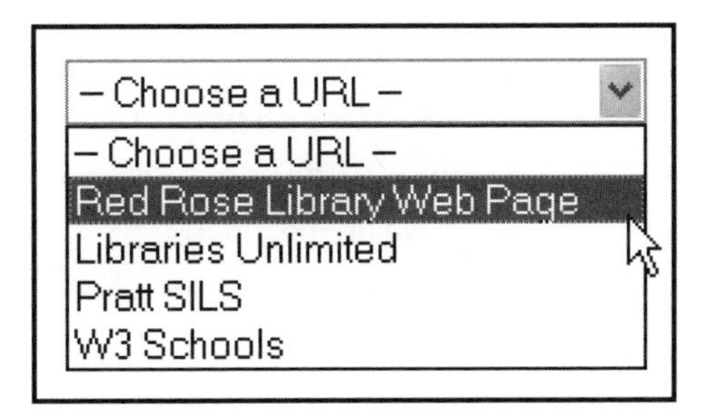

Figure 9.9. Simple JavaScript URL Selection Form (code0909.htm)

Figure 9.9 is the output from a form using Javascript to automatically hyperlink to another Web page or even another Web site. Based on the HTML code in **code0909.htm**, the form and JavaScript are designed to allow a list of URLs to be created and enable your patron to use these for simple Web site navigation.

URL Selection Form Code (see code0909.htm):

```
<html>
<head><title>
Simple Javascript URL Selection Form</title></head>
<body bgcolor="#ffffff">
<script langage="JavaScript">
<!--
function jumpToPage()
{
  if (document.index.url[document.index.url.selectedIndex])
  {
   location.href = document.index.url[document.index.url.selectedIndex].value;
  }
}
//-->
</script>
<form name="index" method=get action="#">
 <select name="url" onChange="jumpToPage()">
     <option value="#" selected>-- Choose a URL --</option>
     <option value="http://www.redroselibrary.com/">Red Rose Library
Web Page</option>
     <option value="http://www.lu.com/">Libraries Unlimited</option>
     <option value="http://www.pratt.edu/sils/">Pratt SILS</option>
     <option value="http://www.w3schools.com/">W3 Schools</option>
  </select>
  </form>
</body></html>
```

As noted previously in this chapter, JavaScript is a very powerful method for accomplishing a variety of animations on your page, but at the expense of having to learn real programming techniques. If the techniques above are useful, use them; if not, perhaps you'll use the calendar techniques in the next section to create attractive calendar pages for your patrons.

Using Forms Graphics in Calendar Pages

Using input button graphics is a simple and convenient way to create simple-looking calendars that can be static, or even have hyperlinks associated with one or more dates to highlight them for events or holidays. I am sure you can find a dozen different ways to use calendars to enhance your Web pages. The calendar can be a quarterly version, such as that in Figure 9.10 for the first quarter of 2006, or the three-month by four-month annual 2007 calendar in Figure 9.11 in portrait printout mode.

2006 Calendar - First Quarter

January

SUN	MON	TUE	WED	THU	FRI	SAT
1	2	3	4	5	6	7
8	9	10	11	12	13	14
15	16	17	18	19	20	21
22	23	24	25	26	27	28
29	30	31				

February

SUN	MON	TUE	WED	THU	FRI	SAT
			1	2	3	4
5	6	7	8	9	10	11
12	13	14	15	16	17	18
19	20	21	22	23	24	25
26	27	28				

March

SUN	MON	TUE	WED	THU	FRI	SAT
			1	2	3	4
5	6	7	8	9	10	11
12	13	14	15	16	17	18
19	20	21	22	23	24	25
26	27	28	29	30	31	

Figure 9.10. 2006 Form Calendar, Quarterly Version (code0910.htm)

2007 Calendar

January

Sun	Mon	Tue	Wed	Thu	Fri	Sat
	1	2	3	4	5	6
7	8	9	10	11	12	13
14	15	16	17	18	19	20
21	22	23	24	25	26	27
28	29	30	31			

February

Sun	Mon	Tue	Wed	Thu	Fri	Sat
				1	2	3
4	5	6	7	8	9	10
11	12	13	14	15	16	17
18	19	20	21	22	23	24
25	26	27	28			

March

Sun	Mon	Tue	Wed	Thu	Fri	Sat
				1	2	3
4	5	6	7	8	9	10
11	12	13	14	15	16	17
18	19	20	21	22	23	24
25	26	27	28	29	30	31

April

Sun	Mon	Tue	Wed	Thu	Fri	Sat
1	2	3	4	5	6	7
8	9	10	11	12	13	14
15	16	17	18	19	20	21
22	23	24	25	26	27	28
29	30					

May

Sun	Mon	Tue	Wed	Thu	Fri	Sat
		1	2	3	4	5
6	7	8	9	10	11	12
13	14	15	16	17	18	19
20	21	22	23	24	25	26
27	28	29	30	31		

June

Sun	Mon	Tue	Wed	Thu	Fri	Sat
					1	2
3	4	5	6	7	8	9
10	11	12	13	14	15	16
17	18	19	20	21	22	23
24	25	26	27	28	29	30

July

Sun	Mon	Tue	Wed	Thu	Fri	Sat
1	2	3	4	5	6	7
8	9	10	11	12	13	14
15	16	17	18	19	20	21
22	23	24	25	26	27	28
29	30	31				

August

Sun	Mon	Tue	Wed	Thu	Fri	Sat
			1	2	3	4
5	6	7	8	9	10	11
12	13	14	15	16	17	18
19	20	21	22	23	24	25
26	27	28	29	30	31	

September

Sun	Mon	Tue	Wed	Thu	Fri	Sat
						1
2	3	4	5	6	7	8
9	10	11	12	13	14	15
16	17	18	19	20	21	22
23	24	25	26	27	28	29
30						

October

Sun	Mon	Tue	Wed	Thu	Fri	Sat
	1	2	3	4	5	6
7	8	9	10	11	12	13
14	15	16	17	18	19	20
21	22	23	24	25	26	27
28	29	30	31			

November

Sun	Mon	Tue	Wed	Thu	Fri	Sat
				1	2	3
4	5	6	7	8	9	10
11	12	13	14	15	16	17
18	19	20	21	22	23	24
25	26	27	28	29	30	

December

Sun	Mon	Tue	Wed	Thu	Fri	Sat
						1
2	3	4	5	6	7	8
9	10	11	12	13	14	15
16	17	18	19	20	21	22
23	24	25	26	27	28	29
30	31					

Figure 9.11. Three-Month by Four-Month 2007 Form Calendar, Portrait Printout Mode (code0911.htm)

Each of these calendars is based on creating a series of tables, with the rows consisting of empty and numbered or text-filled input buttons:

For the Month Name Rows:

```
<tr align="Center"><td><big><big><b>
February</b></big></big><br /> </td></tr>
```

For the Days of the Week table data entries:

```
<td width="14%"><font size="1"><b>MON</b></font></td>
```

For the 25th day of the month button:

```
<td align="center"><input type="button" value="25"></td>
```

For a 'blank' day button to fill in the rows:

```
<td align="center"><input type="button" value="   "></td>
```

Sudoku Anyone?

Another way to enhance your Web pages, especially those in the young adult section, might be to add some sort of Sudoku puzzle. The puzzle is basically a nine-by-nine matrix of numbers configured as nine three-by-three matrices. If you don't know how to play it yet, ask any teenager!

You could merely enter the puzzle as a normal nine row by nine column table (Figure 9.12), or as shown in Figure 9.13, using forms elements to create the puzzle. It will take a bit of effort to work these out, but the codes are all there in the files **code0912.htm** and **code0913.htm** for you to play with.

What's Next?

In Chapter 10 we look at a variety of techniques that you can use to further enhance your Web pages. These include using strings of hypertext and image maps for navigation and how to add marquees and transitions to your pages. We'll also look into a few points on Web page accessibility for patrons with limited sight.

1	2	3	1	2	3	1	2	3
4	5	6	4	5	6	4	5	6
7	8	9	7	8	9	7	8	9
1	2	3	1	2	3	1	2	3
4	5	6	4	5	6	4	5	6
7	8	9	7	8	9	7	8	9
1	2	3	1	2	3	1	2	3
4	5	6	4	5	6	4	5	6
7	8	9	7	8	9	7	8	9

Figure 9.12. Sudoku Puzzle, Large Table (code0912.htm)

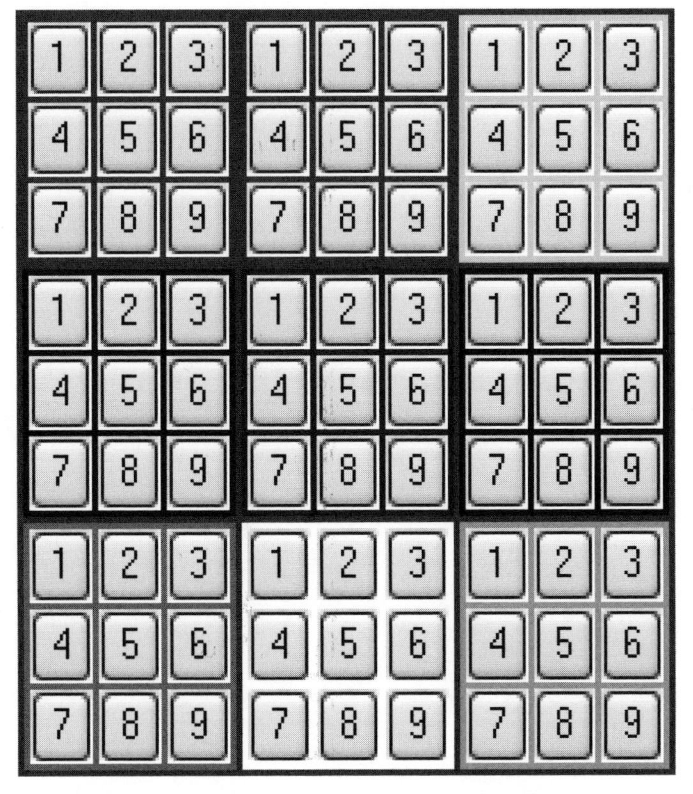

Figure 9.13. Sudoku Puzzle Using Input Buttons and Color (code0913.htm)

Chapter 10

Web Page Navigation, Image Mapping, Marquees, and Transitions

Well, you are nearing the finish line. This, our last chapter, much like Chapter 9, is not for the faint of heart. In this chapter we look at a variety of techniques that you can use to further enhance your Web pages. These include adding image maps to create navigation bars and hypergraphics, as well as adding marquees and transitions to your pages. We also look into a few points on Web page accessibility for patrons with limited sight and how search engine optimization is being used to get your Web pages noticed by Google and other vendor search engines. Most of these techniques require some level of JavaScript computer programming, so you may need to find a local high school student to help you follow these instructions.

Web Page Navigation Techniques

Most Web pages have one or more hyperlinks on them, either to other pages on your site or to other Web sites. Like our Red Rose Library home page, they often have a variety of hypertext links that would be nice to have on all of our Web pages to make it easier for your patron to navigate around in your Web site. This navigation tool can be in a column to the left side of the Web page, at the top, or at the bottom of the page. A common problem with setting up a left-side navigation column is that the column takes up room that could be used for content, and when the page is printed, the column prints, but not the rest of your page.

If you have decided to use a top or bottom navigation tool, there are two approaches to the task. One uses hypertext and the other uses the image map technique discussed in the next section. In each case, clicking on the hyperactive area navigates between the major sections of your Web site.

```
<hr/>
<a href="index.htm">Home</a> |
<a href="hours.htm">Hours</a> |
<a href="staff.htm">Staff</a> |
<a href="board.htm">Board</a> |
<a href="archive.htm" target="_blank">Newsletter</a> |
<a href="children.htm">Children</a> |
<a href="youth.htm">YA</a> |
<a href="av.htm">AV</a> |
<a href="ref.htm" target="_blank">Ref</a> |
<a href="friends.htm">Friends</a> |
<a href="faqs.htm" target="_blank"> FAQs</a>
<hr/>
```

With the code line of Figure 10.1 at the bottom of your Web page, you will have eleven easy-to-find navigation links on your page in a minimum of time and taking up a minimum of precious space on your page.

Home | Hours | Staff | Board | Newsletter | Children | YA | AV | Ref | Friends | FAQs

Figure 10.1 Hypertext Navigation Bar (code1001.htm)

Notice that unless you change the link **style**, to **text-decoration: none**, your hypertext bar will not be as elegant looking as you might like. Surrounding these hypertext codes with horizontal rules (which can also be stylized as **<hr style="color:red" />**) and adding the **style** attribute code

style="text-decoration:none; color=red"

to each anchor element, in line, for example in the FAQs links

<a href="faqs.htm" style="text-decoration:none; color=red;" target="_blank" > FAQs</a>

will remove the blue color and underline associated with typical hypertext. Add a **font** element to the beginning of the code with a **style** attribute for the full text block to include styling the separating vertical bars and setting the overall font **size** to 18 pixels:

<font style="font-size=18; font-weight=bold; color=red" >

and the result is the hypertext navigation bar seen in Figure 10.2 (**code1002.htm**).

Home | Hours | Staff | Board | Newsletter | Children | YA | AV | Ref | Friends | FAQs

Figure 10.2 Stylized Hypertext Navigation Bar (code1002.htm)

You could also add the **style** changes to an internal or external style sheet (as well as change the hover style, etc.), as has been discussed previously.

The Red Rose Library Page of Figure 4.19 (**code0419.htm**) can be enhanced with the text logo designed in Chapter 5 (Figure 5.4; **img002.jpg**), trimmed to **width="300"** and include the bottom navigation hypertext code we designed in Figure 10.1 (**code1001.htm**) to create the Home Page with navigation seen in Figure 10.3 (**code1003.htm**).

Welcome to the
Red Rose Library
18 Rose Street
New York, NY 10010
Telephone +1 212 555 - 7673

Where we are - When we're open

Library Staff	Board of Trustees
Calendar of Events	
Red Rose Newsletter	The History of Red Rose

Our children's RoOm!
Young Adults Section
Audio & Video Collection
Reference & Database Information
Online Public Access Catalog

Friends of the Red Rose Library
Cultural Programs
December 2006: **Radio City Music Hall**
January 2007: **The American Museum of Natural History**
February 2007: **MoMA - The Museum of Modern Art**

FAQs - *Frequently Asked Questions*

For additional information please contact the webmaster
Copyright (c) 2006 C. Rubenstein - RedRoseLibrary.com

Home | Hours | Staff | Board | Newsletter | Children | YA | AV | Ref | Friends | FAQs

Figure 10.3. Home Page with Logo and Hypertext Navigation Bar (code1003.htm)

Clicking on any of the text in the navigation bar would take your patron to the appropriate page on the Red Rose Library Web site. Another way of accomplishing this same action would be to use a graphic and segment the graphic in such a way that each segment works like a single image that exhibits hyperlinking. You could, of course, use individual graphics, but the effect of using a single interactive graphic, although a bit more difficult, requiring image mapping techniques, is quite a bit nicer.

Image Maps

An image map is an interactive graphic that the user interacts with by clicking on predefined "hot spots" that result in client-side (not needing information stored on a Web server) hypertext jumps. You may have seen one or more examples of this type of Web page if you access Web sites looking for cellular telephone service areas, local stores, or representatives of a national firm. Although you will quickly review the concepts here, please remember that image mapping requires a lot of concentration and a software program to create a good map. It is unlikely that you will have time to do this yourself, but you might find one of your library's high school pages with technical experience or a knowledgeable volunteer in the community that has the appropriate technical experience and would be interested in helping you. The basics are covered here so that you can create a navigation bar to place at the top and/or bottom of your Web page. Once more, this section might be too advanced for some. Feel free to jump over to the "Marquees" section of this chapter and know that image mapping is here if you need it.

Once only available through Web server software using CGI Scripts that required high-level programming ability and access to the cgi-bin directory on your Web server, image mapping can be done on your local computer. You'll see how to do it manually here, but client-side mapping software like MapEdit (currently in Version 2.95 and available for free evaluation as a fully functional thirty-day download at **http://www.boutell.com/ mapedit/download.html**) makes the job go faster. This is a shareware program, and you can register it for $10 and get a variety of U.S. and world maps to use on your Web site.

Perhaps the most common of image maps is the navigation bar of Figure 10.4. The navigation bar image **navbar.jpg** consists of several words in a long rectangle with a fuschia (**#ff00ff**) colored background that users can use to navigate your Web site.

Home | Hours | Staff | Board | Newsletter | Children | YA | AV | Ref | Friends | FAQs

Figure 10.4. Navigation Bar Image (navbar.jpg)

Unlike standard graphing that starts with the 0,0 coordinate in the *lower left hand corner* of your page, image mapping begins at the *upper left hand corner* of your graphic. Image mapping relies on the **img** element to identify the image used, but then only cares about the pixel location relative to the upper lefthand corner. **gif**, **jpg**, and even **png** image files can be used.

Image mapping is a powerful method of identifying areas on an image with specific URL links. The empty **map** element's **name** attribute identifies the particular **map** data to match with the **usemap** attribute name of an **img** tag. So we will start with setting up the **img** tag to specify the graphic and the **usemap** attribute name. (This two-part method is similar to the technique used to accomplish relative linking within an HTML document using the anchor tag's **name** attribute.)

Image Map Area Attributes

The image map coding for the 640 pixel width by 26 pixel height **navbar.jpg** image in Figure 10.4 uses the **img** tag with a **usemap** attribute and would look like

```
<img src="images/navbar.jpg" usemap="#navbarmap" />
```

Note that the **#** is used as part of the **usemap="#navbarmap"** attribute value to indicate that the coding for the image map is within the current document at the map name element's **navbarmap** location. Although the corresponding map element coding can be anywhere inside your HTML document, map data are typically placed either directly below the **img** tag or at the very end of your document. Image map elements use the same **name** attribute structure used by the anchor tag's **name** attribute (**<a name="internal_hyperlink_name">**). The image map code looks like

```
<map name="navbarmap">
```

This client-side image map coding uses the **area** element to define each individual clickable hot spot **area** in your image. The **area** attributes of **shape** and **coords** are used to specify hot spots.

Valid **shape** attributes that create hyperactive circle, rectangle, or polygon areas are **rect** or **rectangle**, **circ** or **circle**, and **poly** or **polygon**. The **coords** attribute gives the X,Y coordinates that define these shapes. For a rectangle, these coordinates define the shapes diagonal with two pairs of points: X1,Y1 and X2,Y2. For a circle **shape** the **coords** attribute defines the X,Y center of the circle, with a third value giving the circle's radius. The polygon **shape** requires **coords** with three or more pairs of X,Y points to create any other hyperactive shape.

The **href** attribute is used inside the **area** tag to point to the relative or absolute URL link the browser will use to retrieve the HTML file when the mouse is clicked on that hot spot. If no link is desired in a particular area, the **nohref** attribute can be used to act as a placeholder for future links.

For our navigation bar example we are quite fortunate that each of the shapes is a rectangle and that they all have the same "Y" top and bottom coordinates (at 0 and 26 pixels). Using any art program, you can determine the specific starting and ending coordinates for each of our navigation points. You can also add hyperlinks to all the library departments and items on the navigation bar. The correlation between the text on the home page with the files it links to (where bold text is used for the navbar links) is shown in Figure 10.5.

Text on Page:	File Link to:
18 Rose Street, Where we are	where.htm
When we're open, **Hours**	hours.htm
Library Staff, **Staff**	staff.htm
Library Board of Trustees, **Board**	board.htm
Calendar of Events	calendar.htm
Red Rose Newsletter, **Newsletter**	archive.htm
The History of Red Rose	history.htm
Our Children's Room!, **Children**	children.htm
Simple Online Interactive Quiz	quiz.htm
Young Adults Section, **YA**	youth.htm
Audio & Video Collection, **AV**	av.htm
Reference & Database Information, **Ref**	ref.htm
Online Public Access Catalog	opac.htm
Friends of the Red Rose Library, **Friends**	friends.htm
Cultural Programs	programs.htm
December 2005	0512prog.htm
January 2006	0601prog.htm
February 2006	0602prog.htm
FAQs, **FAQs**	faqs.htm
webmaster	mailto:webmaster@redroselibrary.com
Home Page, **Home**	index.htm

Figure 10.5. Correlation Between Hyperlinks and Files

The **Home** rectangular hot spot link is defined by the upper lefthand coordinate 0,0 and the lower righthand coordinate at 56,26. The X,Y coordinate sets can be separated by commas, semicolons, or spaces.

As you begin setting up the map data for **navbarmap** you will see the first two entries name the map and begin defining the areas:

```
<map name="navbarmap"> ← Note that the # is NOT used here
<area shape="rect" coords="0,0 56,26" href="index.htm" />
```

You would then continue defining the other areas with their coordinates, **alt** values, and link names to create the full map code:

```
<map name="navbarmap">
<area shape="rect" coords="0,0 56,26" href="index.htm"
        alt="Red Rose Library Home Page" />
<area shape="rect" coords="56,0 116,26" href="hours.htm" alt="Hours of operation" />
<area shape="rect" coords="116,0 166,26" href="staff.htm" alt="Library Staff" />
<area shape="rect" coords="166,0 228,26" href="board.htm" alt="Board of Trustees" />
<area shape="rect" coords="228,0 322,26" href="archive.htm"
        alt="Newsletters" target="_blank" />
<area shape="rect" coords="322,0 402,26" href="children.htm" alt="Children's Room" />
<area shape="rect" coords="402,0 436,26" href="youth.htm" alt="Young Adults" />
<area shape="rect" coords="436,0 472,26" href="av.htm" alt="Audio/Visual Collection" />
<area shape="rect" coords="472,0 512,26" href="ref.htm"
        alt="Reference Desk" target="_blank" />
<area shape="rect" coords="512,0 584,26" href="friends.htm"
        alt="Friends of the Red Rose Library" />
<area shape="rect" coords="584,0 640,26" href="faqs.htm" alt="FAQs" tar-
get="_blank" />
</map>
```

Other shapes possible for image maps include the **circle** with **coords="X,Y circle center; radius"**, whose coding for the Staff mapping would look like:

```
<area shape="circle" coords="141,13; 26" href="staff.htm"
alt="Library Staff" />
```

and the general polygon shape value "**poly**" with **coords="X1,Y1; X2,Y1; X2,Y2; X1,Y2"**, where in coding the rectangle for the Young Adults (YA) link area X1,Y1 is the *upper left corner*, X2,Y1 is the *lower left corner*, X2,Y2 is the *upper right corner*, and finally X1,Y2 is the *lower right corner,* as illustrated here:

```
<area shape="poly" coords="402,0; 436,0; 436,26; 402,26" href="youth.htm"
alt="Young Adults" />
```

The **map** ending tag **</map>** signifies that the map data set is complete.

With the **navbar.jpg** image and this **navbarmap** data set in an HTML document, you will have the navigation aid shown in Figure 10.6.

```
<img src="images/navbar.jpg" usemap="#navbarmap" />
... other web page stuff goes here ...
... hidden map data can be placed anywhere ...
<map name="navbarmap">
<area shape="rect" coords="0,0 56,26" href="index.htm" alt="Red Rose Library Home Page" />
<area shape="rect" coords="56,0 116,26" href="hours.htm" alt="Hours of operation" />
<area shape="rect" coords="116,0 166,26" href="staff.htm" alt="Library Staff" />
<area shape="rect" coords="166,0 228,26" href="board.htm" alt="Board of Trustees" />
<area shape="rect" coords="228,0 322,26" href="archive.htm" alt="Newsletters" target="_blank" />
<area shape="rect" coords="322,0 402,26" href="children.htm" alt="Children's Room" />
<area shape="rect" coords="402,0 436,26" href="youth.htm" alt="Young Adults" />
<area shape="rect" coords="436,0 472,26" href="av.htm" alt="Audio/Visual Collection" />
<area shape="rect" coords="472,0 512,26" href="ref.htm" alt="Reference Desk" target="_blank" />
<area shape="rect" coords="512,0 584,26" href="friends.htm" alt="Friends of the Red Rose Library" />
<area shape="rect" coords="584,0 640,26" href="faqs.htm" alt="FAQs" target="_blank" />
</map>
```

... other web page stuff goes here ...
... hidden map data can be placed anywhere ...

Home | Hours | Staff | Board | Newsletter | Children | YA | AV | Ref | Friends | FAQs

Figure 10.6. Image Mapping a Navigation Bar (code1006.htm)

Since the image map technique does not care where the map data are with respect to the image, navigation bar image tags can be repeated more than once inside an HMTL document (e.g., at the top and bottom of the page). Note, too, that you can use **alt** attributes inside the **area** elements so that when the mouse hovers over the image map area, additional information can appear using Internet Explorer. Hovering over the **Ref** area, for example, makes three changes in the Internet Explorer browser display. You see the cursor become a hand, you see the drop down **alt** tag value “Reference Desk,” and at the bottom of the browser screen you see the filename and location that this hot spot is linked to (**ref.htm**). We used relative URLs in this example but could just as easily have used absolute addressing with full URLs. As discussed earlier in this chapter, the **target** attribute can be used to load the linked page or image either into the current window (default is **target="_self"**) or into a new browser window (**target="_blank"**), as we illustrated for the Newsletters, Reference Desk, and FAQs links in this example.

Adding Navigation to the Red Rose Library Page

The home page with image map navigation is shown in Figure 10.7.

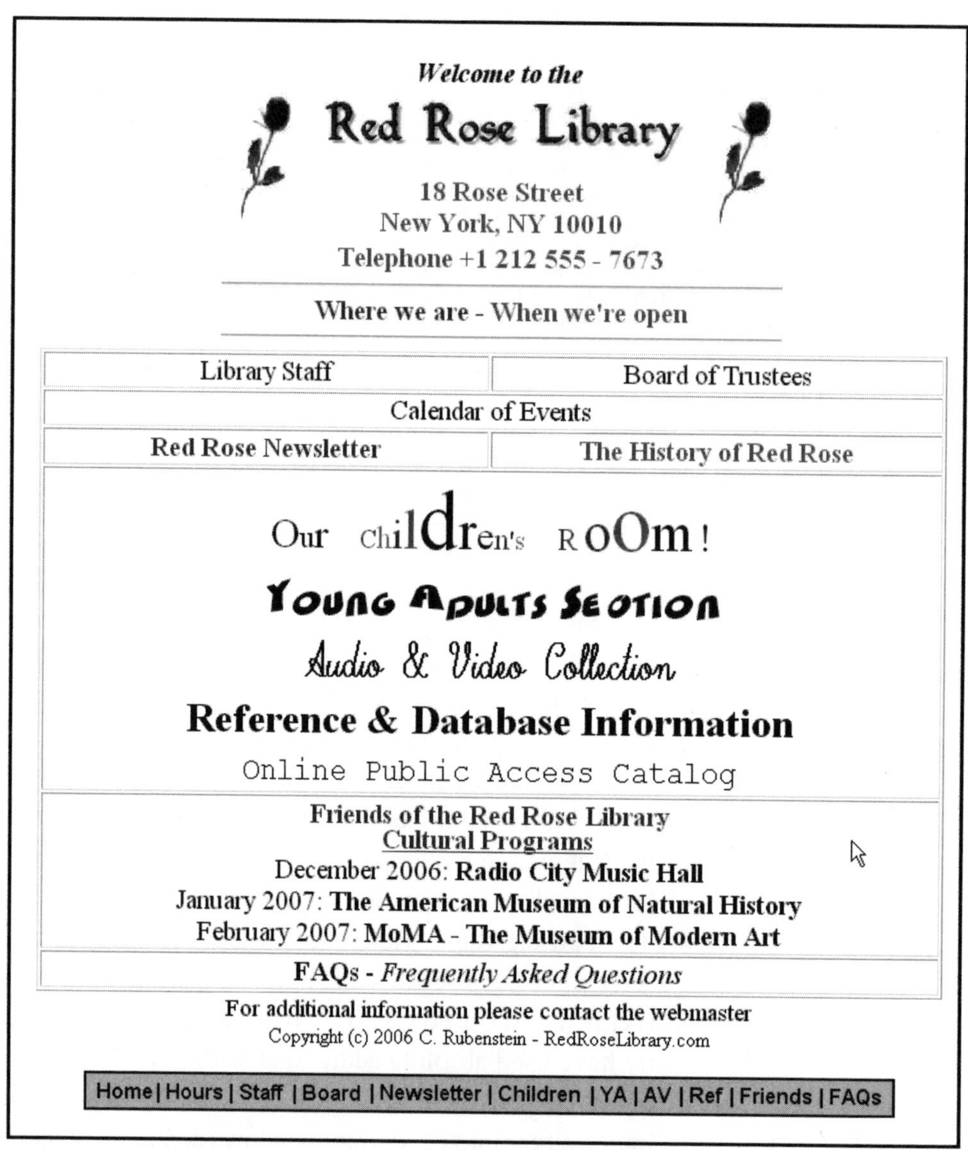

Figure 10.7. Adding Navigation to the Red Rose Library Page (code1007.htm)

You cannot resize the 640-pixel-wide navigation bar using **width** because the image map code does not scale to a resized image. We would have to redesign the navbar image and the image map data set if we wanted to size it to the text above it. The other option is to resize the original Web page. Figure 10.8 resizes the original Web page to fit the

640-pixel navigation bar. And since you know how to create hyperlinks, you can supply all navbar links with real filenames.

As you did with the hypertext version of this code, you can turn off the navbar's **Home** link to this home page using the **nohref** attribute instead of the **href** attribute in its line of code:

<area shape="rect" coords="0,0 56,26" nohref alt="Red Rose Library Home Page" />

Figure 10.8 shows the effect of setting the bottom table's **border** to **"0"** to improve the overall look of the Web page.

Welcome to the

Red Rose Library

18 Rose Street
New York, NY 10010
Telephone +1 212 555 - 7673

Where we are - When we're open

Library Staff | Board of Trustees
Calendar of Events
Red Rose Newsletter | The History of Red Rose

Our children's RoOm!

YOUNG ADULTS SECTION

Audio & Video Collection

Reference & Database Information

Online Public Access Catalog

Friends of the Red Rose Library

Cultural Programs
December 2006: **Radio City Music Hall**
January 2007: **The American Museum of Natural History**
February 2007: **MoMA - The Museum of Modern Art**

FAQs - *Frequently Asked Questions*

For additional information please contact the webmaster

Copyright (c) 2006 C. Rubenstein - RedRoseLibrary.com

Home | Hours | Staff | Board | Newsletter | Children | YA | AV | Ref | Friends | FAQs

Figure 10.8. Adding Hyperlinks and Real Filenames (code1008.htm)

Another trick you can use to enhance the look of this home page is to control the color of text hyperlinks (normally blue with blue underlines) by surrounding the text inside the anchor tag using **font** elements with **color** attributes. This is seen in the text of lines "18 Rose Street", "Our Children's Room", "Friends of the Red Rose Library", and "Cultural Programs" of Figure 10.8 where in each case the underline also takes on the text's font color. Figure 10.9 shows another variation of this finished home page where anchor stylization has resulted in removal of all underlining. In this example, some hypertext enlarges when the mouse hovers over it, in other cases the hypertext becomes bold.

Welcome to the

Red Rose Library

18 Rose Street
New York, NY 10010
Telephone +1 212 555 - 7673

Where we are - When we're open

Library Staff　Board of Trustees
Calendar of Events
Red Rose Newsletter　The History of Red Rose

Our children's ROOm!

Young Adults Section

Audio & Video Collection

Reference & Database Information

Online Public Access Catalog

Friends of the Red Rose Library
Cultural Programs
December 2006: **Radio City Music Hall**
January 2007: **The American Museum of Natural History**
February 2007: **MoMA - The Museum of Modern Art**
FAQs - *Frequently Asked Questions*
For additional information please contact the webmaster
Copyright (c) 2006 C. Rubenstein - RedRoseLibrary.com

Home | Hours | Staff | Board | Newsletter | Children | YA | AV | Ref | Friends | FAQs

Figure 10.9. Restyled Hyperlinks for a "Finished" Look (code1009.htm)

Marquees

You can use the **marquee** element to create a horizontal area in your document that contains scrolling text or characters and is called a marquee. The **marquee** attributes include **align**, **behavior**, **bgcolor**, **direction**, **height**, **hspace**, **loop**, **scrollamount**, **scrolldelay**, **vspace**, and **width**.

The **align** attribute specifies the alignment of the marquee with respect to the surrounding text. Where the **left**, **center**, and **right** attributes create marquees that are independent of the surrounding text, the **top**, **middle**, and **bottom** attributes include the marquee as part of it.

The **behavior** attribute default is **behavior="scroll"**. The text starts at one side of the document, scrolls across it, scrolls off the other side, and repeats. Other variations are **behavior="slide"**, where the text starts at one side, scrolls across, and stops at the opposite margin, staying there, and **behavior="alternate"**, where the text starts at one side, scrolls across, and bounces off the opposite margin. This repeats, with the text traveling back and forth across the page. Treating the text as an image, the **width="n"** or **height="n"** attributes size the marquee. The value of "**n**" here can be a number of pixels (**width="450"**) or a percentage of the screen (**width="75%"**). The **scrolldelay="n"** attribute sets the delay (milliseconds) between each series of scrolling text in the display. These simple marquee codes

```
<marquee behavior="alternate" width="450" scrollDelay="100"
style="color:#ff0000; font-weight:bold; font-size:25; font-style:italic" >
Welcome </marquee>
<marquee behavior="slide" width="450" scrollDelay="100"
style="color:#00ff00; font-weight:bold; font-size:25; font-style:italic" >
to our </marquee>
<marquee behavior="scroll" width="450" scrollDelay="100"
style="color:#0000ff; font-weight:bold; font-size:25; font-style:italic" >
Web Site </marquee>
```

result in the three-line scrolling display shown in Figure 10.10.

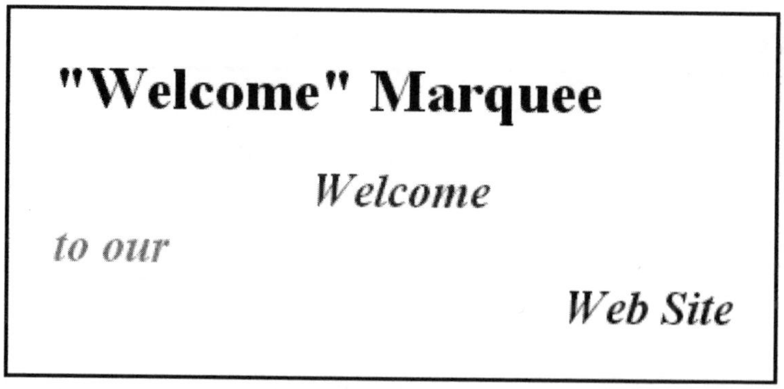

"Welcome" Marquee

Welcome

to our

Web Site

Figure 10.10. Adding Marquee to Your Page (code1010.htm)

Other attributes add a variety of other stylings to the marquee. These include determining the **direction** in which the text scrolls, with the default being **left**, that is, the text begins at the right and scrolls left. This attribute can also have the value **direction="right"**, which reverses the direction of text movement. Much like an image, the marquee uses the **hspace="n"** and **vspace="n"** attributes to provide left and right or top and bottom margins around the marquee.

The scrolled text can be further modified using **scrollamount="n"** to set the space (**pixels**) between each series of scrolling text, or the **loop="n"** attribute can be used to set the number of times the text scrolls through the marquee. For infinite scrolling, use **loop="-1"** or **loop="infinite"**. Marquees can also be generated using JavaScript, but that requires programming.

Web Page Transitions Using http-equiv Attributes

Using http-equiv="refresh"

We saw in Chapter 3 how the **meta** element uses the **name** attribute to insert specific cataloging information (**content** attribute) into a Web page. This information, typically utilizing the Dublin Core specification, assists search engines in categorizing and finding your content. Another use for the **meta** tag noted in Chapter 3 was to use the **http-equiv="refresh"** attribute value to spawn, or jump, to new Web pages, either immediately or after a specified number of seconds, without the user doing any mouse clicking. Many Web users would consider the refresh to be a negative use of the meta tag, as some Web pages have links to advertisers. The "code"

<meta http-equiv="refresh" content = "t">

refreshes the current HTML Web page every **"t"** seconds, during which time a new advertisement would appear (possibly in a new window under the original window so you don't see it until you try to close the browser). This result is often unwanted by the user.

The **refresh** technique also has a very positive use. When a Web page has been moved from one URL or directory to another, the **meta** tag may be used to refresh the page in **"t"** seconds, at which time it automatically hyperlinks or "jumps" to the html page "**next.htm**" on the current Web site. The "code"

<meta http-equiv="refresh" content ="t"; url ="next.htm">

could also be "programmed" to jump to another Web site by substituting the full URL, for example to the www.redroselibrary.com Web site:

<meta http-equiv="refresh" content ="t"; url =
"http://www.redroselibrary.com">

Section 508

Federal regulation Section 508 (of the Rehabilitation Act of 1973, as amended, 29 U.S.C. 794d) defines sixteen accessibility requirements with which government Web sites must comply to be accessible to people with disabilities. If your library is included in this group, or if you are concerned about the accessibility of your Web pages to your patrons, you need to be aware of the Section 508 guidelines at **http://www.section508.gov/final_text.html#Web** You can learn more about this important topic at **http://www.netmechanic.com/accessibility.htm** The pages you designed in this text are pretty much all in compliance with the accessibility guidelines, but the rules should be reviewed before you post your specific pages.

We Covered a Lot of Things, but Not Everything

Many other techniques can be used to dress up your Web page. There are pop-up windows that can be created for emergency announcements (again, like any automated element, can be abused), and you can embed music and videos and special programming scripts in your Web page. All of these are well beyond what you need to set up a good library Web page. The challenge is to keep your pages up to date with current information. Remember, the key to information is content. The most beautiful page doesn't help your library if the content on it is a year old! You need to begin a process of having someone on the staff or a volunteer (possibly the newsletter editor) review materials as they become available and have these materials forwarded to you for posting. You have enough work without having to do the Web page editing, too!

One thing you need to know is that you need to find personal gratification in seeing your Web page go live after all your hard work and testing. True enough, the time you put into the design of your Web site will increase its efficiency for your patrons, but many will appreciate the effort. Don't despair. After all, you designed the published Web page. And now, you've finished the book!

Congratulations!

Index

3368

About the Author

CHARLES P. RUBENSTEIN is a Professor of Information Science and Engineering at Pratt Institute's Graduate School of Information and Library Science in Brooklyn, New York, and a Visiting Professor of Engineering at the Institute for Research and Technology Transfer at Farmingdale State University (SUNY) in Farmingdale, New York. He has a doctorate in bioengineering (Polytechnic Institute of New York) and a master's in library and information science (Pratt Institute). A distinguished lecturer for the IEEE Computer Society and the IEEE Engineering Management Society, he has presented HTML and e-commerce tutorials in Canada, India, Puerto Rico, and the United States.